Strategic Policy Design

Modern organizations, whether public or private, are animated by a universal imperative: to achieve prominent goals that fulfill their mandates and uphold deeply held values and ideals. To realize this imperative, leaders entrusted to pursue organizational missions need to exercise a core set of strategic skills, discern opportunities, identify worthy goals, and implement pursuing actions. *Strategic Policy Design* introduces an integrated architecture for strategic thinking that enhances leadership skills in gauging conditions and crystallizing plans. This framework promotes a structured approach to strategic tasks by offering templates for decision making, from articulating a strategic mission, understanding the environment in which an organization operates, and rallying people and resources toward attaining strategic goals to a portable, versatile framework for the development and writing of strategy-oriented communications.

For practitioners of policy, this book offers clarity of strategic thinking and introduces a new framework with which to perceive policy environments, identify and define goals, and organize strategies. For students, this book explores the skill and art in exercising leadership, encompassing both pragmatism and idealism. By learning and applying the showcased techniques, students will be equipped with a heightened awareness of policy domains, goal construction, and operational planning. Students in public-sector studies will find this book of interest, as will those studying political science, public administration, law, foreign affairs, international development, history, military sciences, and similar majors. The organizational perspective in strategy will also appeal to students in both business and non-profit sectors.

Jack C. Chow served as U.S. Ambassador and Deputy Assistant Secretary of State for global health and science issues during the presidency of George W. Bush, and he subsequently was Assistant Director-General at the World Health Organization. He held posts within the legislative and executive branches of the U.S. government and was a consultant at RAND Corporation and McKinsey & Company. He is a Distinguished Service Professor (adjunct) in the Washington, D.C. program of Carnegie Mellon University, Heinz School of Public Policy and Management.

"*Strategic Policy Design* is a flexible tool for educators and a valuable resource for aspiring leaders at every level. While policymaking processes are the central focus of courses on public policy, we should not overlook that the future quality of those processes begins today—the moment we begin to teach our students to think like leaders. Effective leadership is all about strategy, and this book provides an efficient framework for introducing students to this skillset."

Jangsup Choi, *Texas A&M University-Commerce, USA*

Strategic Policy Design

A Practitioner's Guide to Statecraft

Jack C. Chow

Routledge
Taylor & Francis Group

NEW YORK AND LONDON

First published 2020
byRoutledge
605 Third Avenue, New York, NY 10017

and by Routledge
4 Park Square, Milton Park, Abingdon, Oxon, OX14 4RN

First issued in paperback 2022

Routledge is an imprint of the Taylor & Francis Group, an informa business

Library of Congress Cataloging-in-Publication Data
Names: Chow, Jack C., 1960– author.
Title: Strategic policy design : a practitioners guide to statecraft / Jack
    C. Chow.
Description: New York, NY : Routledge, 2020. | Includes
    bibliographical references and index.
Identifiers: LCCN 2019040340 | ISBN 9781482239928 (hardback) |
    ISBN 9781003009009 (ebook)
Subjects: LCSH: Political planning—United States.
Classification: LCC JK468.P64 C56 2020 | DDC 320.60973—dc23
LC record available at https://lccn.loc.gov/2019040340

ISBN 13: 978-1-03-247469-4 (pbk)
ISBN 13: 978-1-4822-3992-8 (hbk)
ISBN 13: 978-1-003-00900-9 (ebk)

Typeset in Times New Roman
by Apex CoVantage, LLC

To my late parents

Chuen-Tyi and Theresa Tse-Wen Chow,

who both ennobled my brothers and me
to enter public service

in gratitude for all that America has gifted to us.

Contents

Figures

Tables

Preface

I am grateful for the professional opportunities and responsibilities that have been bestowed upon me by leaders of several prominent organizations. The entirety of my experiences enabled me to become a leader in my own right, chiefly in the field of global health diplomacy. My professional origin was that of being a physician specializing in health policy. Training as a doctor reinforced my natural empathic self as well as rooted me in the ways of science and analytics. As I further evolved my skills and thinking in the realms of policy beyond the formal bounds of healthcare, I began to see more clearly how professional training can cause a type of "self-compartmentalization" among practitioners, who, having invested heavily to achieve their statuses and expertise, tended to aggregate into insular, often tribal, communities within organizations.

Through my participation in countless meetings and projects, I came to see how such compartmentalization of expertise and interactions, however unintentional or unnoticed, locked in and shut off value creation across the whole of organizations and across broader sectors. Sometimes groups were divided across their functional roles; to make something work, one group might insist that others take actions that strictly conform to standards that they, or their professional tribes, have defined. At other times, groups undertook hardline positions arising from narrow self-viewpoints that excluded substantive understanding of other parties' interests.

To resolve some of these differences I found myself undertaking bridging roles that required crossing over into different spheres of expertise and expectations. To adapt, I began to create my own sets of rules and approaches, some of which were created on the spur of the occasion.

Over time I kept note of my self-originated recipes for action, many of which are frameworks in a heuristic style, cast in the form of acronyms or alliterations for better mental retrievability during times of intensity. When I began teaching graduate and undergraduate students in public policy, I shared my framework approaches with them to guide them toward structured thinking and writing and found many students especially appreciated having widely applicable methods to frame issues across several disciplines. A former colleague urged me to author a book with my approaches so that students and professionals alike, in wherever part of the world, might benefit and apply them with productive effect in their careers. This book, after a long period of gestation and formulation, is the fulfilling result.

It is my aim and purpose that this book and the tenets contained within serve as a practical form of "intellectual software" for policymaking applicable not only within the public sector, but to any organization—whether public, private, or non-profit—pursuing missions of complexity. While written by a physician, this book is non-technical, with frameworks of generic applicability for readers across a wide spectrum of professions, especially those involved in soft power issues. Furthermore, with modern career tracks becoming increasingly cross-disciplinary, I also hope that this book serves another purpose as an "analytical passport" that enables students and practitioners to cross whatever boundaries, professional or tribal, they might encounter and to unify those communities toward achieving ever-higher levels of value and fulfillment.

Acknowledgements

This book incorporates learnings and insights gleaned from the many responsibilities I've been privileged to experience in my three decades in the public and private sectors, academia, and as an everyday citizen. I am very grateful to have met innumerable professionals and students with talent and dedication to their life missions. From many I have learned valuable lessons that I've applied to fruitful use; to others I've served as a teacher and as a mentor in the confidence that they too will apply their energies for the betterment of society.

There are many people of kindness and wisdom in my life's journey who are deserving of recognition, and my message of gratitude to all of them is that I hope my writings here will enable upcoming generations to enrich their thinking and to embolden their dreams.

I convey sincere gratitude and appreciation to the following individuals with whom my interactions contributed in some way to the content and approaches of this book. In rough chronological order as to when I first had the good fortune of meeting them:

I grew up in the community and public schools of Saegertown, Pennsylvania, and my family and I have never forgotten their support. It was there that I first kindled my interest in public service, even when working in private sector roles. I also thank the following academic mentors: the late Fr. Charles Drexler of Gannon University in Erie, Pennsylvania; the late Alvin Z. Rubinstein and William Kristol, both professors at the University of Pennsylvania; Dr. Peter Budetti and the late Aaron Wildavsky at the University of California at Berkeley; as well as Jonathan Showstack and Dr. Philip R. Lee at the University of California at San Francisco. I also appreciate the influential teachings of Austan Goolsbee at the University of Chicago's business school and those of Philip Zelikow and Robert Blackwill, then at the Harvard Kennedy School of Government. I am grateful for the longstanding encouragement by Brian Higgins, my Kennedy School classmate and now a U.S. congressman, and for the visionary initiative of Rosabeth Moss Kanter, professor at the Harvard Business School. She founded the Harvard Advanced Leadership Initiative, where I was a participating fellow and where I conducted some of the background research for this book.

In particular, I credit Philip Zelikow's article, "Foreign Policy Engineering: From Theory to Practice and Back Again," in a 1994 issue of the journal

International Security, with hooking me into thinking about policy in structured, logical forms. Zelikow's concepts stayed with me throughout my career, and I began to coalesce my thinking about finding common patterns of policy engineering resident across great swaths of institutions and entities, in both public and private sectors. This book serves as an evolution of Zelikow's policy engineering concept to undergird a broader leadership skill toward what I call "organizational statecraft," which I assert goes beyond the traditional concept of diplomatic statecraft to include all entities that engage in the pursuit of a purposeful mission.

In my professional life, I owe enormous gratitude to those who regarded my potential high enough to invite me to contribute to their organizational missions: the late Congressman Silvio O. Conte of Massachusetts; James Kulikowski at the House Appropriations Committee; Bettilou Taylor and Craig Higgins at the Senate Appropriations Committee; Ripley Forbes, then at the House Commerce Committee; the late Senator Arlen Specter of my home state of Pennsylvania; Nancy Killefer at McKinsey & Company; Frank E. Loy, John F. Turner, Anthony "Bud" Rock, Judith Kaufman, Marc Ostfield, William Dilday, David Kramer, and Paula Dobriansky at the State Department; the late J.W. Lee, then Director-General of the World Health Organization, and his chief advisor Jim Yong Kim, former President of the World Bank; Alex Ross, my Chief of Staff at W.H.O.; Melanie Zipperer, Sue Block-Tyrells and Drs. Fatoumata Nafo, Winnie Mpanju, and Mario Raviglione of W.H.O.

I particularly thank Steven Kelmar, then at the U.S. Department of Health and Human Services, who coincidentally also lived in Switzerland when I was working at W.H.O., for his encouragement to me to write a book that incorporates my unique framework approaches. This book is a product of my acting on his good counsel.

I give a special salute of recognition to former Secretary of State Colin L. Powell and his deputy Richard Armitage for appointing me to serve as U.S. Ambassador, leading the diplomatic campaign on their behalf against global HIV/AIDS and other diseases. Even in the post-9/11 era, both Powell and Armitage unwaveringly backed my efforts to establish a new Global Fund against major pandemics and to advance President George W. Bush's historic worldwide initiative to support people living with HIV/AIDS. I am forever grateful for the trust these leaders invested in my team and me to accomplish those profound objectives.

I continue with my march of thanks to: the late Dr. Donald A. Henderson at the White House Office of Science and Technology Policy; the late Philip Schambra at the National Institutes of Health; Edmund Moy, former director of the U.S. Mint; Anthony Ross and Soeren Mattke at the RAND Corporation; Chandresh Harjivan and Dr. Robert Kadlec, both formerly at the consulting firm PRTM/PwC; Wilpen Gorr, Marie Coleman, and Ramayana Krishnan at Carnegie Mellon University's Heinz College; Yanzhong Huang and Courtney Smith at Seton Hall University; and my colleagues and friends Jeannie Perrie, Robert S. Winter, Mark DeSantis, Venkat Venkateswaran, Conrad Lee, Kimberly Reed, Peter and Helen Sjoquist, Michael Cao, and Kent "Ky" Phan.

I express deep appreciation and respect for the students at Carnegie Mellon University's Heinz College and at Seton Hall University's School of Diplomacy and International Relations. Their idealism, smarts, and desire to do good in the world always uplift me whenever I step before them in the classroom. They gave excellent feedback to the framework approaches I introduced, and I've incorporated many of their suggestions for the benefit of the students to follow.

I appreciate the efforts made by the publishing team at Taylor & Francis: Lara Zoble, Laura Stearns, Katie Horsfall, Karen Cain and Ramachandran Vijayaragavan who led the editing and production team. They all earned my gratitude for helping me bring this title into the hands and minds of those who could benefit from the lessons contained within.

Above all I thank my family: my parents, Chuen-Tyi and Theresa Chow, and my two brothers, Kevin and Daniel, and their families for their love, support, and understanding during this project. My father was a college professor and my mother was a nurse, both of whom instilled in me the values of public service. Whereas my parents are now deceased, their light and spirit live on as I teach, write, and act as a humble but determined force for good.

Introduction

This book, *Strategic Policy Design*, advances the premise that organizations are animated by a universal imperative: to achieve prominent goals that fulfill their mandates and uphold deeply held values and ideals. To realize this imperative, the leaders entrusted to pursue their organizational missions need to exercise a core set of strategic skills in what might be called a "strategic craft" to discern opportunities, identify worthy goals, and implement pursuing actions.

To advance this craft, *Strategic Policy Design* introduces an integrated architecture for strategic thinking that enhances leadership skills in gauging conditions and crystallizing plans. As is done in the design of buildings, this framework promotes a structured approach to these tasks by elaborating major categories, or templates, for decision-making. These primary decisions can then lead to subsequent sets of choices involving more detail and consideration of a situation's unique circumstances.

The chief elements of the design are elaborated in four major parts. Each part delves into a framework element, or what might be called a "framelet," in considerable detail. Each part can be studied as a standalone module or in connection to each other. When viewed as a whole, these four parts constitute a continuum from intention to implementation.

Part 1, The Strategic Mission, sets forth the animating reasons why organizations come into being, exist, and are motivated. Leaders establish those enduring purposes that orient the organizations' central tasks and define their activities. Purposeful missions not only motivate people to implement tasks and attain goals, but they also seek to enlist and engage human emotions and to fulfill them through accomplishments.

Part 2, The Strategic Domain, describes the environment in which an organization pursues its mission. Leaders navigate their entities across complex, dynamic realms that may range from the hospitable to the hostile. Ahead of embarking on major goals, leaders should be equipped with the means to assess their domains along with the forces and factors that populate them. This part supplies "lenses," or structured methods by which leaders can organize their views regarding the landscapes ahead of them.

Part 3 introduces a new, practical way to structure and articulate the central aim of organizational mission, **The Strategic Goal**. It is through goals that entities fulfill their mandates in ways meaningful to stakeholders. Goals are established to create targets for performance and to establish a proposition of value that would result from success. In this part, a new four component framework standardizes the essential attributes of a grand goal, thereby promoting the leadership skill of "goal-crafting."

Part 4, The Strategic Plan, advances a new method for conceptualizing action plans that rally people and resources toward attaining strategic goals. The centerpiece of this part is the POSTERS framework, an acronymic description of the different categories of objectives that contribute to strategy formation. A strategic plan not only inlays an operational blueprint for achieving the declared goal, but it also must inform and motivate those people tasked for carrying out the mission. Thus, at the conclusion of this part is a chapter on communications tools that introduces portable, versatile frameworks for writing memoranda and for organizing thoughts in speeches and meetings. Such skills are highly prized within organizations, yet they are often underemphasized in professional training.

Mission

There are four primary aims of this book.

1. Practical Aim

For practitioners of policy, this book aims to bring added clarity to strategic thinking and to introduce a new framework with which to perceive their environments, identify and define goals, and organize strategies. Senior practitioners may find framework elements described within as complementary to the styles and techniques they have used throughout their careers. Younger policymakers rising up their ranks may use these elements to sharpen their thinking and arguments and to organize their memos and speeches. Practitioners in developing regions, especially those in junior ranks, will find this book useful to escalate their strategic thinking skills and become more influential in their interactions with practitioners in industrialized countries, where organizations tend to be large and complex.

2. Academic Aim

For students, this book aims to promote the cause of *strategic education* by aiding young people to learn the skill and art in exercising leadership, encompassing both pragmatism and idealism. By learning and applying the techniques showcased, the student will start to build a strategic sense with a heightened awareness of policy domains, goal construction, and operational planning. From historical examples the student can identify the common challenges involved in policy strategy and tactics.

The natural readership for this book are students in public sector studies such as political science, public administration, law, foreign affairs, international development, history, military sciences, and similar majors. The organizational perspective in strategy would also appeal to students in both business and non-profit sectors. The structured methodology is particularly relevant to business students in consulting, a profession that relies upon organized strategic assessment. Overall, this book would appeal to any student with an interest in leadership and strategy and who aspires to take on roles at the highest levels in their careers.

3. Aspirational Aim

For those supporting societal advancement, this book aims to promote the *democratization of leadership*. In many societies, access to leadership at institutions, governments, and companies is limited to the powerful and privileged. Access to leadership platforms is denied by incumbents to protect their influence and thereby perpetuate their advantages. Many forms of injustice impose barriers to leadership, of which corruption, discrimination, and oppression are prominent. The talents of people in ranks outside the privileged are lost to their societies, and these excluded groups remain mired with little chance for upward mobility. Persistent denial of leadership roles across society deprives the skills and experiences needed to sustain entire tiers of institutions and organizations. By providing an accessible system for strategic thinking and acting, this book looks to equip aspirants to leadership roles and to embolden them to break through the societal barriers that stand in their way.

4. Leadership Aim

For those who aspire to lead and to transform, this book promotes strategic skills toward the broader service of *organizational statecraft*, which is the idea that organizations conduct their own means of diplomacy among or against each other in the pursuit of their respective missions. By training new generations of leaders, the chief framework will empower them to assume and exercise authority in entities across their societies. Akin to the role of armed service academies to train officers to lead military units, this book's mission is to help train new generations of "officers for society," primed to lead at all strata of responsibility. Such a cohort will have the capability to implement consistent policy designs throughout their careers. With widespread adoption, this framework can create a new form of *lingua franca* for policymaking, a common set of concepts and terms that harmonizes dialogue and policy construction. A common standard for policy design, in turn, makes institutions more consistent in their makeup and approaches, conferring more stability and predictability. A common standard also facilitates more efficient interactions among entities and countries when they communicate using widely shared concepts.

The Line Method

A central and distinguishing feature of *Strategic Policy Design* is the introduction of the *line method* in describing components and approaches within the framework. In the English language, the word *line* is at once descriptive and vivid. It succinctly conveys to the reader the vision of a continuous stroke of writing, or in the real world, a continuous marking of a particular usefulness.

In the physical word, lines are often created to produce a contrast and a distinction, creating separation as well as identification. A boundary line, such as a state line, makes clear the end of one province's authority and the start of another. In the world of abstractions, where complexity often clouds clarity, a concept expressed as a line-word can serve as a helpful demarcation device, separating one concept from another, or it can impart a worldly characteristic that makes the idea more understandable. For example, *fault line*, a term borrowed from geology, is often applied in news reports to describe a contentious issue that divides people into conflicting, pro- versus anti- camps.

Line words also communicate a meaning of connections between causes and effects; alignments of people, places, or things; or forward movement from an origin to a destination. *Story line*, *front line*, and *path line* are respective examples of terms conveying these types of meanings.

From the power of the word *line* to convey a clearer descriptive picture, especially in combination with other words, the number and variety of singular and compound words incorporating -*line* proliferated in the English lexicon, including *headline*, *timeline*, *frontline*, *dividing line*, among many others. The wide variety of "line-words" reflects the versatile usefulness of their meanings, or the added vividness of their descriptions. Line-words' ubiquity in English and their instant recognition make them practical, handy building blocks to use in this framework.

As a practical aim, the *Strategic Policy Design* framework makes selective, even creative, use of line-words to spark first-run ideas in situational assessments. Having an analytic toolkit loaded with memorable components aids time-pressured practitioners and inexperienced junior professionals. When facing situations of complexity, urgency, or uncertainty, people often act from "gut reactions," instinctual impulses derived from ingrained habit, values, and acculturation. Their primal feelings often stem from an individualized mental model of the world about them and of the causal relationships within. Yet mental models, like any other aspect of human thought and behavior, can be flawed in many ways and lead to incomplete or erroneous conclusions. Idiosyncratic systems of thought can produce blind spots or excess detachment from the true state of the world, making haphazard decision-making a too frequent outcome.

Heuristic Approach

Strategic Policy Design is dedicated to help those who want to learn a more systematic method of assessing situations and formulating goals. By distilling strategic thought into more concise and even memorable formats, this framework aims to promote alacrity in both thought and deed. To do this, the book makes extensive use of *heuristic techniques*. Heuristics is a method of mental engagement that employs concise rules or formulas to approximate real-world conditions. Some everyday terms that describe heuristic style methods include: *shortcuts, rules of thumb, tried-and-true formulas, pearls of wisdom,* and *back-of-the-envelope calculations.*

The practice of heuristic technique is a recognition that incessant demands and time pressures prevent leaders from obtaining the most optimal information and from formulating the most extensive plans. Heuristics is a method to achieve simpler yet sufficient understanding that is good enough for decision-making. Nobel laureate and economist Herbert A. Simon coined the term *satisficing* to describe how efforts to get "good enough" can lead to better overall results than what is achieved by maximal efforts.[1] Maximum efforts may be too costly in time and resources for the benefits won, whereas satisficing can spare such costs yet yield adequate results. The colloquialism "Don't let the perfect become the enemy of the good" is advice rooted in this concept.

A natural inclination that arises from satisficing, in which some gain is accepted when maximization is too expensive or difficult, is the predilection in taking action rather than standing still. The admonishing command of "Don't just stand there, do something" when nothing is happening during a crisis is belief in blind action irrespective of circumstances. But action taken solely for its own sake, detached from fair judgment about realities at hand, can be risky. Blundering ahead without any gauging of surrounding conditions is fraught with pitfalls. A modicum of insight, however tenuous, might be sufficient to avert the most hazardous of pathways. By recognizing the limited "mind budgets" of leaders under duress, heuristic methods that simplify a complicated situation can clarify matters sufficiently for initial decision-making.

Strategic Policy Design uses heuristic approaches to help leaders grasp fluid situations more easily and clearly. For those well versed in their professions' longstanding paradigms, the frameworks described herein are intended to supplement, rather than supplant, existing mental maps and methods. For those leaders, this book can add fresh approaches to enhance their thinking toolkits. For those new to leadership, who are on the rise in their organizations or who are studying to become leaders, this book offers a system of strategic thinking concise enough to identify key decision factors, precise enough to offer means to assemble a strategic course, yet portable enough to be applied across a wide variety of sectors, situations, and scenarios.

To make these heuristic approaches concrete and useable, the book uses a set of conceptual tools, or devices, that make framework concepts more lucid and memorable and therefore more mentally retrievable when pressing demands arise. Such devices include:

- Alliteration—the use of consecutive words or terms that begin with a particular letter or sound. One example of an alliteration is a favorite saying of James A. Baker III, a former U.S. Secretary of State, attributed to his father as sage career advice in the memorable form given as the Five P's: "Prior Preparation Prevents Poor Performance."[2] An example from this book is the three-element alliteration: Asset—Action—Achievement, describing a basic formula in the design of a plan.

- Acronyms—the creation of a whole word whose constituent letters are the first letter of other words. They work by prompting memory to underlying facts linked together. HOMES, the simple grade school example, stands for the five Great Lakes: Huron, Ontario, Michigan, Erie, and Superior. Acting as a type of verbal package, acronyms hold together related concepts or explanations with one easy "handle." Making use of acronyms' ability to stir memory from their succinctness, this book introduces a number of new acronyms such as SPIGOTS, a quality control checklist for memos.

- Analogies, similes, and metaphors—creating or highlighting a meaning by making a comparative link between the concept and a real-world reference. A real-world reference can serve as a memory prompt that leads to retrieval of an array of concepts. For example, the book makes use of environmental terms, such as *landscape* and *terrain*, to describe how a background might be perceived.

- Parallelism and rhyme—the use of linked concepts that have similar word forms. An example from later pages is a description of three key attributes of a strategic mission: significance, performance, and resonance. Another example is the layers of analysis extending top-down from a skyline point of view to the ground-line: surveillance, reconnaissance, intelligence, experience, and evidence. Grouped words that rhyme make them more memorable and thus more retrievable when needed.

- Formulas and equations—the assembly of factors or variables that describe their interrelationships, or the creation of special-purpose equations that express how inputs could produce an output or outcome. To highlight them, they are set off in capitals such as in the following linked relationship: CAPABILITY = CAPACITY + ABILITY. Although not actual mathematical relationships, these equations are better seen as formulas that describe how a variable is composed of a number of sub-variables. Other equations could be considered recipes, such as MEMO = SOAP + SPIGOTS, the latter two variables being acronyms describing content and quality checklists, respectively, to consult in writing policy memoranda.

- Dichotomous pairs—one analytical technique often employed in this book in creating novel framelets, or mini-frameworks, is the MECE Method. MECE is an acronym that stands for Mutually Exclusive, Collectively Exhaustive. It is a method that deconstructs a set of information into separate categories, and those categories altogether comprise the complete whole.[3] By separating elements, MECE helps to clarify and organize underlying factors that make up a larger, amorphous field of information. A common starting point of this method is the use of dichotomies, the splitting of information into two parts. The dichotomy of tangible vs. intangible is one that is frequently used in the book to describe two major categories of outcomes. Further splitting can create even more subcategories, and a cascade of dichotomous splitting can yield an abundance of constituent pieces.

Definitional Elaborations

The title of this book, *Strategic Policy Design*, is a deliberate choice of those three words. These words, along with the two-word clauses embedded within are worth elaborating here for their basic meaning and usage.

Strategic

Strategic is a widely used descriptor that originates from an elevated point of view, a wide, sweeping perceptual aperture that takes in a broad vista—at a national or international level, for instance—that takes in factors to be considered on a grand scale. That scale can also extend to time horizon: *Strategic* often implies a longtime horizon that may span decades, even centuries, in contrast to the shorter time periods of concern involved in tactical, day-to-day operations.

Here, *strategic* pertains to the calculated line of action taken toward an objective, taking into account key forces and factors. It also ascribes actions or stakes as being substantive, pivotal, or crucial to an overall endeavor. A subtler meaning for *strategic* is the identification of an underlying cause-effect relationship, so that to act strategically is to exert an effort to influence causal relationships to one's benefit. Strategic implies a confidence in certain sets of outcomes arising from chosen actions, or an anticipatory view of the linkage between actions and their implications and consequences.

Strategic is intended as a descriptor of policy elements deemed substantial and necessary to an organization's ongoing mission. It can describe actions and assets deemed mandatory and vital, as well as those that are chosen as discretionary in the pursuit of opportunities.

Policy

In the broad landscape of public and private sector decision-making, policy is a chosen approach toward issues, taking into account the interests of a specified set of stakeholders. Policy is commonly perceived as formal exercises of authority through laws, rules, and regulations in the governance of what currently exists. But policy also involves a stance toward what might exist in the future, whether threats or opportunities. Policy can be considered as an essential "product" that an organization creates in order to execute current responsibilities as well as to formulate and carry out its forward mission. Policy as a product translates and transmits governing principles into well-articulated goals and actions. Policy upholds the premise, the founding rationale for an entity's existence, and puts forth a promise, the commitment toward achieving future gains.

A policy which formulates commands and issues instructions to carry them out could be seen as having two computer-like components: its software and its hardware. A policy's software can be considered as the embedded programming, the executable code that directs actions from an overarching philosophy or ideology. A policy's hardware is the set of organizational mechanisms that converts intent into action. These mechanisms altogether make up an apparatus, the system of personnel and resources designated to implement a task. Without implementation, policy becomes inconsequential. To bolster their ability to implement, nations in particular invest heavily in building capabilities, such as technologies or workforces, as instruments of national power and prestige.

This book aims to help in the crafting of policy by introducing heuristic, fast-framing methods to enhance the overarching functions of governance and to sharpen the executive functions of goal-setting and implementation.

Design

Involving both product and process, design is deliberative integration of selected components into a whole, complete object or system whose functions will perform as intended. Design as product arrives at an end result wherein judgments are incorporated into the object, embedding the decisions made regarding features, forms, and functions. Also expressed in the design product are the assumptions made about how the object will be used, by whom, and under what conditions.

Design as process is an approach that contemplates the object's purpose, functions, and characteristics and anticipates how it will act in its surrounding environment. This process involves a common set of "Five I" steps:

1. **Ideation** is the origination of concepts;
2. **Intention** is the willfulness to act upon those concepts;
3. **Incorporation** is the embedding of concepts into a product or system;
4. **Integration** is the linkage among components that results in the creation of the whole; and
5. **Implementation** is the concept functioning as intended in its expected environment.

Design is conjoined to the parallel crafts of architecture and engineering. Adapted from its original description for the design of physical structures, architecture for policy involves the arrangement of systems that interconnect in reinforcing ways and reflect a preferred style or philosophy. Engineering for policy purposes is a calculated construct of processes so that they produce an intended outcome effectively and efficiently. Altogether, the mission of design, architecture, and engineering could be described as one that converts "entropy into entity": confronting a state of disorder or ambiguity and establishing a clearly defined process or system.

This book offers templates with which to organize understandings of a fluid situational landscape so that ideas for goals and actions can emerge more readily.

Strategic Policy

Strategic policy is the choice of the core goals that are identified as essential to the existence and the identity of a group. Strategic policy is shaped by stakeholders' demands and expectations from groups holding interests in certain outcomes or which possess various abilities that could help or hinder plans. In upholding an organization's mission and its values, deliberative strategic policy considers available choices in light of its capabilities and limits and assesses the operating environment to find the best ways to achieve success. Strategic policy can assume offensive or defensive postures: going on offense to proactively achieve specified objectives or taking on a defensive stance to prevent threats to survival.

Strategic policy weighs possible destinations and the pathways to get there. It then must assess the presentation of the operating environment—the landscape ahead upon which allies and adversaries are acting to achieve their own sets of goals. With complex interactions happening among all parties, strategic policy planning makes assumptions about operating conditions and about how others may react to one's chosen course.

Strategic policy is the conduit between making assumptions and committing resources for implementation. Such a need for coordination spurs the creation of an apparatus to apply such decisions in an institutional manner. An apparatus is the organizational mechanism by which policy is formulated and then promulgated into actions. By serving as an enduring platform of stability spanning time and even generations, an apparatus makes possible institutional memory and fosters cultures of professionalism that are committed to sustaining traditions and the retention of ongoing history.

This book focuses on strategic policy as designed and implemented by organizations and nations. It further examines how strategic policy works as a template for action across and within the whole entity; how leaders weigh their choices, rally resources, and motivate personnel.

Policy Design

Policy design is the configuration of an entity's positions and powers in ways deemed most effective to perform its mission. Whereas the design of physical things focuses upon the creation of a specific object with known properties, the design of policies involves multitudes of complications and complexities. Circumstances can change, sometimes radically, making an earlier policy design obsolete or deficient. Constituencies can shift allegiances, compelling leaders to adapt policies to new demands and needs. Event shocks, such as the 9/11 attacks, have transformed global politics to confront new realities and threats. With such complexity, the conduct of policy design can seem an elusive, frustrating task. In contending with the fluidity of events and interests, the use of models can simplify a universe of factors down to essential components, clarifying understanding of their interactions.

In building a basic model, it helps to conceptualize policy as a whole structure, consisting of working components and systems. For an entity to survive and thrive, all constituent systems have to work well with one another and be coordinated to achieve an intended impact. Policy design aims to improve both processes and products, and to do so in a manner consistent with stakeholder values and needs.

To craft policy as an integral whole, policy design undertakes three primary tasks: analysis, synthesis, and catalysis. Analysis of a policy entails the separation and isolation of components that sufficiently allows for focused attention and evaluation. Synthesis in policy design is the skill of assembling elements into a working, effective whole, guided by a vision of desired outcomes. Catalysis is the provocation that sets the policy into motion through persuasion and motivation. The catalyst can be sparked by outside events, provoking a response. Or the catalyst could originate from within, by ideas or by inspiration that leaders take forward to bring into fruition. The frameworks presented establish a basis for these primary tasks by creating common ways to describe a goal and the components of a plan, standardizing concepts so that acting upon them becomes easier.

Strategic Design

One level higher than policy design is the level of strategic design, at which leaders decide how best to define their organizations' central interests and to position themselves to fulfill their chosen aims. Whereas policy design emphasizes the mechanisms used in the application of organizational power, strategic design involves a broader array of issues pertaining to positioning and influence. Positioning and influence can be directed both inwardly, to shape a group's inner makeup and dynamics, and outwardly, to sway other groups active in a shared sector.

Whereas much effort is invested in pushing forward a drive toward desired goals, strategic design frequently involves looking to strike balances and to stabilize conditions. By and large, organizations seek to exist and function within an environmental equilibrium where conditions are stable and predictable. Such "safe harbor" conditions give organizations the time and stability to assess outbound conditions and to chart an outward course toward a destination.

To achieve stability and balance, strategic design weighs tradeoffs and opportunities for counterbalancing. Whereas the natural inclination of people and groups is to maximize gains and minimize losses, shifting circumstances and unpredictability of future conditions compel the need for hedging, or the anticipatory positioning toward a variety of outcomes. Hedging against uncertainty forces the consideration between optimality and sufficiency.

Another major trade-off in strategic design is that between commitment and optionality. Options are the range of choices available for action. Commitment is the selection of one of those choices with a backing of resources to implement it. Actions taken consume time, energy, and resources. Most consumption is irreversible, and the assets depleted may be hard to replace. The prospect of consumption and irreversibility leads to calculations on how differing options might pay off and what each option would cost.

Shaping perceptions matters in strategic design. Perceptions drive judgments, which in turn drive behaviors. Behaviors, the actions taken by individuals and groups, can either help or hinder progress toward a goal. Knowing the cause and effect linkages and human preferences creates a strategic sense, an ability to discern how humans might react to actions taken. Strategic sense is acquired through two basic skills: perceiving the intentions and actions of others and crafting the perceptions of oneself that are projected toward others. Employing strategic sense in both directions involves the concept of information profit: seeking to gain more information about other players in the environment than what others might gain in learning about you.

Synthesizing the knowledge of one's internal and external environments provides the clarity necessary to mobilize one's organization and to navigate a course among other groups to achieve a valued destination. This synthesis might be described as a three-point question, akin to what a football quarterback might consider in leading a team: Can one "see the play," "call the play," and "run the play"? Seeing the play is knowing enough about the configuration of forces and factors ahead; calling the play is the choice of goal and the action plan; and running the play is implementing the capabilities to achieve the desired end result.

Strategic design is a high art of leadership that entails the commanding grasp of the tangible—assets, operations, goals, and the insight of the intangible— values, preferences, intentions. The complexities and uncertainties involved in achieving this grasp can be overwhelming. By simplifying a dynamic environment into common elements more easily understood, one would benefit from using a working model with which to ask pertinent, high-payoff questions and to craft optimal strategies. The succeeding parts of this book will build out such a model.

Explanatory Notes

The book's concepts are meant to be applied broadly, across all types of groups spanning from small NGOs to nations to international organizations. For economy of space, this book's chief unit of analysis will be the *entity*, a proxy word for the range of organizations and authorities that exist—spanning public and private sectors, small and large groups, nations and corporations.

This book's main point of view is that of the leader at the head of an organization. This point of view is taken to give the reader an overarching, "high altitude" perspective. The big picture viewpoint affords an appreciation of the grand factors that interact amongst each other, some in concert to each other and many in conflict against one another. From seeing the patterns of forces and factors gained from a skyline point of view, a leader can define the organization's best way forward, avoiding foreseen pitfalls or alighting on newly opened avenues of opportunity.

This book seeks to empower all who aspire to responsible leadership, welcoming all readers and their gender identities. The book strives for gender neutrality in as balanced and efficient manner as possible. In those instances where the pronoun *he* or *she* is used by itself, such usage is not meant to be exclusive but is intended to encompass all gender identities.

Notes

1. Herbert A. Simon, "Rational Choice and the Structure of the Environment," *Psychological Review*, 63(2) (Mar. 1956): 136. doi:10.1037/h0042769.
2. James A. Baker, III with Steve Fiffer, *Work Hard, Study . . . and Keep Out of Politics!* (New York: G.P. Putnam's Sons, 2006), 5.
3. Barbara Minto, *The Pyramid Principle: Logic in Writing and Thinking*, 3rd ed. (London, UK: Pearson, 2009).

Part 1
The Strategic Mission

1   The VIPs of Leadership

Strategic mission is a calling that activates people toward achieving a set of meaningful outcomes that fulfill their own needs and interests. It motivates as a call to action, summoning believers and followers, and enlisting their allegiances and energies to embark upon a particular quest, which can be arduous and even dangerous. Strategic mission animates an overarching, enduring purpose that resonates in the mindsets of adherents. By holding forth that its purpose persists even beyond a lifetime, many a strategic mission is perpetuated by supporters across successive generations.

Frequently articulated in the form of an organizational mission statement, strategic mission also expresses the values and principles of prime importance endorsed by the group. In contrast to a mission of a tactical or operational nature, a mission that is strategic backs a prevailing cause that defines a group's core identity, essential aspirations, and ultimate goals.

A fundamental divide among organizational missions is that which separates the for-profit and non-profit sectors, which are also commonly classified as being private or public sectors, respectively. For-profit entities, mainly businesses, are formed with the specific purpose of creating and selling a good or a service and in so doing, produce a financial gain that is then shared among those involved in the enterprise, such as shareholders, employees, and managers. The central quest of companies is to compete and ultimately prevail in the marketplace and thereby earn a profit.

The primary mission of non-profit organizations is to serve and create value for the citizenry at large and to better particular constituencies. Prominent among non-profit organizations are those that are created by governments with the sovereign authority to create, operate, and disband them. Most government agencies and departments are focused on serving intra-national, or domestic, populations, but a notable number, such as the international organizations of the United Nations system, makes use of authorities conferred by nations to operate regionally or globally to pursue their missions. A modern trend is the growth of privately constituted non-profit groups apart from government, commonly known as NGOs or non-governmental organizations. NGOs and other non-profits, such as philanthropies and civic organizations, are dedicated to missions that are rooted in raising the public good independently, often in concert with, but sometimes at odds against, government.

The central quest by public organizations is to improve the common needs and space shared by broad swaths of people, or to confront many types of problems or conflicts affecting them. The strategic mission of the public sector is focused more upon creating value across various categories, such as social, cultural, political, and broadly shared economic benefits, rather than financial profit. Still, in the pursuit of their missions, public sector organizations must contend with prevailing economic conditions to assure their own financial viability and may even participate in markets to support their core functions.

One mnemonic way to think about the difference between the strategic missions of private versus public sector organizations is to consider that private companies seek to produce profits in the form of "income" whereas public groups seek to produce a particular "outcome." The complexities and intractabilities of many modern problems have given rise to alliances, partnerships, and coalitions that combine efforts from public as well as private sectors, based on shared interests and diversity of capabilities.[1] A commonality shared by both sectors is the pursuit of a sustainable reward, a benefit that contributes to and is part of a prevailing purpose. Entities from both sectors seek to produce a gain that is meaningful and represents an evolution of the accounting identity common in the private sector, standardly known as ROE or the return-on-equity invested, to a newly coined form of ROE: "Return-on-Effort," with the effort incorporating both tangible and intangible forms of inputs, not solely financial. Examples of intangible forms of input might include social media influence or trading of political capital.

The quest held forth by a strategic mission, whether of a private or public nature, is a prospective journey having an origin, a destination, a pathway, and the means for pursuit. An origin may be literal, such as a physical starting point for a journey across air, land, sea, or space. Origins can be also figurative, such as a historical or cultural reference that establishes what a force is changing. The choice of the starting point is significant because it becomes the reference point against which progress is gauged as the mission unfolds. How an origin of an issue is defined and expressed establishes the opening narrative of a storyline.

The organizational journey transits a pathway, or the necessary action steps and sequences to reach the destination. A set of means is the assets, such as personnel, tools, instruments, even vehicles, available to implement steps on the pathway. The mission culminates in its destination, the endpoint that achieves a desired result. For enduring missions, a high ideal can be upheld as a perpetual task, or it can be set forth as a series of goals for every generation to achieve.

All four attributes of the journey—origins, destinations, pathways, and means—involve options, or choices among available alternatives. Leaders making these choices often do so on the basis of trying to maximize a benefit or to minimize a cost. Some choices are made on the basis of expediency, whereas others are made on the basis of calculation and anticipation. In particular, how a journey is framed and described—defining the original problem, promoting a preferred remedy, and declaring a desired goal—is frequently slanted toward shaping perceptions and evoking certain emotions.

If a strategic mission of organizations can be described as a journey, then what motivates people to join? People are motivated by their interests, what they perceive to be their primary needs and wants. Often those interests can be personal and internalized—needing to eat, earning a living, paying debts. Human are also emotional beings, endowed from birth with feelings and primal motivations. Inner drives seek a fulfillment, a satisfaction that comes about from achievement. To achieve these ends and derive satisfaction, people often join groups to pursue interests that are above and beyond themselves. When people with different skills band together, it allows them to attain goals that are more difficult and complex than what individuals could achieve by themselves. Affiliations also contribute to people's sense of identity and provide an added means to give substance to their beliefs. At its best, a strategic mission sustains a human motivation to participate in a higher purpose that goes beyond one's own concerns to enlist in a grander cause that promises meaning and fulfillment.

Once constituted, the organization itself assimilates the emotional as well as rational motives of its human authors. To pursue its assigned cause, the entity is organized and formulated to implement pragmatic duties, such as meeting payrolls and paying bills. The embedded risk is that over time these prosaic functions will demand more time and attention of senior leaders and, if not managed, the collective force of everyday tasks can overcome and drain the expressive, advocacy functions of the organization to the point of discouragement and even disillusionment.[2] Bureaucracy becomes the twin sibling who countervails its emotional partner. Consequentially, a leader must harness and master two primal forces arising in organizations, that of its rational, task-oriented functions and that of its emotional, mission-animating functions.

In moving an organization forward on its mission, a leader must further contend with two primary forces involving people and their interests: the inherent self-interest of individuals and the collective interest of the group at large. Self-interest can act as a dis-associative, or distractive, force whereby the interests of individuals tend to pull them away from the interests of the group, whereas a collective interest can act as an associative, or attractive, force that draws people inward to work together. These two motivating forces can either be in alignment or be in conflict. When self-interest is in alignment with the group's interests, morale can be uplifting and implementation can be synchronous. But when self-interest varies from the interests of the whole, morale can plummet from dissension, and operations can degrade from strife or departures. The challenge for the leader is to recognize individuals' natural proclivity to act in their own self-interest and to find ways to align them toward mutual interests.

When presented with a leader's directive, many individuals think instinctively and ask in self-interest: "What's in it for me?" To nudge those tendencies toward a common cause, the leader can appeal to a higher level of motive by declaring three propositions:

What Lies Above Us
What Lies Ahead of Us
What Lies Within Us

For each of these propositions, a useful mnemonic, or memory prompt, to use are three sets of leadership "VIPs:"

1. What Lies Above Us

Values—the standards of behavior and of status deemed venerable to uphold
Ideals—the ultimate, supreme standards one aspires to reach
Principles—the maxims that guide action on a pragmatic level

The Lift: *The Appeal to a Higher Cause*

2. What Lies Ahead of Us

Vision—a clear definition on what changes could happen and what a future might look like through action
Ideas—thoughts on how a vision could come about through the actions and assets of people
Purpose—the potential benefits that arise when a vision is finally and fully attained

The Drive: *The Appeal to a Better Future*

3. What Lies Within Us

Valor and Virtue—the courage and integrity with which to recognize a higher cause and to act toward a purpose
Inspiration and Imagination—the wellspring of thought and motivation that generates new ideas
Passion and Perseverance—the emotional drive, enthusiasm, and resilience with which to overcome challenges and to achieve a goal

The Spark: *The Appeal to Inner Strengths*

These three VIP groupings can be summarized as the Lift, the Drive, and the Spark: the mission that uplifts spirits, the forward motion toward a fulfilling future, and the catalyst that instigates the journey.

These three sets of VIPs in an acronymic format is a modern reworking of Aristotle's classic rhetorical strategy of deploying *ethos*, *logos*, and *pathos*. The ancient Greek philosopher's three principles concisely capture how a leader's ability to understand the audience's standing, reasoning, and feeling are the basis for argument and persuasion.[3] Just as Aristotle advanced his concepts to promote better oration, these sets of VIPs are a memorable way to formulate a unifying message.

Notes

1. Elisabetta Iossa and David Martimort, "Risk Allocation and the Costs and Benefits of Public-Private Partnerships," *The RAND Journal of Economics*, 43(3) (2012): 442–474. doi:10.1111/j.1756–2171.2012.00181.x (accessed July 15, 2019).
2. Linda Putnam and Dennis Mumby, "Organizations, Emotion and the Myth of Rationality," in S. Fineman (Ed.), *Emotion in Organizations* (London: Sage, 1993), 36–57.
3 Purdue University Online Writing Lab, "Aristotle's Rhetorical Situation." https://owl.purdue.edu/owl/general_writing/academic_writing/rhetorical_situation/aristotles_rhetorical_situation.html (accessed Oct. 19, 2018).

2   The Strategic Mission Cycle

An organization's strategic mission is its commitment to an enduring purpose that is meaningful and fulfilling. Such a commitment means that the particular purpose holds an important core value to the group worthy of its time, energy, and resources. An enduring purpose is one that is lasting and holds its meaning over time. An enduring purpose is also sustainable in that it also holds its value over time.

To accomplish long-lasting and complex aims, groups assemble in order to harness the specialized talents of individuals and deploy them in particular roles through coordination and leadership. As many purposes take time to realize, different kinds of groups are formed to last beyond the lifetimes of individuals and achieve continuity, even permanency in their pursuits. Corporations, institutions, and governments are examples of embodiments formed in the pursuit of purpose that can span generations.

Over time, the conditions a group faces in achieving goals in keeping with its mission will vary, and often dramatically so. Economic competition, technological transformations, political revolutions, and social upheavals are among the many forces that can upend an organization's operating environment. For an organization to be successful in fulfilling its central purpose, it must be resilient and adaptive enough to change its tactics and strategies.

Amid the complexities and uncertainties, it becomes easy for leaders to become distracted or overwhelmed. A vision of the way forward can become fractioned by problems, breakdowns, and crises. Divided attention then can open new vulnerabilities, which leads to further fractionation of a leader's energies. Consequent frustration and failure may doom the mission, and even the organization.

To guide the active leader, it helps to have a roadmap, or a working model, with which to formulate a strategic mission and to determine the major tasks that build and shape the mission.

What follows is the Strategic Mission Cycle, a new model that incorporates critical components that are linked and mutually supportive. What makes this model unique is its use of twelve contributory concepts that start with the letter "I," arrayed within a circle like the hours on a clock (Figure 2.1).

What follows is an elaboration of each of these twelve *I* concepts in turn.

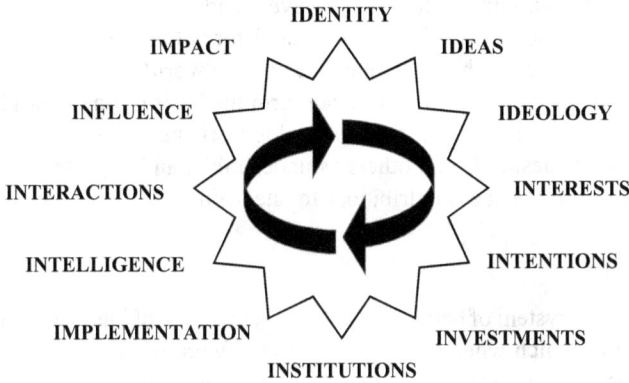

Figure 2.1 Twelve I's of the mission cycle

1. Identity

The mission cycle starts with Identity, the self-definition of oneself and any group to which one belongs. Identity is the answer given by oneself to the questions "Who am I?" or "Who are we?" Identity is fundamental to one's self-regard and self-esteem. Identity establishes one's core sense of place in the world and one's relationship to others. Extending from a person's core identity are the person's bonds and attachments to others with similar interests and outlooks. This web of attachments gives shape to the affiliations among people, giving rise to group identities.

2. Ideas

Within a mission cycle, ideas are the conceptual building blocks with which one formulates an agenda and the means to pursue it. They are the thoughts generated about possible goals, along with the strategies and tactics needed to attain them. Identity influences which kinds of ideas are surfaced and acted upon, in keeping with expectations that ideas are generated in kinship with one's identity rather than in conflict. For instance, one who identifies as an adherent to a particular political orientation, perhaps as a liberal, would be inclined to originate and support ideas that are consistent with liberalism rather than conservatism. Another source for ideas is one's intuition, the insight gleaned from past experience and a "gut sense." Such innate feelings often lead to fresh insights toward an issue or problem and ways to address it.

3. Ideology

One's identity and ideas conjointly contribute to one's outlook of the world. Ideology is the system of belief regarding the state of that world and one's role in it, as perceived as expressed by the individual or group. Ideology involves emotions and opinions about what is desirable or undesirable about the world, and about what should be done to achieve an ideal. Ideology is the answer in reply to the question, "What do we stand for?" Once answered, ideology becomes the system with which one discerns the world for events that affirm ideals over those that refute them. It can form the basis of one's own behavior and of one's affiliations. Ultimately, ideology orients the individual to view certain goals as desirable and others as undesirable, and to prefer those methods and strategies seen as contributory to one's aims.

4. Interests

An ideological system of belief then determines a range of interests, or the array of necessities which when attained would satisfy an overarching ambition. In basic terms, interests can be described as falling into two primary categories: acquisitive and preventative. Interests are the answer to the question, "What must we have?" Interests of an acquisitive nature are those that one strives to attain, namely objects, situations, or processes that one currently lacks. Conversely, interests of a preventative, or defensive, nature are those situations that one wants to avoid. The importance of both acquisitive and preventative interests can be tiered in cascading levels from those of the highest category deemed as vital, essential interests down to those that are of lesser importance, namely those interests that are discretionary, or optional to pursue. In this manner, acquisitive interests can be ranked in order of necessity: situations that one must have, ought to have, should have, or could have. Likewise, the intensity of preventative interests could range from those situations that one must avoid, ought to avoid, should avoid, or could avoid.

5. Intentions

As interests are sets of wants and needs that one seeks to fulfill, intentions are the actions considered in tandem with the necessary willfulness to achieve such interests. Intentions are the answer to the question, "What must we do?" As interests and intentions are linked together by the relationship between a higher purpose and necessary action, it follows that there is a strong tie between the importance of an interest and an urgency to act. A vital interest leads to essential, urgent actions, whereas a discretionary interest leads to a set of actions that are more deliberative and voluntary in character. As willpower is likewise tied to the gravity of interests, a vital interest would be correlated to a strong willingness to take action, whereas a discretionary interest would be associated with more moderate willingness. Furthermore, complicated, ambiguous conditions surrounding an interest may cloud or weaken intentions in ways that lead to an ambivalence, or even an aversion, to taking action.

6. Investments

Actions utilize resources, those necessary ingredients that a strategy consumes. Resources encompass the different forms of capital such as money, tools, personnel, and time. They can also encompass the less tangible forms of capital such as social connections, political favors, and cultural affinities. To equip intentions, these assets must be assembled, organized, and deployed. Investments are the answer to the question, "What assets or supplies must we acquire for our strategy to work?"

Investments are important in establishing a basis for setting expectations. The greater amounts of resources committed to a strategy, the higher the results expected of that endeavor. The correlation between interests, intentions, and investments is further extended as vital interests spur an urgency, a stronger willingness to act, and an accompanying drive to amass essential inputs. By showing off one's arsenal of assets, as what many countries do with military parades, one can set expectations that both intentions and resolve can be backed by capabilities.

7. Institutions

In order to translate investments into forward progress, a mission must have the means with which to activate assets and deploy them in an organized, purposeful manner. Yet assets cannot do work by themselves; they require human capital to bring them to life. Individual people often choose to congregate in organizations to concentrate expertise and allocate tasks, with multitudes of people joining together in emulation of a singular organism functioning on a larger scale. Organizations with long-standing missions are often called institutions, but they can exist under other similar names, such as *foundation, entity*, or *alliance.*

Institutions answer the question, "Who do we need to pursue our mission?" Institutions convert investments into three primary intermediates: the tools to do work effectively, the techniques to use tools efficiently, and the talent to use them judiciously. Institutions house internal capabilities and provide a structure governing their long-term evolution. They also embody the mission's intellectual home from which goals and strategies originate.

People not only serve institutions, but institutions serve their constituents by providing services beyond what an individual could do on one's own, particularly those that require specialized expertise and continuity. This mutual inter-reliance between the individual and the institution is a symbiosis that is beneficial to all participants.

8. Implementation

Institutions then dedicate their resources into purposeful plans of action that exert influence into surrounding environments. Implementation is the phase of a mission that involves a series of action steps that are executed under a supervising authority. It answers the question, "What actions must be taken to achieve our goals?" Implementation can involve various degrees of sophistication ranging from simple tasks to complex, multiphase, multiparty campaigns.

A fundamental unit of implementation is the operation. Operations are coherent, coordinated plans of action that aim to accomplish a specific objective on the pathway toward an ultimate goal. Operations can feed into larger campaigns, which themselves can feed into stages, phases, and theaters, each with their own designated target for achievement. The ultimate endpoint of implementation is the strategic goal, the structure and design of which will be described in another part of this volume.

9. Intelligence

Success or failure in implementation can pivot upon prevailing conditions surrounding operations and campaigns. Like weather conditions, policy conditions can range from large, diffuse "macro" factors such as broad political, social, and economic trends to local, on-the-ground, "micro" factors such as the actions and preferences of specific individuals. The forces and factors that could impact implementation can range from the predictable and knowable to that of the volatile and unknowable.

As implementation is about deploying investments in a risk-filled environment, gaining knowledge about surrounding circumstances is crucial for sound judgment and decision-making. Intelligence strives to answer the question, "What do we need to know?" ahead of and during implementation. Acquiring a state of knowledge involves not only collecting facts; it also involves the much more complicated task of assessing the strategic interests and intentions of pivotal leaders and their organizations. Such intelligence gauges other players' likely behavior within a range of expected circumstances, incorporating assumptions of their past and present actions. An intelligence apparatus acts akin to an analytical radar that illuminates the policy landscape and provides a leader with a clearer understanding of both dangers and opportunities ahead.

10. Interactions

Implementing strategy inevitably leads to encounters with the other players active in the operating environment. Some players will be allies, others adversaries, still others neutral or inactive. Links among them all could be fickle, even capricious: Allegiances can be switched, bought, or betrayed. Establishing links, agreements, and understandings involves a full set of political investments, or the efforts made to secure an alignment of power relationships favorable to one's own interests, or conversely, unfavorable to opponents' interests.

The choice of interactions answers the question, "Who do we need to achieve our goals and how do we work with them?" Avenues of engagement involve a wide array of formal and informal channels, ranging from those of an alliance-building nature such as cooperation and collaboration, to those with neutral overtones such arms-length transactions and negotiations, to those of an adversarial nature, such as competition, confrontation, and coercion. The question on choice of interactions may also be posed inward, directed to those acting within and for the organization. Internal interactions involving employees, board members, and management are just as critical to smooth and effective implementation as those involving external organizations, and involve issues of communication, coordination, and collaboration, along with the many factors adding to group cohesion.

Interactions can fall into one of three primary groups—the first being those of an assertive, offensive, or aggressive in nature. These interactions seek to win. The second group is interactions of a preventive, defensive, or protective nature. These interactions seek to avoid losing. The third group is interactions of a pre-emptive, disruptive, or dispersive nature. These interactions seek to avert threats before they arise. Phrases and terms coined within a military context, such as *The best defense is a good offense, pre-emptive strike, The enemy of my enemy is my friend,* and *divide and conquer* are examples of such hybrid offense-defense interactions.

11. Influence

Within a web of player interactions, influence is the ability to shape events toward a favored outcome. It is the exercise of a power to achieve a desired behavior, perception, or result. The choice of an act of influence answers the question, "How do we get what we want and by what means?" Often deemed "grand strategy" or the "calculus of power," this body of strategic thinking considers how players act to convert their realm of interests and intentions into actions and outcomes that matter to them.

In executing a plan, acts of influence are directed at those players deemed central and necessary to the progression of events. Those players assert their roles within complex political ecosystems that host many intricate balances of power. To reach their goals within crowded strategic terrains, players will seek to shape or alter others' perceptions and behaviors in ways thought to enhance their own prospects for success. Such ways of influence include negotiations, incentives, alliance building, public relations, favor trading, and many other forms of engagement.

The design of strategies and tactics relies on the use of assumptions, the set of chosen beliefs regarding the state of the world, particularly how people, processes, and objects behave and how they might act and react in particular circumstances. A well-elaborated plan invests in working assumptions about which factors and trends are active within an operating environment, including the configurations of other players' capabilities, their thought processes, and particular behaviors of important individuals and groups.

What engenders assumptions is a "theory of causality," a system of belief regarding the cause-and-effect relationships pertinent to achieving desired ends. It is a belief on how an action will produce a desired post-action result and can be described as a series of "if-then" propositions: "If action A is taken, then result B will happen." As contextual factors also matter in success or failure of an action, planning also includes presumptions regarding the conditions expected to surround a chain of actions, such as economic drivers, political overtones, or social attitudes.

Given the fickleness of human events, however, any theory of causality ought to build in a capacity for resilience. Even robust plans can encounter unanticipated obstacles or dramatically transformed circumstances that upend fervently held assumptions. To recognize new realities, a theory of causality should be re-assessed for changes among cause-and-effect relationships and be recast to include revised "if-then" assumptions.

Building one's influence involves attaining higher degrees of potency and optionality: expanding one's capabilities with which to assert power as well as widening the menu of tactical choices available to implement a strategy. This can drive multi-player behavior along starkly different tracks. In cooperative situations, players with like interests may join forces to pool capabilities and to combine their available options. In competitive situations, allied players are likely to coordinate in ways to constrain their opponents' capabilities and options.

The application of influence in either cooperative or competitive situations can fall into two primary approaches: by direct (or linear) means or by indirect (or nonlinear) means. The direct-linear approach makes immediate use of cause-effect relationships, typically by applying a force implementing an asset or asserting an argument. In contrast, the indirect-nonlinear style takes a more circuitous route toward goals by shaping events in the background, seeking to influence outcomes through contextual factors, and creating favorable conditions deemed "ripe" enough for a strategy to take place.

As societies change, how power is acquired and applied also evolves. Many studies have captured dynamics within this evolution, among the most notable are works about new ways in shaping behavior and a new taxonomy for the sources of power.

A major school of thought, advanced by Richard Thaler and Cass Sunstein, introduced the use of "nudging" behaviors that impart influence through the creation of various "choice architectures" that channel people to make choices among carefully selected options, a menu that incorporates benefits for both the individual and the sponsoring organization.[1] The nudging philosophy emphasizes the exercise of influence through judiciously crafted inducements and the illumination of choices over that of binary if-then, either-or propositions.

Another paradigm, originated by Joseph Nye, bifurcates the sources of influence into that of hard-power or soft-power, with hard-power being centered over the application of force and other means of coercion, in contrast to soft-power means of imparting influence through indirect means or through transmittal through shared, communal factors, such as through culture or by societal trends.[2]

The study of influence, in both formal and informal settings, continues to grow along with the expansion of technologies and tools being invented at a relentless pace and with ever-expanding scale. Changing cultural factors add to the complexity in how influence is attained and wielded in individual societies, compounding upcoming challenges to be faced by practitioners of global statecraft.

12. Impact

The physical sense of the word *impact* implies that a force is imparted upon an object, which then moves to a new position or is changed in some way. In the context of policymaking, impact also describes how a force, or influence, is exerted to achieve an effect. Unlike what occurs in the world of physical matter, impact in responsible policymaking is the intentional change sought to benefit people and the environs about them. Policy impact is the desired, purposeful result that defines the success of a strategy.

The preceding elements of the strategic mission cycle culminate in creating an impact, purposely attaining an ultimate outcome. The assemblage of resources, motivation of personnel, entangling interactions, and assertion of power are all mission actions converging upon a desired end-state. The end-state is the terminus of a campaign, and answers the question, "What do we seek to achieve?" The end-state can be defined as a single objective or it can be defined as a set of multiple objectives; it can be grouped across any number of themes or sectors. A sporting team, for example, would have a single primary objective of winning a game, but it can also have a secondary series of objectives that might include attaining key offensive and defensive statistics. The team may also have non-game related objectives, such as contributing in charitable ways throughout the community or simply earning a profit by season's end. Whether singular or plural, end-state objectives are what a strategic campaign seeks to reach with its efforts.

Impact is not only about attaining a specific set of outcomes; it is also about achieving results that matter. To be worthy of effort and risk, the objectives of the end-state must create benefits that improve upon the original state or that protect against a worse outcome. Furthermore, it also matters to stakeholders that a strategic campaign wins benefits above and commensurate to the effort and investment expended. The primal question in war and peace, *Was it worth the blood and treasure?* refers to the high and compelling standard by which the price of conflict in lives and resources might be judged relative to its achievements.

Whereas the word *objective* implies those goals that are observable and tangible, many achievements have non-objective, or subjective, outcomes in mind. Chief among subjective outcomes are those with psychological or emotional impact. As campaigns work to achieve objective outcomes, they can also seek to achieve subjective outcomes by either attaining a positive emotional end-state or avoiding a negative emotional end-state. Positive emotional impact includes such feelings as satisfaction, fulfillment, elation, and euphoria. Negative emotional states include demoralization, despair, dejection, and depression.

Sometimes the price paid psychologically can exceed what was gained objectively, especially when a campaign has been long and arduous, depleting the willpower among those who fought to soldier on. Yet there have been many historical instances, for instance during wars and disasters, in which people confronting hardship gain an emotional fortitude that sustains them to carry forward.

The degree of psychological impact is mediated by the role of expectations. Expectations are the projected outcomes for actions and situations based on past experience or an accepted standard. Expectations set the reference point by which an actual result is judged to be a success or a failure. In general, meeting or surpassing expectations is deemed a success, whereas falling short is typically considered a failure. Yet there are notable exceptions in which smaller than expected wins are perceived as losses and smaller than expected losses are perceived as wins. This has happened frequently in election results across a variety of countries when an underdog over-performs or when the favorite wins by an unexpectedly narrow margin. Thus forms the "expectations game," the struggle by parties to establish preferred sets of expectations as the chief referee in deciding, by psychological means, how an outcome is called either a victory or a defeat.

Psychological impact can arise from surprises, the intrusion of the unexpected. Surprises can fall into the two groups: those that are welcome, positive, and serendipitous or those that are unwelcome, negative, and deleterious. Surprises can stem from plain luck, good or bad, but they can also be imposed intentionally when one party foists a situation onto others. Surprise attack is a universally known military stratagem designed to achieve victory through sudden, unexpected aggression. Yet surprises of a positive and dramatic character have transformed situations previously weighted by past expectations and old enmities: Richard Nixon's visit to China in 1972 or Anwar Sadat's visit to Jerusalem in 1977 are landmark historical events whereby those leaders seized the diplomatic initiative to recast the strategic landscape toward peace and stability.

Even upon achieving a desired outcome, newly won benefits may prove ephemeral. End-state conditions are rarely static as surrounding factors can all change—from physical conditions in the environment to psychological conditions in the mindsets of people. Winners may move on to new priorities whereas losers may mount comeback attempts. Random factors can intrude and alter existing dynamics. An achievement itself may be disruptive: A new end-state may provoke reactions that then ripple into new conditions, perhaps disturbing or even erasing all prior assumptions. Thus, impact leads to implications, those reverberating consequences that arise from the reactions and adjustments made by other players. Consequences provoke new circumstances that can complicate the landscape enough to alter standing assumptions and affect the conduct of future campaigns. The prospect of post-goal situational transformation adds further complexity to strategic thinking.

The drive to "achieve what one believes" completes the full mission cycle from identity to impact. A mission fulfilled creates an impact, a result that is meaningful and beneficial. Achievements can set off a chain effect extending into future dynamics. Winning can affirm one's identity, and that can lead to new ambitions and goals. On the other hand, losing can also set off a reexamination of one's priorities, and defeated parties may be determined to bounce back to pose as an even stronger threat.

Heuristic Analysis of Impact

A convenient way to think about impact is to consider it divisible into two prime factors: results and valuation. Results are the change that is created from the original set of conditions into a new set of improved conditions. Valuation is the change in value from a baseline to a higher level. To summarize, the following heuristic equation is proposed:

IMPACT = RESULTS × VALUATION

with supporting equations:

RESULTS = (IMPROVED CONDITION − ORIGINAL CONDITION)
VALUATION = (IMPROVED VALUE − ORIGINAL VALUE)

Consider a simple example from business: If a hypothetical maker of "widgets" currently produces 100,000 units at $1 each per month, then its monthly revenue is $100,000. If the maker now wishes to invest for growth and seeks to expand double output (results) and improve its product so that it can fetch a higher price, say 50%, in the market (valuation), then its financial impact equation could look like this:

IMPACT = (HIGHER LEVEL OF OUTPUT − ORIGINAL OUTPUT) ×
     (HIGHER PRICE − ORIGINAL PRICE)
   = (200,000 − 100,000) × ($1.50 − $1.00), or
   = 100,000 × $0.50,

so that IMPACT from investment project = $50,000 in higher revenues per month.

Yet many campaigns that achieve impact produce intangible results and intangible value, especially in the realms of public policy and businesses involved in social impact projects.

Tangible results are typically those that can be quantified or identified in some objective way. In contrast, intangible results are subjective, or regarded by the judgment of opinion. Emotions are a prime example of an intangible factor that can shift as a result of a strategic campaign. Emotions are also the basis for intangible valuation by creating opinion that either appreciates or depreciates the new situation. An organizing matrix can be constructed that encompasses these interactions.

Table 2.1 guides a fundamental assessment for identifying outcomes and their valuations. A company producing a good or service would be primarily be found within the tangible category. Its results would be objective—quantities of items or transactions sold, for example, and the financial valuation would be calculated through standard accounting measures. The company could also have intangible results resulting from its efforts, very possibly from heightened

Table 2.1 Matrix of results-valuation vs. tangible-intangible

	TANGIBLE	INTANGIBLE
RESULTS:	Objective Quantifiable and Identifiable	Subjective Emotional and Psychological
VALUATION:	Calculable or Estimatable	Opinion-based or Judgmental

morale and an emotional sense of accomplishment and belonging. Valuation of such intangible results, however, is more difficult to assess than tangible results and would be a matter of one's judgment, an innate sense of the implications for the company's future prospects.

By comparison, a social impact campaign, perhaps a non-profit entity, may have a primary aim of supporting a high ideal through its mission. That mission may involve achieving sets of tangible results, such as the numbers of needy individuals given hot meals and shelter. Valuation of this laudable project can involve a tangible valuation—dollar savings to society at large from the prevention of worse outcomes—as well as an intangible valuation—the strong sense of community and humaneness in helping the less fortunate as well as the beneficiaries' sense of appreciation and gratitude for that help.

Still, for times when the difficulty of assigning numerical values to results or discerning observable outcomes for intangible factors is too complex or challenging, intermediate proxies might be used to gauge impact. For example, polling of public opinion is a common method for discerning how communities have responded to a particular public relations campaign. The stock market uses a measure called the volatility index, known by the initials VIX, to gauge the level of pessimism and fear embedded in stock and options prices.[3]

A heuristic equation is not a strictly functional mathematical equation, but acts to simplify complex ideas into a compact, more readily understandable form. Here, the multiplying operation could work for quantifiable results, such as those in the world of finance. For non-quantifiable outcomes, the impact equation could be simplified to yield an additional insight that complements the RESULTS × VALUATION equation:

$$\text{IMPACT} = (\text{TANGIBLE} + \text{INTANGIBLE})\ \text{OUTCOMES}$$

Making this equation additive invites the consideration of the set of circumstances and outcomes that lie within the realm of human nature, in addition to those that are objective and observable. As psychological impact can affect states of mind, intangible factors are worthy of further elaboration to assess how they might shape underlying motivations.

One way to consider this is to assume that success is not only pursued for the benefit of tangible outcomes but is sought to enhance one's own reputation, or leadership track record. Reputation as a form of intangible gain is desired as it confers upon the individual a "halo effect" that might translate into promotions and other forms of advancement. Reputations are further heightened when they occur in the form of surprises that exceed conventional expectations. Conversely, reputations may not rise as much, or may even weaken, when achievements are perceived as falling short of prevailing expectations. These dynamics can be incorporated into the following equation:

$$\text{REPUTATION} = \text{RESULTS} - \text{EXPECTATIONS}$$

This relationship implies that one's professional and social standing are tied to achieving results beyond those which have been already anticipated; that is, a halo effect is earned when one is able to create improvements from an original state of affairs that exceed an existing level of expectations. The equation emphasizes two leadership imperatives: to seek positive change and concomitantly to influence the sphere of expectations surrounding one's performance. Shaping expectations then becomes a necessity as an investment to enhance one's set of intangible assets. This may involve playing down one's prospects for success so that if achievements do happen, they are seen in the context of modest expectations. If one is to injudiciously brag or unnecessarily talk up one's prospects, then success, even if outstanding, might become discounted or even ignored when results are compared against excess expectations.

Notes

1. Richard Thaler and Cass Sunstein, *Nudge: Improving Decisions About Health, Wealth, and Happiness* (New York: Penguin, 2009), 83–102.
2. Joseph S. Nye, Jr., *Soft Power: The Means to Success in World Politics* (New York: PublicAffairs, 2004), 11–18.
3. Chicago Board Options Exchange, "What Is the Cboe Volatility Index (VIX Index)?" www.cboe.com/products/vix-index-volatility/vix-options-and-futures/vix-index/vix-faqs#1 (accessed Oct. 18, 2018).

3   The Strategic Mission Triads

In formulating missions for their organizations, leaders must "gauge and engage": they must assess situations, make judgments, and then motivate stakeholders. They must take stock of strengths and weaknesses, make sense of their organizations' surrounding environments, and declare an effort to achieve desirable goals. To do this, leaders must manage through varying levels of detail, from the macroscopic (where large issues loom) to the microscopic (where particular, specialized characteristics prevail).

The complexities and intricacies of their organizations and their environments can be overwhelming, and the demands of daily activities can easily consume time and attention. Delegation and organization help to simplify and to clarify the universe of activities, but even with help, the fact remains that leaders' own thinking about forward strategic issues can become clouded by obligations to existing problems.

To guide thinking about an organization's forward agenda, the following sets of strategic mission triads with three interconnected elements give an overarching perspective with which to identify and then design future missions. These triads help to simplify a dynamic environment into smaller, clearer frames.

Each of the three elements in a triad can provoke questions about the right way forward or which underlying tensions, problems, and dilemmas need to be confronted. For example, a leader using the Three D Triad could ask: What is our organization's overall sense of direction? What is our ultimate destiny? What specific destinations, or arrival points, can we achieve with available resources? Like other frameworks, triads jumpstart a thinking process about major issues to weigh, and using them consistently creates an instinctual habit for methodical deliberation.

The Three D Triad: Direction, Destination, Destiny

1. Direction

From the myriad of options available to them, leaders are expected to chart specific directions for their organizations. From their stature and authority, they are entrusted to gauge situations, apply judgment, and then make decisions, big and small. In deliberating choices, leaders adopt their own styles of decision-making, relying upon a personalized set of criteria and processes. Each person's style is rooted in an individual's experiences from the past and values in looking toward the future. These factors, among many others, add up to a leader's sense of direction, or a primary orientation in how they approach situations. This sense of direction is an acquired perceptual posture toward the world, and it becomes expressed as a person's leanings and inclinations in choosing what to think and how to act. In other words, a sense of direction emanates from a person's preferences and predilections.

A sense of direction can be further refined into two basic apertures, or the broadness of scale with which to perceive the world at large. The first is a narrow sense of direction, which is typically involved when issuing directives, exercising command authority, and giving specific orders. The narrow sense is carried out in situations with a high degree of understanding about what is going on and what can be done. In particular, specialists within a profession seek to thoroughly comprehend a body of knowledge and master the essential if-then and cause-and-effect relationships, often to exacting detail. Equipped with this knowledge, the specialist has high confidence in making recommendations for a specific set of actions.

The second sense of direction is a much broader one, one that can involve intuition, a subjective "gut-sense" about situations. In contrast to the microcosmic world of the specialist, the panoramic world of a globalist teems with ever-shifting dynamics, portraying a grand picture of major forces in motion.

Without the anchorage of what is familiar, leaders must rely upon other personal sources of insight and inspiration to make decisions. Three major contributors to a leader's sense of direction are *preference, precedence*, and *allegiance.*

Preference is made up of the tastes, biases, and inclinations that result in certain choices being made consistently, even reflexively.

Precedence is the reliance upon past experiences and historical examples for lessons learned and for applying them toward similar situations.

Allegiance is the set of affinities and bonds to particular people, ideas, and organizations in ways that steer a leader's actions to be more in alignment with favored entities and ideologies.

These factors contribute to an intuitive mindset that views the world in a more convoluted manner and that involves emotions to a higher degree than the linear, analytical approach of specialists.

Pre-disposition of viewpoint then influences the inclination to act or react according to preferences. In assessing choices, pre-disposition can lead to biases in favoring one set of facts over another, or in preferring to work toward outcomes more in line with one's philosophy over that which is antithetical. In addition, ongoing ties and affinities to outside groups further shape leanings and biases in forming external alliances and partnerships.

A leader's well-formed sense of direction is a strategic skill that assesses the internal and external factors in the environment in making choices. Direction grants the initial impetus toward certain methods and pathways, and the agility with which one decides promotes a perception of confidence in their actions. To outsiders, leaders who express their sense of direction clearly and consistently project an additional sense of predictability about future actions. Predictability, in turn, gives added comfort to backers contributing various forms of capital. An articulated sense of direction then shapes overall expectations about how events are perceived, which goals are pursued, and what means are applied.

2. Destination

A direction is an orientation toward preferred sets of outcomes and the pathways to attain them. Typically, the expression of leadership direction is cast in varying degrees of generality, ranging from broad swaths of aspirations to narrow lanes for specific actions. For direction to become a motivating driver, there need to be additional propositions: that a direction leads to a specified reward, or benefit; that the reward is meaningful and compelling enough; and that there is a clear path of actions leading to that reward.

A direction needs a culmination, a fulfillment of the promise. Metaphorically, a direction points to a "promised land," a point of arrival that holds out the prospect for a gainful set of rewards. A declaration of the direction forward conjures up a journey, from a current state of affairs toward a new, more desirable end-state. It is the destination that specifies the particular arrival point, or terminus, for the journey. Often that journey is fraught with risk and uncertainty, or even involves grave danger, such as undertaking a military campaign. To motivate followers to endure hardship and sacrifice along the journey, leaders need to specify both the accomplishment and the gains to be won in clear and appealing terms. Defining the destination with high specificity allows others to judge the ultimate value of a campaign and the desirability to participate in it.

A casual hypothetical example: If a professor was to reward a classroom of high-performing college students a free trip from the U.S. east coast, with their only direct expense being that of their time, one would expect a room full of murmuring anticipation. If the destination were to be revealed in a progressively specified manner from vague to detailed, such as: "somewhere out west," "west coast," "California," "San Francisco," and finally "Pier 39 at Fisherman's Wharf," one can expect more takers, some no doubt with expressed glee, as the destination becomes clearer and clearer. The declaration of the final destination makes the value of the destination most apparent as visions of strolling along Fisherman's Wharf, riding cable cars, and viewing the majesty of the Golden Gate Bridge becomes more vivid and appealing. But specification may also lead to disappointment for some: perhaps some hail from the Bay Area, some may have visited previously, and still others may prefer to go to other places. The specification of destination clarifies the value of the proposition, and therefore allows those to make choices according to their interests and needs.

Extending this example to public affairs, a candidate for a prominent office typically makes statements of a general nature that appeal to a broad range of

voters, such as that person's promise to "improve education" and other posi-
tively worded but vague pledges. If the candidate were to promote a highly
specified destination, perhaps the provision of free college tuition for all quali-
fied students, the electorate now has an ability to make a judgment about the
desirability of such a goal: Some may become wildly enthusiastic, whereas
others more reticent, given the prospective costs of the endeavor. Specification
invites consideration on a more concrete basis, but providing such clarity can
be a matter of judgment as divisions may arise from doing so.

For leaders with operational responsibility, the specification of destination
is at the core of their duties. To fulfill an organization's mission, the leader is
entrusted to translate its mandate and to convert resources and efforts into substantive accomplishments. To do that, the leaders set a direction, a broad-based
charter indicative of esteemed values, and then identify a destination that makes
clear a desired outcome. The head of an educational agency, for example, might
translate a presidential mandate to improve education into a specific destination,
such as raising a national test score among college-bound high schoolers by 5%
over ten years or raising the teacher-to-student ratio by a minimum of 20% in
Miami, Florida. The destination identifies the target for achievement and, assuming that it is accepted as meaningful, beneficial, and attainable, provides a motivation for internal teams and external stakeholders to work toward it.

In the exercise of leadership, the declaration of destination crystallizes the
promise of an organization's mission into proposed achievements in keeping
with its mandate and overarching values. Destination is also central to how a
leader refines a broad-based call of direction into specific operational targets
and a proposition of benefits. The clarity provided, however, may spark debate
and conflict, as some parties may find a destination highly motivating whereas
others may find it unappealing. The choice of destination and the degree of
clarity with which it is described become a matter of discernment for a leader
to contemplate with care and acumen.

3. Destiny

Within this triad, direction is the orientation toward chosen preferences or certain ways of interacting with the world at large. That direction points toward
a horizon of possible opportunities consistent with the set of values of the
group. Leaders look out toward the horizon and specify destinations, the designated points of accomplishment within the scope of an organization's capabilities. Reaching those destinations unlocks the value that can be enjoyed by the
group's stakeholders.

Upon reaching a point of arrival after spending time and effort, leaders and
followers alike would likely ask themselves and each other, "What's next?" A
destination is an endpoint, a termination of a journey, yet an accomplishment
can leave participants asking what else lies ahead and yearning for even big-
ger challenges. For an organization to sustain its mission beyond short-term
goals, it needs to express a longer-term promise that is motivating and meaningful. That promise is embodied in a calling toward a *destiny*, the appeal that

a perpetuity of grander horizons and a multiplicity of desirable destinations lie ahead.

Whereas sharing the common linguistic root of *destin-*, the words *destination* and *destiny* diverge into two separate yet complementary concepts. Destination can be seen as a definite endpoint at "ground level," an accomplishment that yields practical benefits. Destiny can be considered as an indefinite upper realm, at "cloud level," where achievements fulfill emotional aspirations. Because people possess values, they wish to achieve goals in accordance with their beliefs and preferences. Whereas goals can be defined down to singular points, human values and beliefs can live on for generations, and can change and evolve in boundless fashion. Thus, what fulfills those values and beliefs will likewise change. Declaring a destiny is claiming that the future holds forth a promise of emotional fulfillment, whether by achievement or by affirmation of one's values.

Destiny entwines both a premise and a promise. Destiny advances a proposition that for any set of human characteristics, virtues, ideals, and identities there are sets of expressions in the real world that affirm it. The proposition of destiny further holds that virtues and ideals are long enduring and worthy of sustenance. Destiny also advances a promise that people, by subscribing to a cause or by supporting a particular leader, will find authentic satisfaction of their needs and aspirations. Destiny's chief promise is the emotional resonance that suffuses throughout a stakeholder group, whether it be a community, country, culture or civilization, when destinations are reached and goals are achieved.

It is emotional resonance that differentiates destiny from fate. Whereas both ideas presume that identity and ideals have an underlying predisposition to future outcomes, each diverges toward different directions. Destiny embeds the concept that innate characteristics of people or a cause will lead to a higher, better state of affairs in the future. Appeal to a destiny leads to a call for action to realize the cause. In contrast, fate pre-ordains a bleaker, even fatalistic, outcome in spite of all efforts. Proclaiming a destiny enlists action that is necessary for the cause to succeed, whereas accepting fate is to passively resign oneself to adversity believed to be pre-ordained.

With these starkly divergent outcomes, it is readily apparent that leaders would choose to invoke destiny as a motivating call rather than resignation to fate, as appeals to action are engaging and energized by optimism. Invocation of a destiny is an appeal to higher, lasting purposes and ever-wider horizons of opportunities.

As destiny calls forth a journey toward an idealized future that can be long, arduous, and even hazardous, a leader needs to strike an emotional resonance with followers by articulating the deep satisfaction, even elation, that can come about in reaching the goal after hard work and sacrifice.

With the sweeping promises that a destiny can call forth, it is not surprising that destiny is invoked frequently in the history of peoples and nations. In American history, the first half of the 19th century when the United States rapidly expanded westward to the Pacific coast became known as the era of Manifest Destiny. At the time, it was a widely held social and political belief that the unique ideals of the U.S., a country promoting freedom as an inherent right, should naturally be expressed by an expansion to go as far west as possible. This emotionally resonant justification created the momentum for settlers to populate new U.S. states and territories from the Great Plains of the American heartland to the Pacific coast.[1]

Once the physical span of the United States was settled and Manifest Destiny fulfilled, American aspirations extended into a broader notion of common values, national allegiance, and even lifestyle standards. Known as the American Dream, this set of ideals connected the positive elements of American character and historical experience to daily practicalities that included earning a higher standard of living, replete with autos, homes, and leisure time.[2]

A continent away, China's rapid rise to become the world's second-largest economy spurred a parallel notion of a "Chinese Dream," which fused aspirations of both people and the socialist nation-state.[3] This idea, still in evolution, combines some of the American consumer-oriented desires with a much higher degree of government-driven goals, such as industrial advancement and societal stability. Consistent with the differences between the American and Chinese sources of political authority, the Chinese Dream expresses a destiny still in line with collective willpower, in contrast to the American Dream, which expresses a destiny of success through individual achievement.

Destiny is a formulation of an idealized vision about the future state of a society or nation. The motivational power of destiny lies in a promised affirmation of common values and core identity through a progressive series of accomplishments that leads to an ideal. The shared effort creates a special emotional bond among adherents, and the achievements along the way reinforce the mission and justify endured hardship.

Figure 3.1 summarizes the complex interrelationships between Direction, Destination, and Destiny and the key attributes of each. Direction is the orientation

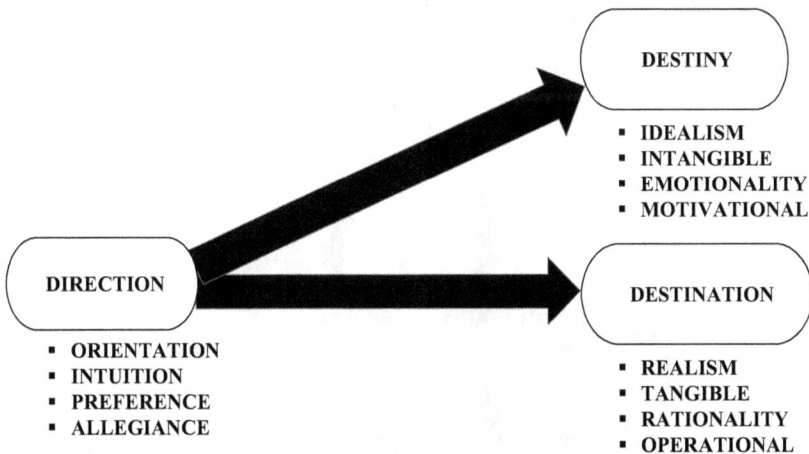

- **DESTINY**
  - **IDEALISM**
  - **INTANGIBLE**
  - **EMOTIONALITY**
  - **MOTIVATIONAL**

- **DIRECTION**
  - **ORIENTATION**
  - **INTUITION**
  - **PREFERENCE**
  - **ALLEGIANCE**

- **DESTINATION**
  - **REALISM**
  - **TANGIBLE**
  - **RATIONALITY**
  - **OPERATIONAL**

Figure 3.1 3D: Direction—Destination—Destiny

toward sets of preferences derived from held values; Destination is the specific point of arrival that upholds a held value; and Destiny is the notion that held values can be further perpetuated in emotionally resonant ways.

The Three S Triad: Strategic, Systemic, Specific

If one were to simplify a view of any human-run entity, such as an organization or a nation, and model its behavior as to how a single organism might act, one could identify major patterns in how it is made up and what motivates it. An entity, like any living being, would act to secure its essential needs in order to survive, would rely upon a series of support systems, and would implement its particular role within a niche bristling with competitors. An organizational entity works as an integrated whole, possessing an outlook and exercising an array of functions toward a purposeful role. The business terms *corporation*, *incorporation*, *company*, and the legal term *corpus* express this sense of the embodiment of people banding together to form a unified whole. Each member contributes an individual role in the functioning of the whole entity. Leaders who act on behalf of the whole are imbued with a consciousness of its mission and of its surrounding environment, and make judgments regarding desirable goals and strategies. The entity acts according to a given deliberated design, incorporating beliefs of how it should be organized and how it should operate.

A simple breakdown of this holistic viewpoint is to think of an organization as having three functional levels: *Strategic*, *Systemic*, and *Specific*. Each can be considered by itself, or in combination with the other two.

Figure 3.2 shows the general hierarchy of the three levels, with the Strategic having the broadest view of the opportunities, Systemic serving internal needs through interconnections, and Specific exercising assigned functions and actions. The dynamic is two-way: Not only do strategic decisions flow down to orders for specific actions, but the intelligence acquired from those actions flows up to those in command, closing a feedback loop that enables further refinement for future decisions.

What follows is an elaboration of each level in turn.

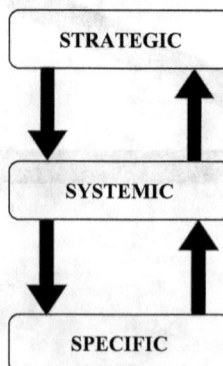

Figure 3.2 3S: Strategic—Systemic—Specific

1. Strategic

It is at this level in which leadership assumes the authority to take command and to make choices that engage the entire organization. The strategic viewpoint is the primary outlook on how the entity survives, how it functions, and how it would succeed in its chosen environment. At the core is an understanding of its identity, its mission, and its capabilities. A strategic viewpoint not only is about one's own standing, but it is also about formulating a judgment about the trends at play, the actions and reactions of its allies and rivals, and about possible future states of its environment. A strategic viewpoint integrates both tactical moves necessary for short-term success with anticipatory, deliberative moves, which position the entity for longer-term gains. This "macro" outlook balances immediacy, the need to act on today's priorities, with that of optionality, the retention of future possibilities.

The strategic viewpoint contemplates what would be the best and full interests of the organization as a whole. The first priority is assuring the very survival of the entity and, consequently, how to go about securing vital needs and creating optimal conditions for its existence. A high priority is identifying essential goals that create the value, which is both sustaining and affirming. Furthermore, the strategic viewpoint also considers what could be the lifespan achievements of the entity: that is, how to establish a lasting, historical legacy that can bridge generations. The strategic viewpoint then becomes a transgenerational responsibility, one that melds the immediate demands of leadership with the long-range considerations of stewardship so that experience, knowledge, and values are passed on.

This duty to sustain the relevance of an institution extends to uplifting those in the ranks of "followership," including employees, beneficiaries of the group's work, and societal supporters. Without implementers, an organization could not move forward toward goals. Without the fruits of work done, an organization cannot create value for those who need it. And without a social impact that is appreciated by broader stakeholders, an organization becomes aimless.

The strategic outlook encompasses the interests of the entity in its entirety: its founding mission, its structural makeup, and its functional capabilities. This outlook is integrative, formulating a commanding vision of what exists and what could be done through the assemblage of experience, perception, and information. As situational complexities and uncertainties abound, formulating a strategic outlook is as much a matter of subjective judgment and nuanced interpretations as it is of objective analysis of prevailing conditions.

2. Systemic

An entity, like any living organism, acts as a whole and is made up of a confluence of systems within itself. Systems are the arrangement of functional units working in conjunction with each other to produce a useful result, product, or action. They work in three basic steps: by collecting necessary inputs, converting them through a process, and producing an intended output, which could feed yet another system in sequence. Healthy, well-functioning systems, whether resident within a being or organization, work in harmony with each other and produce vital, essential needs as well as secondary supportive functions.

A simple, binary way to classify systems is to consider them as either internal or external to the entity. Internal systems are how entities are constituted as individual beings. External systems are the arrangements that might arise through the entity's interactions with other individuals or organizations within a particular field. External systems form various webs of interactions, in various degrees of cooperation or competition, and might be seen as a broad eco-system in which a stable equilibrium might be formed among all participants. Industrial sectors, comprised of networks of producers and suppliers, are often analyzed as a dynamic system responding to multitudes of market signals and competitive pressures. International relations are frequently seen from an external system perspective, assessing national actions through models of state behavior.

Systems arise from the driving force of specialization, whereby particular functions are exercised by units, akin to an organ in a living being, that are effective in implementing a role and efficient in doing so. How systems and their constituent components come about and are arranged can be attributed to three primary sources: *advantage, assignment,* and *association.*

Advantage is a unit's superiority in the performance of a task or in the efficient usage of resources; such an edge creates an incentive for the perpetuation of that unit in that role.

Assignment is the discretionary distribution by leadership of individuals or groups into niches within a system. An example is how a military command might order its soldiers to serve in various forces or functions, subject to individual skills and overall needs.

Association is the degree of linkages, whether deliberative or fortuitous, between units within a system, or even across systems and entire entities themselves. Such cross-linkages can be forged by communication, coordination, and collaboration among systems and underlying units. These linkages can range in strength from near full integration, as might be seen among specialized industrial supply chains, to loose, informal affiliations, such as community sporting leagues.

For leaders considering strategic moves, assessing systems is important for two reasons: design and diagnosis. How well an organization's internal systems are arranged determines its overall ability to function and to achieve its intended mission. How its external environment is configured by prevailing factors and by the actions of other players influences the organization's degree of difficulty in reaching its goals. In planning, judgments about internal and external systems and how they might perform under real world conditions add to the design of a campaign by instigating questions of operational and tactical nature, such as: What internal functions need improving, and what persuasion efforts are needed to enlist allies or deter adversaries?

The intricacies of critical systems can create points of vulnerabilities that, if stressed during operations, could lead to breakdowns. The understanding of systems is essential for diagnosing causes of a failure, as the knowledge of how components work individually and in unison informs choices on fixes and preventive measures. Likewise, awareness of the interplay of systems in the external environment when things go wrong provides an ability to reshape the landscape of actors and factors toward repairing or restoring a situation.

3. Specific

The strategist often contends with the ever-present tension between striving for idealism and struggling with the realism of the everyday world. An organization's mission may proclaim its dedication to bold and lofty principles, yet their worldly fulfillment is constrained by the reality of limited resources and by the plethora of complicating interests and actions of other parties. At the core of this tension is that idealistic aims are typically couched in broad, generalizing, and sometimes simplistic terms, whereas getting specific things done can be thwarted by the realities of the everyday world. Optimism at the start of a campaign can become depleted when mistakes are made, when accidents happen, and when fickle supporters defect. Misplaced, excessive faith in the performance of others can disappoint when they fail to perform in some way. The aphorisms "The devil is in the details" and "Be sure to read the fine print" express seasoned advice about diligence ahead of commitments.

The values pursued by adherents can be divergent in nature, with broad appeal and open-ended promises for opportunity. When advocated, values and ideals can be unbounded, without strictures or structures to guide their meaning toward specific outcomes. Strategic leaders interpret mission values and make definitive choices on how to best reach goals. They must exercise a skill in convergence: shaping the intent of their values into workable solutions. To do so, they need to be proficient at making their ideas and strategies pragmatically specific, distilling them into identifiable cause-effect relationships.

The act of specification is to provide a sharper degree of clarity and higher degree of precision, honing the original, rough-cut idea down to a clearer level of understanding. By narrowing and shaping broader concepts into discrete, better-understood meanings, specification makes both knowledge and intentions more actionable. Engineering specifications, for example, would convert planning sketches for an object such as a satellite into elaborated blueprints laden with numeric measurements and precise assembly instructions.

Adapting a specification approach in strategic affairs may not ever be as mathematically intricate as what is done in engineering, yet specification can produce a clearer, much-needed picture of the task ahead. Whereas some aspects of a problem can be treated quantitatively, specifying the qualitative, non-tangible features of strategic issues can be challenging. A means to do this is to first break down an undefined aim into sub-dimensions or classifications that are better understood by a particular community and to continue the specification process as needed, down to even more exacting terms.

An example is to consider the simple two-term cause-effect paradigm in which both terms, *cause* and *effect*, are generic in form. If a hypothetical group is working in education with the mission to improve test scores among disadvantaged youth, it might begin with an assessment of a desired outcome within its capabilities. A basic specification process could reveal some options and help the group gauge which one it could implement. The cause-and-effect relationship could be disaggregated into simpler elements that make up an equation in this form:

ACTOR + ASSET + AIM + ACTION = ACHIEVEMENT

If a desired educational achievement is specified, say the group believes in working toward a goal of improving a science test score by 10% over five years in the state of Florida, then a specifying analysis can be done for the other side of the cause-effect equation to see how each link in the Actor—Asset—Aim—Action chain could be further specified in ways that make sense.

To extend the example, the Actor might be designated as being an industry or social sector, the organization itself, or its internal departments, all the way down to roles or even named individuals. The Asset could be defined as a capability, such as proven skill-set in online communications, or as a particular tool, such as web-based video coaching. The Aim is the intention to work toward a beneficial purpose or outcome, namely more skilled and knowledgeable students. The Action could be defined in a range from a generalized national launch to a narrow rollout to designated school districts and implemented according to a certain timetable.

Through specification, a baseline strategy can be proposed with sufficient clarity so that its value can be judged, debated, or modified. Specification is a means of objectifying issues and concepts in such a way that all those involved in a matter can comprehended them. Specification is a critical path for the crafting of *objectives*, the intended outcomes defined by commonly accepted characteristics.

The Idealism—Realism—Pragmatism Triad

An organizational mission is typically suffused with the values of adherents who work toward real-world objectives deemed meaningful and emotionally resonant. The animating set of values is a composition of ideals, or the zenith of aspirations that orient stakeholders in line with their desired destiny. *Idealism* is the state of allegiance toward reaching the purest of values, sometimes in defiance of conventional wisdom or the presenting reality. Idealism can incorporate a sense of optimism by adopting a belief that an outcome can be attained and the effort be proven worthwhile. As such, Idealism is the natural home for the realm of emotionality shared by an organization's stakeholders.

Achieving worldly objectives compels action within the realm of what exists at present, among people and parties whose interests may or may not be aligned with one's own. Idealism's natural counterpart, *Realism*, is the state of allegiance toward engaging the world as it exists and as it is expected to become. It takes into account the interests and motives of people and the organizations they inhabit, and it forms the basis of calculation and strategy in the pursuit of objectives. As a viewpoint that discounts emotions and emphasizes raw interests, Realism often perceives actions and intentions with a pessimistic or even cynical perspective. In contrast to Idealism, Realism is a doctrine of rationality about cause-effect relationships and how they might be influenced in order to win a particular goal.

Each half of the Realism-Idealism dichotomy is a necessary but incomplete partner to the other. Realism acted upon for its own sake, detached from ideals, attains objectives but does so without sentiment or emotional overtones. Idealism implemented without regards to realism can lead to a zealotry that disregards true costs or constraints. Yet Idealism is the necessary and innate drive to win objectives not only for tangible gain but also for emotional satisfaction, whereas Realism is the prism needed to focus upon real-life factors for accurate and effective implementation.

Pragmatism is the functional bridge between Idealism and Realism. It is an approach that seeks to achieve tangible, substantive results and to do so in the service of emotionally fulfilling, higher ideals. It recognizes and weighs the costs and compromises that abound and seeks the most practical pathways that ultimately lead to fulfillment of the grand mission.

In the pursuit of objectives, there can be a persistent tradeoff between an unyielding adherence to Idealism and the dispassionate operations within Realism. A prime challenge for pragmatists within this tradeoff is striking the right balance of specificity in objectives. Vague yet appealing idealistic notions, especially those connected to positive values, attract a broad range of support for a cause. But specifying high degrees of exactness within that same cause may create divided opinions about what is feasible. Reasonable people can sincerely differ about which routes, among many choices, are best in reaching a destination. One way may be quicker, but riskier. Another path may be the cheapest, but is the most time-consuming. Yet another may be calculated to be the most cost-effective, but may provoke political complications. With all possible combinations and complications, it is not a surprise that working toward an ideal can be frustrated, even thwarted, by the reality of intervening factors.

The contrast between Idealism and Realism creates tensions between campaigners, those who persuade others to enlist in a cause, and operators, those who implement a plan toward defined objectives. Leaders who transition from winning based on ideals to assuming operational responsibilities must interpret their mandates and translate them into a specific plan of action. Whereas details may provoke arguments, they are crucial in vivifying how theory can come to life. They also bring to the surface underlying assumptions gone unspoken, spurring the debate necessary for a decision on the acceptance or rejection of a plan.

The pragmatic skill of judicious, calibrated specification is a nuanced task of leadership, as it entails knowing the ways in which an organization's idealism relates to the realism in which it exists and further, knowing how to refine broad aims into clear goals and knowing how systems, both internal and external to an entity, function and what specific outputs or actions they produce. That skill also requires knowing how not to over-specify matters and sensing when providing too much information overwhelms or confuses. If there is a tendency to push too much information, the use of organizing structures, such as frameworks, helps prune down proliferating data points.

Gaining a command of relevant details aids in the design of systems and in the diagnosis of problems. Details of structure and function supply logic in assembling a system, a forward-oriented task. Details of problems supply the clues to how systems have failed and how they could be fixed, analogous to how a detective or a doctor might make inferences and deductions as to what happened. Yet another value of knowing the details is defensive: Knowing more reduces the ability of others to exploit information gaps, and knowing more about how vulnerabilities might arise from specific weaknesses leads to preventive measures.

A practical guideline in exercising specification skills is to undertake a "recipe book" approach. In taking action within a situation, the guidance given to implementers should take the form of a directive, with enough clarity and precision for them to follow on their own. A recipe is a model directive from the culinary world that offers widely understood components adaptable to the policy world: ingredients, quantities, conditions, steps, timing, and result. Implementing a strategy involves pointing to a desired outcome, assembling ingredients such as supplies, specifying the amount and qualities needed, following a sequence of steps, adhering to time limits, and making beneficial use of the result.

The usefulness of the recipe model is its concrete simplicity for communicating needed actions in a way that is both precise and concise. Precision is needed to define the correct measures, such as weights and temperatures, whereas conciseness conveys appropriate information economically. Without precision, directives become too vague to be followed consistently; wide interpretations of unclear orders in turn lead to outcomes that stray far from an intended result. Without conciseness, directives can delve into unnecessary complexities that fatigue and frustrate. Recipes are distillations of information and can serve as a commonplace model for organizing a process and acquiring the necessary "ingredients" for a line of action.

Part Summary

Strategic mission is the pursuit toward an enduring cause by people motivated by shared values and who choose to organize themselves into entities that can embody the key skills and knowledge needed to undertake the mission across time, even generations. The shared challenge for leaders and followers alike is navigating the complex interchange between the idealism of their mutual values and the realism of working in everyday life. The emotional uplift from ideals often is tugged downward by the gravitational pull of everyday realities, creating a conflict between striving to attain ideals to the utmost and having to contend with world filled with rivalries, obstructions, and limits. By deconstructing the elements of mission and the task of strategic leadership, one can appreciate the intricacies between the emotional resonance of an idealistic dream with the imperative to fulfill the dream through concrete achievements.

In determining ways to move the mission forward, the strategic leader assesses the systemic makeup of the organization and its operational performance in its external environment, among kindred actors sharing its strategic terrain. From these judgments, the leader undertakes campaigns that tread across landscapes filled with actors and factors. To do this successfully, leaders need to be proficient in understanding the elements of strategic policy design to follow, namely the domain, the goal, and the plan.

Notes

1. James Knox Polk, *Presidential Inaugural Address*, Mar. 4, 1845, paragraph 26 on "the right of the United States to that portion of our territory which lies beyond the Rocky Mountains." http://avalon.law.yale.edu/19th_century/polk.asp (accessed Oct. 18, 2018).
2. Jim Cullen, *The American Dream: A Short History of an Idea that Shaped a Nation* (New York: Oxford University Press, 2004), 1–9.
3. "Chasing the Chinese Dream," *The Economist*, May 4, 2013. www.economist.com/briefing/2013/05/04/chasing-the-chinese-dream (accessed Oct. 18, 2018).

Part 2
The Strategic Domain

4   Assessing Actors and Factors

Strategic mission is fulfilled by organizations achieving goals in keeping with the values of the group. Their leaders are authorized to make decisions on how to reach these goals, both choices made for internal arrangements as well as those made to interact in the external environment. Tangible goals also imply the consumption of tangible resources, for example, money, energy, labor, equipment, and time. Actions taken to reach the goal, in various forms such as projects or operations, consume resources, which are irreversibly used up. For example, fuel burned by an engine forever disappears when it is ignited into heat, light, and exhaust.

The direct implication of resource consumption is that there are costs, losses, and risks inherent in the pursuit of goals, and the failure to reach them can leave behind "deadweight losses." Whereas many classes of tangible losses theoretically can be replaced, such as broken machinery or departed personnel, replenishment can escalate costs and take time. What is irreversible is the loss of time spent when a project goes awry. Not only time spent is irretrievable, but so are other plausible options that might have been exercised. Opportunities foregone when one option is undertaken to the exclusion of other options, known as opportunity costs, multiply the stakes in decision-making, placing a premium on understanding what options exist and the pros and cons of each.

It is not just the prospect of tangible losses and opportunity costs, which loom when efforts fall short, but that of intangible losses as well. Intangible resources are those that are primarily non-physical in nature and can include intellectual property, social links, and political power. For leadership, the failure to achieve strategic goals puts at risk a critical intangible asset: reputation. For leaders, their license to lead stems not only from formal, conferred authority but also from informal authority earned from ethical, personal, and professional attributes. A reputation for past success, a track record, adds to a leader's allure, which in turn attracts more backing. Success begets confidence, which emboldens oneself to do even more and spurs a virtuous cycle of ever-higher deeds coupled with the esteem of accomplishment.[1]

Conversely, failure depletes confidence by raising doubt and second-guessing from detractors. A spotty track record scares away backers, and those who are in a position to help may demand more for their aid. Failure and mediocrity can set off a destructive cycle of de-investment and deconstruction, leaving an organization depleted and demoralized.

The allure of reward is mirrored by the realities of risk, both known and unknown. Complexities can arise from the variability of factors, the volatility of events and people, and the vulnerability of internal weaknesses. Hazards can surprise at any time. Allegiances can shift and past allies might now become foes, or vice versa. Furthermore, jeopardy to life and limb is a central risk within many professions: Military, intelligence, and law enforcement professionals routinely place themselves in front of dangerous risks, even death, in the course of their duties.

To act within the bounds of realism is to plan and act deliberatively and to make reasoned choices about risk and reward that fit the situation as it currently exists and as it might become in the future. Ignoring the realities of risk across its full totality is to blind oneself as to how failure can happen and what it could cost. Acting upon whims, without rudimentary thought given to the panorama of risk and danger, is to blunder forward onto a figurative minefield and make the missteps that could endanger resources and life.

To avoid acting with blinders, leaders should act with an outward mindset that seeks to perceive all pertinent factors in their realm as objectively as possible, not just those that favor their cause. Such a mindset also seeks to enhance their perceptual powers by acquiring tools and techniques that add to and organize knowledge. Above all, a leader's mindset is strategic in purpose, seeking a grand point of view that captures the major dynamics in which the organization acts. Being strategic anticipates and accepts that a dynamic world changes ceaselessly, in ways understood or mysterious.

However challenging it is to see the world in its full complexity, the leader's duty is to equip oneself to confront the realities ahead and, even amid the tumult of breaking events, to discern the key factors that could enable or disable the drive toward a goal. What strategists need are conceptual tools to simplify complexities, to clarify essential matters, and to organize their understanding so that they can decide upon the best path toward the goal.

One conceptual tool is to define the boundaries of the world in which an organization exists. Simple, everyday boundaries include border lines for the physical demarcation between different political states, or time zone lines defining areas that observe a particular time of day in relation to the global standard, Greenwich Mean Time. As organizations are dynamic bodies endowed with assets for use in the pursuit of a goal, their own functionality is the most widely understood way for identifying a group category. Organizations with similar functions, such as oil companies, make up a particular industrial sector. Specialty functions, like deep sea drilling, constitute an even smaller sub-sector, with additional specialties and subdivisions possible. Because similarities of function and purpose are subject to common prevailing forces, such as the market price of oil or the retail price of fuel, those kindred entities act within a shared sphere of activity, often termed its *functional environment*.

A functional environment for an organization is a conceptual space in which it acts as one denizen among others who also act in various roles and in which it is subject to particular forces, or drivers. The presence of other occupants and prevailing pressures establish the setting that confronts the organization as it considers its options and actions. Intangible yet inescapable cultural factors such as emotions, customs, and attitudes add to the environment. This enwrapping environment, also known as a milieu, commingles behavioral factors with those tangible factors of operational importance.

Like an ecosystem in the natural world, the functional environment for organizations shapes the actions and perceptions of its inhabitants. It does so by presenting opportunities for organizations to share interactions among each other, often in transactions common to a specialty or an industry. Some interactions may be cooperative, whereas some competitive; others may be short-term transactional, whereas other interactions may last generations, even centuries.

An environment is also influential for the sets of exposures cast upon its members, namely the forces that can act in ways beneficial or detrimental. A bank, for instance, acts within its functional environment, the financial system, to earn its profit; in pursuit of its mission, it is exposed to interest rates, foreign exchange rates, banking rules and regulations, political pressures, and numerous other financial forces exerted by other members in the industry.

The degree to which an organization responds to particular exposures in its functional environment is keyed to its sensitivities, or the reactiveness or the lack thereof, to its sets of exposures. The aforementioned bank would have different sets of sensitivities depending upon its positioning, perhaps as a mortgage lender, and its posture, perhaps holding a loan portfolio with a richer mix of residential loans than its peers. Thus, that bank would be keenly attuned to the behavior of the benchmark thirty-year interest rate as the bulk of home loans are tied to that maturity length. In contrast, that same bank, because of its chosen lending posture, would be less sensitive to movements of ten-year interest rates, upon which many shorter-term consumer loan rates are based.

Sensitivities shape the sets of actions and reactions by organizations in response to exposures, such as defensive measures taken against exacerbating factors or pro-active measures embarked upon to take advantage of beneficial changes in the environment. The example bank, anticipating rising 30-year rates and higher profits, may choose to increase its marketing efforts and attract more customers, who in turn are more likely to act upon their own sensitivities to act quickly and borrow ahead of rate hikes. If the bank thinks long-term rates will fall faster than short-term rates, it may choose to dial back on home loans and expand its marketing of short-term consumer loans instead.

A functional environment, by presenting exposures, touching upon sensitivities, and provoking actions and reactions, narrows down the expanse of a world with infinite detail into a more practical, finite arena where the forces and factors are more readily identifiable. Once the players and driving factors are clarified, it becomes possible to assess their own motivations and how they behave, giving rise to ideas about how best to interact with them or how best to defend against them, should they be threats.

In developing a strategy toward fulfilling major goals, a motivated, purposeful entity considers its own influence within its functional environment. Each entity has a unique configuration of assets and skills that it uses to achieve desired ends. Exercise of those skills, in interaction with others, creates changes in the functional environment, influencing other parties to react and adapt. A ripple effect of changes can makeover an entire environment into a wholly new setting, with some opportunities closed off and new ones arising.

The power and reach of one's capabilities define the span of influence within the functional environment, informally marking the outer limits of one's impact. Whereas ripple effects, those rings of secondary changes that radiate outward from a primary change, make it difficult to precisely determine a definitive boundary of reach, the capabilities for direct, first-order impact are a useful gauge of clout.

As organizations and nations undertake actions to achieve strategic goals, the prime objectives that fulfill their missions, they assess their functional environments and their own internal capabilities to create desired impact. The integrated view of one's functional environment and one's influential reach constitute the entity's *strategic domain.*

The strategic domain is an outcome from conceptualizing a working representation, or a mental model, of the configuration of forces between oneself and a particular goal. The strategic domain is a bounded realm that reduces the myriads of details down to the essential understanding of the "lay of the land," a visual metaphor for the terrain populated by participants acting toward their own interests. By better understanding the prevailing climate of factors and what is actually happening within the realm of concern, one can gain the situational awareness necessary to act in offense or defense and to argue knowingly and authoritatively about a preferred course of action.

The extent of a strategic domain can range from being wide and expansive, such as the classic geopolitical concept of the "spheres of influence" wherein the great powers of the 19th century, Victorian Great Britain and Napoleonic France for example, lorded over entire continents, down to the narrow and specific, such as what a real estate investor might face in managing a multi-asset portfolio within a particular city like Chicago. The strategic domain for an individual can be highly detailed, including one's workplace, webs of relationships, and professional platforms.

The strategic domain, by setting the stage for the dynamics at play, helps to focus one's attention upon those that matter in reaching a central goal. There are two categories, conveniently paired in rhyme so as to be more memorable, that are consistently present within a domain: *actors* and *factors.*

Actors, like those in the performing arts, are people who undertake roles in the domain, either as individuals or as part of a larger ensemble, such as working within a company or serving in a government. The word *actors* is apt because it expresses the essence that "an actor *acts*." Actors exercise their own personal and professional abilities and can work either in alliance with or in rivalry to others.

Factors are the prevailing forces that affect the actors in how they perceive the world and how they might behave. Factors can be specific to a particular sector, such as metal prices within an industrial sector like car-making, or systemic in nature that affects players more broadly, such as a prevailing political climate in a country. A memorable hook is to consider that "factors embed *facts*," the evidence that can be demonstrated objectively. By understanding both actors and factors, a strategist is better informed about what choices exist and what influential actions might be taken toward a goal.

Once the strategic domain is populated with the leading actors and factors, one can consider the challenges ahead using a basic three-element approach: *Content, Context,* and *Contest.*

The first of these, Content, refers to the substance at the core of an issue, whether it be a set of problems, a body of knowledge, or ongoing challenges. *Content* can also imply the organization of information in objective forms, such as data, charts, and maps that are understandable by those involved.

The second element, Context, refers to the circumstances in which the organization finds itself, including the history of the situation, backdrop of culture and values, and the meaning of winning or losing a particular goal. Context surrounds a situation with additional perspectives of other actors, providing further information about their interests and intentions.

The third element, Contest, points to the challenges ahead in the form of strains, struggles, and overt conflicts. The contest refers to upcoming conflicts that must be fought on the pathway to the goal. Entrenched interests will resist change and pursue counter-strategies. Natural barriers need to be overcome to build large infrastructure projects. Long standing cultural attitudes may harden communities against new ideas. By defining the conflict in terms of how one's own aims contrast against those of others, which actors and factors might oppose them and in what ways, one can begin to formulate a strategy and rally resources needed to win.

Defining one's strategic domain entails attaining a holistic understanding of the existing situation that is populated by the cast of interest-driven actors and by the environment of prevailing factors and how they altogether help or hinder one's own interests, capabilities, and aspirations. Gaining such a situational awareness equips one to fulfill one's own interests more intelligently, by discerning opportunities worth seizing or new dangers arising. Illuminating a clear vision of the landscape of surrounding dynamics enables one to design a more purposeful game plan and to make more effective and efficient use of assets than if such a vision was absent.

As any situational analysis can become overrun by complexities and be muddled further by perceptual biases, what helps are tools and techniques that winnow down to the key factors. To cut through the clutter and achieve valuable clarity, *frameworks* and *lenses* comprise a ready set of conceptual tools designed to aid the "optics" of perceiving prevailing dynamics and focusing on essential developments.

Frames are a way of defining issues and organizing information by the use of including and excluding criteria. Frames are used to spotlight issues of central importance while excluding or limiting those of peripheral importance. A basic, simple frame is to pose an issue in a binary way, such as pro-con, for-or-against, it-is-not-this, but-rather-that propositions. Frames are frequently used in the crafting of decision memoranda, in which a proposed action is posed as a yes-no, go-no go, approve-disapprove question. Even simple frames can surface conflicting viewpoints and bring about open debate about underlying rationales. Above all, frames help shape a judgment about the value of a goal and the implications of taking a particular course of action toward it.

A system of frames, taken to a wider scale, can be considered as a *framework*. In the leadership setting, a strategic or policy framework sets out major categories of issues, ideas, or principles that are linked together by a common theme, working purpose, or a specified relationship among them. Like a framework for a house under construction that provides the skeleton for further customization and embellishments, a policy framework also provides points of anchorage, or common foci, for issues to be structured in a customized manner. Additionally, frameworks can serve as an outline for the key issues needing to be addressed or as a checklist of requirements to be fulfilled.

A well-known business framework is Michael Porter's Five Forces Framework describing the interplay of competitive pressures in an industry: 1) buyers of a company's product; 2) suppliers of components of the product; 3) substitutes for the product that allow customers to switch away; 4) barriers to entry into the product's market that deter new producers; and 5) intra-sector rivalries among all companies encompassing all their interactions.[2] This analytical system highlights the major factors at play when a company considers whether or not to enter a market. Further research into each factor can create a mosaic of information with which to make a definitive decision. An additional benefit of a framework with generic components is its use as a template for analyzing a broad variety of situations. Porter's five forces, generic as they are, can be applied toward any number of business sectors such as industrial, technological, and financial.

Elements that make up a framework are typically broad categories, and what is needed are ways to assess and judge what is found within them. What are needed within frameworks are analytical tools with which to parse information and to make judgments toward decision-making. Such tools metaphorically act in the way of prisms and lenses—prisms by which to differentiate incoming information and lenses by which to "zero-in" upon desired details through an inclusion-exclusion process. Together they act to promote a higher degree of clarity than what casual observation might obtain. As frameworks typically encompass a larger swath of issues, lenses can be applied for more specific uses, such as defining the actors and factors in particular industries.

By bringing situationally pertinent features to the foreground and fading those of lesser relevance into the background, conceptual lenses simplify what is being perceived and magnify the specific features worthy of attention. In this way, preliminary judgments can be made based on the most prominent factors, whereas secondary factors can be reserved for future consideration.

A real camera is adjustable to capture a scene either broadly or narrowly, by manipulating its aperture, the opening for inbound light. In an analogous way, conceptual apertures for strategic thinking can be honed for the "precision decision" by setting a range of focus from a broad angled "macroscopic" perspective down to a sharply detailed "microscopic" pinpoint. The conceptual aperture, the mental perception for inbound information, can be set to the macroscopic, capturing the broad, sweeping vistas of an issue, such as the overall strategic interests of a nation, or the systemic strengths and weaknesses of a complex system. Obversely, the conceptual aperture could also be set to the microscopic, narrowing attention to the detailed intricacies of functions and interactions.

To extend the metaphor even further, analytical lenses sharpen the boundaries of a field of knowledge through four functions: *confine, define, refine*, and *streamline*.

The confine function is setting the inclusionary vs. exclusionary boundary that encloses a particular topic.

The define function is applying a specific, distinct meaning in a situation.

The refine function is adjusting definitions to take into account recent events or new knowledge.

The streamline function is enhancing effectiveness, efficiency, and aesthetics through selective pruning of features or adding emphasis to those most noteworthy.

On a cautionary note, lenses can distort, leading to a clouded view of an issue—some elements may become exaggerated beyond their true value, whereas other factors of high importance may become overly discounted. Furthermore as models in their own nature are exercises in simplification, they might cut out too much of what is relevant or include too much of what is not. A flawed vision about an issue can lead to misjudgments about the actors and factors involved and subsequently can result in wrong or ineffective measures being applied.

Frameworks indiscriminately applied or fervently subscribed because of past success can lead to decisions that are blind to current realities. It is especially hard to forego vivid tropes and themes pulled from history and applied to modern ills. For example, the presidential scandal of Watergate spawned countless iterations of new "scandal-gates" to describe corruptive events and malfeasances big and small and became used in other countries and languages, such as "deflategate" in American football or even a Spanish language "valija-gate" about a cash-stuffed suitcase smuggled and confiscated in Argentina.[3] More serious are visually appealing descriptors as well as historically anchored frameworks that are used to paint a similar picture for an ongoing crisis. In the 1960s, the tropes "containment" and "domino theory" was used in part to justify U.S. intervention policy in Southeast Asia, as an effort to establish a bulwark against further spread of communism especially in Vietnam. Ironically, Vietnam itself became an anchor-term for foreign policy quagmires, and was once wielded incessantly by veteran diplomat Richard Holbrooke during the Obama administration to describe the unfolding of the U.S.-Afghanistan war, so much so that his advocacy soon became discounted.[4]

A primary risk of a popular framework is that it can lead to "group-think," an excessively convergent style of perception that creates a predominant point of view. When immutable, conventional wisdom crowds out both diversity and dissent, it results in vulnerability to unseen or underappreciated factors. To stay relevant, frameworks and conceptual lenses should be evaluated and validated over time, and amended and refined as new conditions warrant. A track record of how well a conceptual tool performed in the past imparts a measure of confidence about its current usefulness, but vigilance and care should be taken to refresh and update it when circumstances change.

What follows within this chapter are three new frameworks (MEALS, Four G, and Vigilance-Diligence) that in different ways organize the strategic domain into discrete components that are mutually interlinked. Each in its own way supplies a head start in assessing a complex situation and identifying important factors, especially those that are not immediately obvious in a first-run assessment. They may affirm well-known factors, but they may also enrich existing paradigms by offering alternative factors to weigh. These three systems can be introduced within organizations to complement or supplement any analytic process already being used.

Chapter 5 introduces a conceptual toolkit that is comprised of a system of "line" words describing various elements of the landscape. This set of common, everyday line-words serves as a prompter on how to populate one's own understanding about the domain.

In addition to frameworks to gauge the strategic domain, there are additional new frameworks to be described in the book parts regarding the strategic goal and the strategic plan that organize ways to analyze the capabilities needed to reach a goal and how to assemble a series of linked objectives toward that goal.

The MEALS Framework

To parse a complex strategic domain, frameworks highlight patterns of facts and actions within pertinent categories of interest. As attention spans are pressured by constraints of time and by expectations to win objectives, frameworks should be concise, with a selective set of categories. An added value is if framework concepts can be made memorable in some way so as to be instantly retrievable during times of urgency. Compact frameworks with vivid "hooks," or gimmicks that use rhyme, alliteration, or acronyms, are more widely adopted than those that are too lengthy or are dryly prosaic. Useful frameworks act as *domain descriptors*, or mental prompts to jar one's thinking about important points that may be forgotten in the rush of business.

What follows are an introductory series of featured frameworks, followed by a series of featured lenses that focus on a single dimension of a domain. The frameworks emphasize the overarching concepts that a statesman could typically deem as necessary in the conduct of diplomacy, or that a military leader might consider in positioning forces in a contested region. In particular, the frameworks spotlight how actors and factors are arranged and some ways to approach them. The lenses are singularly focused on the use of "delineation," which is being introduced as the foundation of the line method of domain analysis.

Descriptors of our physical environment provide a rich menu of terms that have been adapted for ways to describe dynamics in the human universe. This is a five-element series of domain descriptors that share the suffix *-scape*, connoting that which exists upon or within a panoramic realm. Three "scapes" are novel descriptors: *Mind-scape*, *Eco-scape*, and *Air-scape*. The remaining two are familiar terms from the physical realm: *Landscape* and *Seascape*. Altogether they prompt consideration about the forces and factors at large, encompassing both external dynamics and the internal motives and behaviors of participants. A description of this series begins with the most conventional of the five descriptors: landscape.

1. Landscape

Landscape is an everyday word that pertains to the notable features residing upon a swath of ground. A strategic landscape is an adaptation of that idea to identify the configuration of forces and factors that may influence a desired course of action within a policy arena. A strategic landscape can be populated with features that might overlay upon an actual physical landscape, such as the arrays of military forces on a continent or the movements of humanitarian aid convoys in a drought-stricken area.

Using the concept of landscape as a setting for domain analysis aids in the visualization of any physical placement of forces and associated assets on a geographic stage. Topographic presentations make clear the configuration of one's own assets and of those of other players upon a terrain and can portray the relative value of their placement. By example, a basic military tenet for infantrymen is to seek and to control the high ground. Upon viewing a battle map that shows forces deployed in low lands, a commanding officer should be prompted immediately to move those forces to higher ground or to displace any enemy occupying them.

Landscape descriptors have become ingrained in the ways strategists and analysts think and communicate about how tangible assets are configured. The landscape is the backdrop for the concept of *footprint*, the descriptor for the dispersement of items across a geographical region. Among business analysts, *footprint* has become a common way to describe the distribution of operational units, such as stores within a retail chain. The footprint has become an object itself, serving as a visual marker in descriptions of strategic moves, as in these hypothetical statements: "The company is expanding its footprint of grocery stores in the sunbelt, anticipating revenue growth as the region's population grows," or "The company is shutting down its mall stores in the snowbelt region, reducing its footprint as online sales accelerate."

The landscape term *horizon* prompts thinking about prospects that lie ahead in the future. Motivational leaders frequently invoke a call for followers to strive toward a "horizon of opportunity," a vista filled with promising goals worthy of achieving. But a horizon might also portend incoming trouble: defense analysts might describe future dangers as lurking on a "threat horizon," suggesting the hazards' inbound direction and the need to confront them in time. Diplomats engaging in a grand review of the roster of issues or mutual interests at stake use the elegant French term *tour d'horizon*, whose literal meaning in English is a "tour of the horizon," or the survey of the full breadth of topics of importance to parties.

2. Air-Scape

In contrast to the tangible, contextual feel of the hard ground as conveyed by landscape, air-scape adds the dimension of major prevailing forces that envelop the strategic domain. The two heuristic prompters within this realm are *atmospherics* and *wind factors*.

Atmospherics refer to that which prevails on an emotional basis: broad-based opinions, cultural and social norms, the overall climate of attitudes and values among a society. Atmospherics can also extend into a more confined, pedestrian settings, such as a conference forum, business hotel, or a negotiating room. Often negotiators seek to control the atmospherics, the degree of tone running from cheerfulness down to tense hostility, as a means of attaining some advantage in the talks. In Henry Kissinger's extensive memoirs he describes many instances of his foreign counterparts either feting him or carrying out theatrical pre-talk histrionics, efforts aimed at influencing his conduct and content of the American position.[5] His recognition of the tactical use of atmospherics as a negotiating lever prepared him to stay focused on the specifics rather than to become overly beguiled by flattery or insincere courtesies.

As emotional tenor can tilt negotiators into a stance of cooperation or confrontation and gradations in between, elaborated "dances," or pre-talk maneuverings, have evolved to contribute to a favorable tone at the start. Confidence-building measures, or reciprocated steps taken to reduce tensions or enhance cooperation, are commonly undertaken to demonstrate a willingness to bargain in good faith. In 2018, ahead of the first leadership summit between the United States and North Korea, Kim Jong-un, the North Korean leader, authorized the release of imprisoned Americans, returned remains of war dead, and shut down certain nuclear bomb-making capabilities, measures which were hailed by President Donald Trump as being a boost to the atmospherics of their bilateral summit.[6,7]

The wind-factor "framelet" is a set of three main direction-oriented elements: *headwinds*, *tailwinds*, and *crosswinds*.

Headwinds are the prevalent factors that act in opposition to an intended aim. These factors are often systemic in nature, affecting most parties in a particular specialty or broad sector, and exert themselves consistently and persistently over the course of time.

Tailwinds, as to be expected, are those factors acting to enhance one's agenda, figuratively pushing the mission from behind, adding momentum toward one's ultimate goal.

Crosswinds are those factors that act in cross purposes to one's intended direction, turbulent enough to complicate, yet permeable enough to withstand. In 2004, Alan Greenspan, then chair of the U.S. Federal Reserve Board, delivered a speech that identified "headwinds of financial restraint" that crimped many businesses' ability to lend and to borrow.[8] His adept use of *headwinds* as a vivid climatic descriptor in the aseptic world of banking became widely accepted in the industry lexicon and is now used frequently among financial commentators to describe other economic drivers surrounding companies and industries.

3. Seascape

Descriptors involving water and its manifestations provide a variety of terms applicable to parsing the strategic domain. Like the prevailing winds, water can flow in a favorable or unfavorable direction, giving rise to "rising or falling with the tide," "being caught in an undertow," "understanding the undercurrents of unexpressed emotions," and "being subjected to cross currents." One's financial standing can be described as being "above or below water," or as "treading water" for those barely keeping apace, foreboding a situation whereby they might "sink or swim." Prepaid, unretrievable costs are known as "sunk costs," which are disregarded in economic calculations for future investment choices. Similarly, "deadweight losses" result from foregone efficiencies when economic actors work astray from orthodox principles in trade and taxation. Indicating stability and affiliation, *anchorage* and *moorings* are seascape words used to describe how people might become attached to certain beliefs or how they might be centered upon and take comfort in the values of meaning to them.

4. Mind-Scape

Distinguished from descriptors drawn from the external world, *mind-scape* is a newly adapted term to describe the inner world of human thoughts, ideas, and attitudes. *Mind-scape*, simply put, is a mental landscape that hosts the range of human behavior and motives. Because leadership is an exercise of beliefs, appraising how such convictions arise and to what extent they become entrenched in a society is a form of "behavioral intelligence." As new credos can take hold of entire populations, as what has happened during revolutions, understanding how thought leaders develop their insurgencies and propagate their doctrines becomes valuable knowledge for strategies aimed at preventing and mitigating risks from groups advocating violent means of change. Within this realm, intertwining psychological portraiture of authority figures with that of population psychology forms a more unified mind-scape of how a nation might react to a charismatic leader.

If mind-scape is the distribution of psychological dynamics across populations, then mindset is its unit of analysis, concentrating an understanding of the intersection between culture, religion, social trends and how they affect behavior. Furthermore, by discerning the mindsets of leaders, a working model could be developed that might predict how certain individuals make decisions and how they might react during crises. Of particular importance is what psychological processes are undertaken in forming strategic decisions, that is, what are their own heuristic patterns of thought—how they themselves assess a domain, choose a goal, and carry out a plan.

Central to mindset analysis would be the elements of *perceptions*, how they choose to view the world; *intentions*, how they form their goals; *assumptions*, how they invest their beliefs; and *expectations*, how they develop their outlooks. Mindset analysis can also delve into pathologies of thought, ranging from cognitive distortions such as blind spots, overgeneralization, and various forms of fallacious logic to psychiatric dysfunctions involving delusions, paranoia, aggrandizement, and many other illnesses of the mind. A newly emerging field of crisis psychology is examining ways in which the boundaries between rationality and irrationality can be breached, as otherwise normal individuals, when stressed, might exhibit higher degrees of irrationality, possibly leading to impulsiveness, panic, and even mental collapse.[9]

In strategic affairs, the importance of the mind-scape in the engagement of international conflict became embodied in the phrase "winning hearts and minds," a ground-line approach that was touted by Lyndon B. Johnson as a strategy in the Vietnam War.[10] His idea was to win over villagers' allegiances with goodwill projects, demonstrating a beneficence of American intentions. Although Johnson's approach ultimately failed with the North's victory in 1975, world powers continue to attempt the "hearts and minds" strategy through various soft-power guises, ranging from concessionary economic packages, goodwill projects, to humanitarian aid. It remains an open question as to whether or not such efforts substantively shape the mind-scapes of recipient communities, and attempts perceived as psychological ploys could very well incite an opposite reaction: communities could reject or denigrate efforts designed to win them over, negating both the original intent and the value of goods and services delivered.

5. Eco-Scape

Of the five scapes, eco-scape surveys the domain with the widest-angle lens, taking in the broadest panorama of scenery involving not only actors and factors interacting within a sphere of interests, but entire systems and their own dynamics amongst each other. Such a wide aperture perceptual camera not only takes in the "big picture" but goes a magnitude higher and captures the "grander scheme of things." In this regard, biologists study classes of living species and how their niche roles comprise a wider ecosystem, geologists hold a macro-view of the globe as a series of tectonic plates grinding atop the earth's crust over eons, and astronomers behold the universe as galaxies upon galaxies forever expanding into space. Indeed, the versatile term *ecosystem* has been widely adopted in describing overviews of organizations, their particular roles, and their interactions with each other.

The big picture portrays the aggregation of forces and factors at play. For policymakers, representation of such forces creates mental "handles" that expedite their thinking of ongoing interplay. Geopolitical diplomacy aggregates countries into blocs, a convenient grouping for allies with shared interests, ideology, and proximity. The Cold War, the bipolar U.S.-U.S.S.R struggle for influence, was an arena for the bloc vs. bloc rivalry between NATO (backed by the Americans) and the Warsaw Pact (sponsored by the Russians). Countries continue to self-assemble to unionize their interests: the European Union, African Union, the Group of 7 and G-20 among industrial powers, ASEAN for Southeast Asian nations, and Mercosur for South American trade, all amid many other blocs in both formal and informal alliances. Going a step higher than the dynamics of countries, political historian Samuel P. Huntington, pontificating on the long-term outlook for international relations, described a foreboding "clash of civilizations" that would shape a new world order centered more heavily upon culture, language, and religion than upon traditional nation-states.[11]

The "ecoscopic" viewpoint raises strategic assessment onto a higher plane of issues, going above the busyness of detail, appreciating systematic dynamics on a grander scale where equilibria take hold and where changes can happen over evolutionary scales of time. In confronting larger scale dynamics, the grand strategist has two primary challenges: (1) how to influence matters within immense universes filled with tectonic-sized forces and (2) how to exert aggregates of power over spans of time exceeding lifetimes, even generations and beyond. Given the finites of time and resources, any human is ultimately constrained from attaining all possible ambitions, but a lifetime can be sufficient for achieving goals that radiate impact within a generation and across eras. A prime motivation is the establishment of a legacy, leaving a marker of reputation and lasting accomplishments that further inspire those who follow.

To acquire insights at higher vantage points, two "meta-" based approaches have emerged, meta-analysis and meta-gaming. Meta-analysis is a statistical technique that collects data from multiple studies on a particular subject, say a promising cancer treatment, and combines them into a larger data set from which broader inferences can be made about the treatment's ultimate effectiveness.[12]

More pertinent to strategic deliberations, meta-gaming is the conduct of a strategy that bifurcates, or splits into, two levels with one "lower level" game played within an original specified rule-set and the second, a parallel "upper level" or "meta-game" played for a different set of objectives. The upper-level game might arise upon the players' realization, after interacting within the lower-level game, of the existence of other stakes worth winning. Trade talks, for instance, might be negotiated within a standard lower-level game of exchanging concessions dealing with tariffs and regulations, but a more strategic upper-level game might emerge in which negotiators take on new and different objectives in order to win points in a political game. One side may want a new politically oriented objective and is willing to concede in another arena, even outside the trade talk realm. Or that side may include enhancers, or sweeteners, to induce one side to make concessions they normally might not make in the normal game. The core idea is that a meta-game, when it comes about, can fundamentally alter players' strategies as they elevate their game to take on new layers of issues and goals.

The Four G Framework

Yet another perspective in viewing the dynamics upon a domain is to conceptualize it in terms of a game, with particular rules on how to play it, with players striving to win, and with specified ways to advance and to achieve victory. Incorporating those parallels to strategic affairs, a framework that models those dynamics can be expressed as the *Four Gs*: the *Game*, the *Goal*, the *Gain*, and the *Gamble*.

1. Game

The strategic domain is where entities and individuals set out to achieve their objectives, interacting with each other as conditions warrant, sometimes in cooperation but at other times in competition. Their actions and interactions when viewed from an overall perspective is likened to the ongoings of a game, in which players compete with a set of "rules and tools" within a defined context. In fact, the origins of many games, particularly conflict-oriented games like chess, are emulations of real world situations. Although games at large are played for mostly recreational purposes, they can serve serious ends as a laboratory in testing human behavior and as a template for strategy development.

Games correlate well with strategic thought, as games have underlying generic properties similar to live competitive processes. Games can simulate, or model, the actions of players seeking to win objectives of value to them. In games, players are bequeathed a set of assets, or game pieces, which are anointed with various forms of power and/or mobility. Players abide by a given set of rules, which specify both allowed and disallowed behavior along with penalties for breaches. Also specified are the objectives, or end points, that determine the winners and losers. Whereas recreational games are played for fun, other games, notably professional sports, offer chances for large tangible prizes such as money or for intangible rewards such as fame, glory, and recognition.

Researchers have studied game behavior for insights on how to conduct some strategic decisions. In groundbreaking work that won him a Nobel Prize,

John Nash sparked a blossoming of insightful learnings from game behavior with his development of the Nash Equilibrium, a theory about the stability that can arise when all players act in accordance to their knowledge of the strategies of the others.[13] Applications of Nash and other game-derived theories have underpinned analyses of historical events, such as Graham Allison portrayal of the Cuban missile crisis in his book *The Essence of Decision*, and of potential crisis scenarios, as addressed in Thomas Schelling's seminal book *The Strategy of Conflict*, which describes the calculation of dances among players in choosing either cooperation or conflict.[14,15] With these and other portrayals of game behavior, terms such as *gamesmanship* and *brinksmanship*, describing the posturing of players for advantage, have become mainstream labels for similar behaviors in everyday life.

Game insights have been woven into the planning by governments and companies with major stakes in multi-player industries. Militaries conduct war games to test tactics and discover weaknesses, disaster planners play roles in table-top exercises, or mini-games, to elicit their responses under crisis conditions, and corporate chieftains run intricate scenarios modeling how their firms might fare in an economic downturn. In the aftermath of the 2008 global financial crisis, which severely strained the U.S. banking system, the Federal Reserve mandated that major banks undergo "stress tests" of their capital structures using financial disaster scenarios, and those who fail must undertake remedies.[16] As game insight has become ingrained in organizational planning, the practice of conducting rehearsals through game-like simulations has become widespread, revealing hidden vulnerabilities well before a true threat is realized.

But many strategic situations might not easily fit into a game-like structure or are otherwise hard to model; some situations may be too fast-paced to be able to be defined, some may be unique with unprecedented features, and still others may be too large or complex and beyond modeling by existing analytical capabilities. Still, there are ways to structure fluid situations in ways which improve clarity sufficiently enough for a working strategy to be developed.

One method to create structure is to apply a template upon an ambiguous or complex situation and identify the following four game-oriented characteristics: *Players*, *Positions*, *Powers*, and *Purposes*.

Players are those participants, both active and passive, who seek to influence or who are subjected to being influenced by the conduct of the game.

Positions is a term with two basic meanings: the first referring to the situational status of the players, i.e. their strengths and weaknesses, resource levels, and other indicators of condition and circumstance; the second referring to the outlook, or opinions, by the player regarding an issue or person, i.e. being for or against a particular candidate for office.

Powers are the players' repertoire of assets, authorities, and abilities to exert actions effectively within the sphere of contention.

Purposes are the players' mission and motivation to achieve objectives of central importance, centering over their core values and beliefs, giving justification to their actions and energizing their determination.

Identification of these four elements can condense a large, unbounded situation into a more concise and defined micro-system with game characteristics, thereby illuminating some basic tactical and strategic choices for the protagonist player.

2. Goal

The culmination of purpose within a game is the attainment of a specified goal. Of course, most games define the goal as simply winning, with one player prevailing by earning an identifiable condition ahead or above all others. How players achieve the goal, whether by shooting a ball into a basket or checkmating an opposing king, is what differentiates games and sports from each other.

In games, the attainment of the goal, along with the declaration of the winner, is the simple end point, after which all action ceases. If players wish to play again, the starting conditions for all new games are identical and are impervious to all previous outcomes. Also uniform are the fruits of victory that accrue to the winner of a recreational game: being congratulated as the winner and savoring a fleeting satisfaction.

In this way, games are self-contained, independent units, with their processes and outcomes standardized for predictability and comparability. For example, a baseball game is started and conducted in a specified manner, with the innings defined always as having three outs per side, and many other particular rules on runs, base advancement, errors, and the like. Sports, like other forms of games, share generic characteristics that establish a predictable set of challenges and conditions for participants.

By contrast, in strategic affairs a goal is customized, shaped by organizational mission, correlated to capabilities, and ultimately specified by leadership. Here a goal is malleable and is often subjected to intensive debate by any number of internal and external parties. A strategy in pursuit of an original goal may encounter unexpected and unfavorable conditions, forcing a change in either the pathway or to the goal itself.

In contrast to the standardized outcomes of games, the goals of strategic policy can be conceived and formulated to yield any array of desired outcomes. Two primary categories of rewards that emanate from goals are those benefits that are either *tangible* or *intangible*.

Tangible benefits include those that are readily recognizable particularly to the physical senses, most notably the visible and tactile senses. They also include the physical changes to the world, along with observable and verifiable changes in the world of humans. As a simple example, a company's aim to increase financial profits by a certain percentage within a year could be verified by accountants supervising the firm's financial statements.

The second category, intangible benefits, is a more complex, ambiguous set of outcomes, typically difficult to quantify and difficult to objectify. The intangibles involve the world of abstract ideas and ideals, emotions, perceptions, and reputations. These psychological outcomes are more elusive to define precisely and to verify convincingly, as opinions among professionals can vary as to what constitutes such concepts as "consumer confidence" or "enhanced prestige." Changes in the intangible human dimensions extend into the broader realms of politics, sociology, and culture where impacts can either be direct or indirect, subtle, even debatable.

With the plethora of possibilities across the universe of tangible and intangible outcomes, it becomes readily apparent that specifying a goal and desired rewards is a matter of judgment and discernment amid the vast expanse of choices.

Furthermore, in contrast to games where the outcomes are independent and compartmentalized, goals in strategic policy and the actions taken in pursuit of them can set off iterative behavior among other players, provoking chain reactions along offensive or defensive lines. Some of the secondary actions may be anticipated, but many are not, yielding a set of unintended consequences, which may or may not benefit the originating player.

A historical case in point in which a victory in one event may spur a rival to reply in strength in later stages of bilateral competition is the Cuban Missile Crisis. That contentious showdown in October 1962 between the U.S. and the Soviet Union over discovered Russian nuclear-tipped missiles in Cuba instigated John F. Kennedy's intensive diplomatic and military maneuvering to get the missiles out. President Kennedy wanted to achieve a vital and complex American strategic goal of compelling the Russians to remove their existing missiles and stop any new emplacements in a way that would avert misunderstandings, armed conflict, and a fatal escalation to nuclear war.

Through deliberation, consultation, and calculation, Kennedy achieved both aims with a measured and nuanced set of actions centered upon a highly visible blockade of Russian ships conjoined with a less visible tactic to leave "the back door open" to allow the Russians to dismantle and remove the existing missile force. Kennedy's moves de-escalated the crisis through a stepwise, verifiable process, including a secret U.S. concession to remove its missiles from Turkey.[17]

Kennedy's win over the missiles in Cuba, however, was a humiliating loss to the Soviet regime, undercutting its aim to be seen and treated as a superpower coequal to the United States. If its military inferiority led to diplomatic concession in this instance, then Russia wanted to assure itself of the power needed to back its claims in the future. The consequential pathway taken by the Russians was a massive two-decade buildup of its nuclear arsenal, an unprecedented weaponization campaign that first attained parity with the U.S. arsenal, and then continued to exceed it in raw numbers and destructive power.[18] Such an upswell of Russian power empowered the Soviet regime to engage the U.S. in the SALT I and II series of nuclear arms talks from many positions of strength, holding a stockpile of advantages with which it bargained as a coequal superpower.[19]

Success by one party can provoke another party to set new goals for itself, including retaliatory objectives intended to offset or erase the gains won by the original winner. Those new goals, in turn, awaken still more parties to alter their perceptions and assumptions in response to the new realities, and so forth in an open-ended cycle.

3. *Gain*

Players of a recreational game win objectives to try out their skills and luck, and ultimately to derive amusement and fun. In the mission of policymaking, winning objectives is the essential duty to fulfill the needs and ambitions of stakeholders. The results can be complex, involving tangible and intangible gains, or outcomes in which gains in one dimension are offset by losses in another. In such serious matters goal attainment should produce a net gain, taking into account all costs of pursuit.

Whereas tangible costs can be tallied, the intangible costs are much more difficult to assess. Emotion, reputation, stature, and the unlimited varieties of human characteristics are all inherently incalculable. Human life is invaluable as human worthiness and dignity escapes any attempts to delimit them.

Amid so many intangible, incalculable factors, such decisions often come down to a judgment of conscience and character, rather than from a dry summation of a cost-benefit analysis.

Still, as incalculable as human life can be, high-risk decisions involving issues of war and peace are assessed for their implications of "blood and treasure." When lives are at stake, the strategic goals being considered must be compelling, involving the highest and most vital of interests.

The strategic aims of nations cover immense swaths of responsibilities: a nation's economy, culture, society, international linkages, and indeed all the substantive elements that it needs to exist and to function. Furthermore, these constitutive sectors evolve with time, revealing new opportunities or exposing new vulnerabilities. Nations and entities alike possess interests, the range of possessions and conditions necessary or desired for their survival or for fulfillment of their aims. Interests are the substantive concerns of sufficient value high enough to enlist the attention of decision-makers.

More plainly, interests are the mix of *wishes*, *wants*, and *needs* that anybody, from specific individuals to entire civilizations, holds as valuable to their existence. Some interests are concerned with preserving current assets or capabilities; other interests are concerned with acquiring something that is lacking. Still other interests involve defending oneself from the encroachments and threats from others.

An acronym that condenses the meaning of interests is *PAWN LAWS*, which stands for:

Protection and Advancement of Wants and Needs

taking into account one's

Liabilities, Assets, Weaknesses, and Strengths.

PAWN represents the impetus to take action on behalf of one's interests. LAWS represents the "balance sheet" that lays out the scope of both opportunities and vulnerabilities. LAWS is an evolution to the SWOT matrix, a widely known acronym denoting Strengths, Weaknesses, Opportunities, and Threats. Altogether PAWN LAWS integrates the balance between offense and defense, choice and limits, and between the immediate needs of today and of those forward into the future.

Interests are the motivation for survival, defense, and even aggression, as they underpin an entity's very survival. Interests establish the basis for achieving a "gain" that is sustaining and satisfying. In pursuit of such gains, organizations keep track of their progress through the use of a variety of tools, such as numeric indicators or visual scoreboards that keep running tallies of effort spent. Gains in international development, for example, are tracked through the widespread use of a matrix table called "logframes," which is short for "logical frameworks" and which compactly intersects goals with activities and outputs, along with other planning elements.[20] From knowing whether gains are being made or not, a leader can make needed adjustments to a strategy.

4. *Gamble*

In physics, a Newtonian law states that for every action there is an equal and opposite reaction. In thinking about risk and reward in the strategic world, a similar action-reaction dynamic is a type of "political law" to consider when planning goals and strategies. In an interactive, intertwined domain with many actors and factors at play, a leader must consider broadly how the human forces of inertia, tension, and friction might complicate strategies. These forces animate the action-reaction cycle when people and organizations respond to provocations by defending the status quo or by resisting with fierce opposition. Because many goals are zero-sum in character, meaning that a win for one party means others must lose, those at risk for losing are motivated to resist and fight back. Zero-sum goals are frequently fought over limited, tangible resources such as territory, money, and material goods.

Like remora fish, which attach themselves to ocean predators and opportunistically feed off scraps, risk factors act like an invasive species throughout the strategic domain, attaching themselves to all endeavors, lying in wait to the detriment of the entity. This metaphor stems from the recognition that there are no guarantees that any goal can be won. Risk is inherently linked to randomness and probabilities, which in turn can lead to either favorable or unfavorable conditions becoming realized.

Risk of failure can also lead to risk of losses when operations break down or campaigns fall short: expenditures of time and resources are often irreversible. The real possibilities for failure and consequent costs should be identified to the extent possible by activating one's own "risk radar," scanning ahead to fill in blind spots and avoid becoming blindsided by surprises.

In contemplating strategies toward important goals, the leader should recognize that surprise and randomness can ensnare any campaign. The leader should consider potential costs and losses in their entirety and designate the risks as a whole to be the "gamble." The gamble considered would include both identifiable, tangible costs, as well as the amorphous, intangible costs such as possible injury to one's reputation, morale, and prestige.

As they acknowledge that strategies incorporate a gamble, planners can create contingencies and options for when events go awry. Space missions, for example, are rife with backup plans and detailed problem-shooting checklists for the myriad of things that could go wrong. Many multi-stage projects and campaigns incorporate "go or no-go" checkpoints that enable or disable further action depending upon progress achieved or the presence or absence of certain enabling conditions.

A nuanced form of the gamble is the *gambit*, a calculated form of risk-taking that works off a hunch about how other players would act in response to an offer or concession. Gambits are discrete, upfront propositions of sufficient attractiveness to incur a reaction by another party, ultimately leading to an outcome more favorable than if the gambit had not been tried.

Case in point: President Barack Obama in 2013 threatened missile strikes against Syria in punishment for Syria's use of chemical weapons against civilians after he warned Bashar Assad a year before that any such attacks would be considered crossing an inviolate "red line" that would trigger a forceful U.S. response. Secretary of State John Kerry advanced the presidential intent by delivering an ominous warning to Syria, demanding that it dispose of its chemical weapons within a week, barely disguising a forthcoming U.S. strike if no action was taken. At a press conference, in response to a reporter's question Kerry left an opening: Syria could avert a strike if they agreed to place their chemical weapons under international control.[21]

Upon hearing of Kerry's opening that there could be an exit ramp leading to a no-strike destination for the U.S., Russian foreign minister Sergey Lavrov immediately called Kerry and ran his gambit by him: If the Russians were to broker a deal for Syria to remove all chemical weapon stockpiles in the way Kerry expressed in the news conference, would the U.S. hold off its attack?[22] Kerry and Obama suspended the attack and chose instead to negotiate with Russia, ultimately reaching an overall agreement for the disposal of the stockpile.[23] Lavrov's gambit worked to Russia's and Syria's benefit, as averting the U.S. missile strikes preserved the Assad regime, and Syria's survival ensured that Russia retained its major foothold of influence in the Middle East (later, in 2018 Syria again used chemical weapons against civilians, incurring a punitive strike by a U.S.-led coalition ordered by President Donald Trump).[24]

One form of risk control is to produce and possess a set of viable *options*, keeping open a range of choices when needed. Having more choices adds flexibility to decision-making by providing different ways to solve a problem. In negotiations, more options among parties lead to a higher chance of reaching agreement as there are more transactional combinations available for a deal to be struck.

In diplomacy, a state possessing more options than a rival has the advantage in maneuvering during a crisis, as when Kennedy confronted Khrushchev during the Cuban missile crisis. The U.S. superiority in military power and its geographical proximity to Cuba gave Kennedy many configurations of assets and tactics from which to choose.[25] Kennedy's moves to enforce a naval blockade and then secretly link the removal of the Russian missiles with a quiet withdrawal of American missiles from Turkey were a product of his access to a rich arsenal of options, much more so than what Khrushchev possessed. Having both "more carrots and more sticks" allows for a wide range of persuasive approaches, from blunt to nuanced, from immediate to long-term, and from intense to measured, making possible an ultimate approach that fits well to a particular situation. If Kennedy had fewer options, he could have been forced to activate a blunter, more aggressive approach that could have escalated risk to the point of war.

Amid the multitudes of ways in which risk can be manifested, the gamble at large can be segmented into discrete categories. One memorable way is to anticipate risk from three basic categories:

1. *Unfortunate happenstances* are the detrimental facets of a current situation, such as intractable problems or chronic deficiencies.
2. *Unforeseen circumstances* are the unexpected, adverse conditions and surprises encountered during pursuit of the goal.
3. *Unintended consequences* are the reverberations, either positive or negative to one's interests, that may follow success or failure.

As a series, they mark risks within the fundamental phases of strategy: at the start, during action, and upon completion.

In considering a forward strategy, the degree of a gamble taken is not only dependent upon external conditions, but also upon one's own "risk appetite," the internal tolerance of, or the desire for higher degrees of risk. Once all of the proverbial "low-hanging fruit" have been swept off the tree, what rewards remain are those that are higher and more difficult to reach. Fruit on the next higher branch may only need a little extra effort, perhaps accessible with a short ladder, but those on higher levels may require added lengths of ladder, and those highest may need specialized tools and techniques to bring them down, making the task more costly and more hazardous.

That is a basic example of the incremental effect much explained in economics, that incremental benefits will be reaped until a point when the added, marginal costs begin to exceed the marginal benefit of the captured fruit. The escalating degrees of effort, resources, and risk winnow the ranks of harvesters to those who have the means to extract high-hanging fruit safely and economically, as well as those who possess the tolerance and fortitude to take on the most difficult challenges.

By analogous extension, this simple example points out a basic correlation between ambition and risk: The pursuit of ever-higher-level aims entails added risks, which may proliferate and escalate to a point beyond one's capabilities and risk tolerances, soon forcing a judgment that the highest prizes, however tempting, may be out of reach and deemed not worth the effort.

The 4G framework is a method with which to condense and simplify a strategic domain of high complexity and ambiguity. It provides a template for the "gamification" of a situation, distilling the dynamics of a situation to the confines similar to a game, with players, powers, and purposes. The gaming model enhances clarity by spotlighting the overall configuration of players and what possible moves could be made. Still, one must recognize the limits of applying game models to strategic affairs, as winning and losing in the real world can have broader, more volatile repercussions than what happens within the static confines of a true game.

The Vigilance-Diligence Framework

If risk is a pervasive and persistent factor throughout the strategic domain, then how might it be surfaced and identified? World history is replete with devastating wars, grand revolutions, financial collapses, and other forms of societal shocks. Some shock factors are accidental or non-intentional in character, such as natural disasters or disease epidemics. Other shock factors arise from human intent, expressed through surprise aggression and other destabilizing behaviors.

The risk that shock factors, whether of nature or of mankind, could provoke widespread loss and suffering has given impetus to efforts to detect problems and systemic stresses early enough so they might be ameliorated or averted. The danger of surprise nuclear strikes during the U.S.-Soviet Cold War compelled the building of early warning systems to detect missile launches.[26]

Since then, technological powers have advanced so that early warning systems are embedded in many non-military sectors. Telecom and utilities survey their networks with centralized command centers that brim with electronic maps. Environmental sensors are networked worldwide to detect earthquakes, tsunamis, and hurricanes. More challenging are ways to detect the early signs of malevolent intentions originated by people. The September 11 attacks were a culmination of hidden planning by plotters led by Osama bin Laden, whose intentions to wreak devastation went undetected for several years until they were carried out.[27]

If risk factors are indeed prevalent, they should be identifiable through underlying generic characteristics, and then further specified to formulate a judgment about their potency. To better "interrogate" the strategic domain and illuminate those risk factors worthy of further analysis, the Vigilance-Diligence model is introduced. Vigilance is a commitment to perpetual alertness toward the advent of risk and maleficent intent. Diligence is a parallel commitment to pursue leads doggedly down to the necessary level of detail required to inform a reasoned judgment.

Modern nations, whose survival are reliant upon deterrence and threat reduction, invest heavily in an array of intelligence assets and technologies to conduct Vigilance-Diligence actions in order to detect signs of aggression and to discern true intentions of other countries. Commercial firms, too, have recently built similar market intelligence capabilities to monitor conditions keyed to their core activities, such as airlines monitoring energy markets for movements in jet fuel prices.

The Vigilance-Diligence framework is an eight-component design allocated over two primary functions in confronting risk: *signal acquisition* and *risk prevention.*

Signal acquisition, with five components, is the function encompassing the detection and substantiation of emerging information, which can emanate from a source as a signal. It might be said to be similar to piecing together a puzzle with fragments of data clued by intuition and insight on what the emerging picture might ultimately look like. Depending on circumstances, acquisition can be a game of patience, with data pieces accumulated over a long period of time, or an urgent task requiring immediate recall to avert a looming crisis.

Risk prevention, with three components, is the function of establishing the capabilities and activities in countering risk and averting dangers, with an action scale that runs from non-confrontational and nuanced (diplomatic outreach) to confrontational, even brutish (pre-emptive strikes).

Components of Signal Acquisition

These components span a perceptual aperture, flexibly seeing the strategic terrain from a wide perspective down to narrow, detailed specifics. In his study of Henry Kissinger's negotiation style, James Sebenius identified the Kissingerian diplomatic method as a skillful use of a "zoom-out, zoom-in" technique, describing how Kissinger took stock of the big picture of power play and how he then used that knowledge to execute his strategy in intricate, individualized detail upon his counterparts at the bargaining table.[28] The five components that make up the Acquisition function hew roughly to a skyline-to-ground-line, wide-to-narrow angled lens approach, with components sharing some overlap and cross-contributory functions.

The five components of signal acquisition and their main tasks can be summarized in Figure 4.1. Figure 4.1 highlights an approximate layering of functions from highest of perches, or the "macroscopic" viewpoint, where the levels of detail can be fuzzy and coarse, down to the ground level where the level of detail can range from the plainly observable down to finely detailed, "microscopic" level. Of course, such layering is not literal, as there is much overlap among functions, but it helps to organize a deliberative approach to their characteristics.

1. Surveillance

This function gains information from the skyline perspective from a high vantage point that overlooks the domain. This overarching view shows overall patterns of movement, emerging concentrations or their dispersals, or warning indicators portending a more powerful event. Space satellite networks, for example, apply specialized sensors to monitor and detect patterns and

SKYLINE "MACRO-SCOPIC"	
SURVEILLANCE	DETECT SIGNAL
RECONNAISSANCE	INVESTIGATE SIGNAL
INTELLIGENCE	UNDERSTAND SIGNAL
EXPERIENCE	ENGAGE SIGNAL
EVIDENCE	VALIDATE SIGNAL
GROUND LINE "MICRO–SCOPIC"	

Figure 4.1 Skyline to groundline

movements, interrogating the world beneath with their technological queries. Online surveillance acts in cyberspace, monitoring data streams and extracting patterns of interest. An ongoing double challenge in surveillance is separating a useful signal from useless background noise and a parallel purpose: weeding out false information presented as truth, often in the form of tactics as feints, decoys, and aggrandizements. Flaws in detecting a valid signal can lead to the wrongful discounting of a true occurrence or to the erroneous acceptance of a false representation. Actions based on either flaw can lead to compounding errors in judgment and wasted efforts.

2. Reconnaissance

If a captured signal is deemed intriguing enough, further investigation is often warranted to confirm its validity and to obtain additional details and surrounding circumstances. The reconnaissance function is a selective pursuit of those signals of interest that involves a closer approach, but with sufficient hedging to avoid high degrees of risk and not overcommit resources. Military reconnaissance units are deployed to ferret out the extent of enemy lines, or to gather additional intelligence about a detected incident. Retailers might conduct walk-throughs of competitors' stores to gain insight on what retail tactics are being used. Reconnaissance units probe what is happening in the strategic domain, obtaining a closer look with added detail, but still retaining sufficient distance, physical and perceptual, to buffer risks and maintain a detached point of view.

3. Intelligence

Once a signal or action is verified as being true and pertinent to one's interests, intelligence functions to bring a network of knowledge to bear upon the situation. Intelligence adds descriptive color commentary regarding the actors and factors in play, delves into motives, predicts likely next moves, and assesses probabilities of success or failure. Simply stated, intelligence is "getting smart" about what is active upon the strategic terrain, drawing upon existing bodies of knowledge but also interpreting acquired information and deriving implications about what might happen.

From these and many other tasks, intelligence is central to the formation of judgment and the development of options. Intelligence integrates a "look-back" function, drawn upon accumulated knowledge and history, with its complement, a "look-forward" function, centered upon the predictive use of logic and intuition. The craft of intelligence also melds the polar perspectives between the "macroscopic and the microscopic" by creating a contextual rationale about an event or person of interest and adding descriptive detail when necessary to make a characteristic or a personality better understood.

4. Experience

Information is not only gleaned from facts and figures derived in detached technological ways, but also from the direct engagement, or interaction, with people and situations. In understanding motives and aims of people, any history of past interactions can yield useful insights about underlying values and personal characteristics. Experience adds to a nuanced view about behavior and system dynamics, showing different shades of a mercurial personality, for instance, or how individuals decide within crisis situations. Interpersonal experience also employs many forms of behavioral heuristics, which are working distillations about the action-reaction tendencies of people, giving clues as to how people might respond in certain situations.

Situational experience, the engagement in activities and scenarios, confers a "descriptive authority" to the participant, empowering them to tell their stories from a unique first-person perspective. Historian Edgar Snow's writings about the rise of Communist China and its leader, Mao Zedong, gave Western readers a first-hand account about the inner workings of the revolutionaries.[29] Diplomat George F. Kennan's time spent in the Soviet Union as a young, foreign-service officer injected him into the intrigues of the Stalin era, but also immersed him with the everyday struggles of ordinary Russians. His direct ground-line perspective enriched his thinking about the aims of Soviet power in the immediate aftermath of World War II. Kennan's pinnacle of influence, his famous "X" article in *Foreign Affairs* about the origins and implications of Soviet international conduct, was underscored by the descriptive authority derived from his personal learnings there.[30]

In similar regards, direct experience is a powerful, authoritative wellspring for the crafting of descriptive and persuasive narratives, storylines that resonate from their vivid portraitures of real persons and situations. Leadership scholars Ernest May and Richard Neustadt wrote in their book, *Thinking in Time*, of the ways in which narrative histories are shaped, framed, repurposed, even distorted, to befit the storytelling by leaders.[31] A contemporary example of refreshed narratives is the constant evolution of the history of the Vietnam War as it is enriched with new avenues for storytelling by those who fought, protested, and suffered, in modern media forms such as online documentaries and specialized YouTube channels.

5. Evidence

Truthful representation is the congruence of a fact with its perception, illusion is perceiving something that does not exist, and evasion is hiding an existence from becoming perceived. Furthermore, the lack of capabilities to perceive certain realities, such as worldly phenomena, results in being blinded to what truly exists or is happening: Without a microscope, one cannot perceive either the presence or absence of disease-causing bacteria on a slide. To ascertain a state of truth, the human has a compelling need to capture the validating characteristics that emanate from that which exists, such as its basic appearance. To do so, a person makes use of the endowed senses and mental abilities, supplemented and complemented by arrays of tools and instruments created for specialized functions.

The iconic insight embedded by Thomas Jefferson into the preamble of the American Declaration of Independence, "We hold these truths to be self-evident," and asserting the ideals of equality and the right to "life, liberty and the pursuit of happiness," galvanized a revolutionary movement toward popular self-government. Modern realities in the realm of strategic affairs are often at odds with the appreciation for or the exposition of truth in the manner Jefferson nobly upheld. Deception, denials, and the maligning of truth have undermined trust among leaders and nations, and have ignited conflicts large and small throughout history. Even nations who consider themselves highly principled have found it necessary for self-protection to conceal intentions, cloak capabilities, run feinting maneuvers, or conduct covert operations. By shielding the truth in tactical and strategic ways, countries act in acknowledgement that truth holds power and that rivals who can acquire intelligence more readily than others can gain advantage and can even weaponize such knowledge.

Strategic actions, particularly those taken against other parties or are risky on their own accord, typically require justification, a reinforcement of rationale and reasoning. Justification relies upon the gathering of evidence, a body of exhibits that supplies sufficient proof about an identified condition or situation. Direct evidence is chiefly in the form of tangible objects or observable events. Antiques, for instance, are more valuable when they have a robust provenance, or a "paper trail" of confirmable, irrefutable documents establishing lines of ownership.

Indirect evidence can be elicited from indicators, which are secondary layers of facts and information that hint at, or allude to, an underlying truth. One piece of circumstantial evidence may not be strong enough to corroborate a fact, but a collection of various pieces of information can produce a web of inferences that bolster confidence about a fact. The "smoking gun" is an apt metaphor for the discovery of circumstantial evidence strongly tied to a specific act, just short of witnessing the actual event itself.

As many strategic actors shield themselves with secrecy or project propagandistic self-images, gaining insight about their true intentions and capabilities may require patient, sophisticated, and skilled gathering of evidence. Evidence can be gathered by the effort of humans, often referred to as HUMINT, which stands for *human-sourced intelligence*, or by the use of various technologies, centered upon SIGINT, or *signal-acquired intelligence*.[32] The evidence acquired from these methods is processed, organized, and interpreted so as to either support or refute a posed question, or hypothesis, about the existence or absence of a condition.

Gathered evidence may be assessed in secret to avoid tipping off rivals, or it may be released in a public forum to rally support or to build a case for an official action. In law enforcement, prosecutors justify their charges against a person accused of a crime by presenting tangible forms of evidence that link the person with the infraction. Such evidence can include photographs, physical traces, telephone logs, laboratory findings, and digital information. In international forums, collective action by member-states typically requires by custom or by demand an exposition of evidence that ties an alleged transgressor to a violation of a norm or a law. As many issues between nations involve evading or denying various forms of proscribed conflict, evidence of such violations may be of a higher order of sophistication, requiring chemical, biological, or cyber forms of forensics.

Components of Risk Prevention

Possessing knowledge about risks and threats present on the strategic domain must be tied to the ability to reduce such threats. These three components—*competence, resilience*, and *deterrence*—are predicated upon having two primary strengths: capabilities and posture. These strengths underpin the ability to take effective actions and reinforce a credible stance of preparedness and readiness.

6. Competence

Any actor who wishes to survive and succeed on the strategic domain must possess a basic level of skill and ability to undertake tasks of importance, and to do it in an effective, timely manner. Competence is the basic ability to implement tasks with sufficient knowledge and skill. Competence is a quality not only of individuals but also of any organization. Reaching goals of importance entails the effective and efficient use of assets in a tactical manner, but reaching those goals also entails competence in strategic skills, such as conducting diplomatic relations or communicating clearly during a crisis.

Competence along both fronts, that for tactical functions and that for higher order strategy, requires the acquisition of skills, opportunities to apply them, and means of transmitting learnings to next generations. Institutions arise to provide for organized stewardship of a body of knowledge and skills, and they serve to uphold and advance sets of values within broader cultural and social environments. Without the existence of longstanding institutions, competence across time and generations can be degraded and lost.

7. Resilience

With competence, entities exercise their core abilities to achieve their stated aims. As they interact with other actors and factors, they will be confronted with innumerable changes and surprises. As many of these unexpected circumstances will work in complication or in opposition to their goals, any organization will need to have an internal ability to adapt and adjust. Resilience is the capability by persons or institutions to absorb shocks and disruptions in various guises and magnitudes and be able to substantially revert to the original level of performance. It is the ability to bounce back from difficulties and still be able to function with effectiveness and efficiency.

Resilience is a competence in its own right. Enduring major breakdowns can be demoralizing and can result in compounding confusion and a downward spiral toward organizational collapse. Contingency planning and crisis training are two methods for organizations to protect themselves as a whole when troubles strike. Building resilience capabilities from within, as managers tasked with risk control might do, is a form of insurance against the unexpected. Furthermore, *overt resilience*, or a demonstrated robustness openly and widely known, affords another dimension of protection: Rivals may be less willing to try to attack if they perceive their target as having deep reserves of retaliatory capacity. Along Darwinistic lines, rivals may instead choose to "go down the path of the least resilient" and attack those whose reserves are the most shallow.

Overt, demonstrable resilience then becomes a form of deterrence, which incentivizes the buildup of internal capabilities even when nominal risks are present. Switzerland, for example, in spite of being landlocked and surrounded by non-hostile E.U. countries, has still invested in sustaining its armed forces at a level that belies its international image as a neutral, non-aggressive country, with compulsory service and training requirements in support of mechanized brigades implanted in mountainous regions.[33]

8. Deterrence

Of the two military postures, offense and defense, offense is the mode that intuitively involves a higher degree of risk and cost than that of defense. Offense entails an outbound excursion into unfamiliar territory, with many uncharted obstacles and likely hostile populations to encounter. Attacking columns stretch supply lines and compel complicated logistics. In contrast, defense of homelands is a more sessile, less logistically fraught mission. Familiarity confers advantage in applying local knowledge on where and how to mount a defense. It is no surprise to think that defense is a more "natural" stance than taking the riskier, costlier posture of offense. By extending this line of reasoning, the prevention of crises is preferable to the instigation of them, as stability and security are likely to be retained at less risk and cost by deflecting conflicts rather by undertaking them.

Deterrence is the posture of choice for most nations, as it is the stance that accords oneself with built-in, "home court" advantages. It is also politically easier to justify a defensive posture than an offensive one, as the mission of protecting one's homeland, community, and family is universally irrefutable. Deterrence is reliant upon having sufficient and effective capabilities that are exercised for a dissuasive effect. As previously noted, deterrence is also served by a show of force that makes clear a commitment to fight back when needed and to bounce back from any inflicted damage.

Ultimately, deterrence is integral to the workings of the Vigilance-Diligence model and the integrated use of intelligence streams. Apart from having sufficient capabilities in equipment and manpower, deterrence is also a compound function of demonstrating credible commitment to act in defense of one's interests, and of highlighting one's own "resilience reserves." An interlocking system of "mutually assured deterrence" promotes stability in the strategic domain and dampens predilections for aggression.

The strategic domain is the universe of actors and factors in interaction amongst each other. Even with bounds placed upon a particular world to narrow its scope and shape its conceptual contours, the domain remains complicated, with actors' motions often concealed and their motives often sublimated, creating halting uncertainties for all players within it. The preceding frameworks help simplify what is perceived and what is understood so that one's own goals can be achieved with more clarity and speed on what to do, with whom to engage, and in what ways. The choice of framework is a matter of preference and of circumstance, but they each propose categories that are generic enough to be applied across a variety of settings, situations, and sectors.

A compact *Four INT framework* acts to summarize this chapter, and is a selectively concise version of the twelve-point strategic mission cycle described in Part 1. As these components have been described earlier, they are presented here in linked fashion, with emphasis on how each progresses to the next.

Figure 4.2 arranges these four components along the points of a diamond, with Interests at the peak and driving the dynamic clockwise.

1. Players are motivated to protect and advance their own *Interests*, their range of possessions and stakes across their own domains. This can also be described as the set of their wishes, wants, and needs.

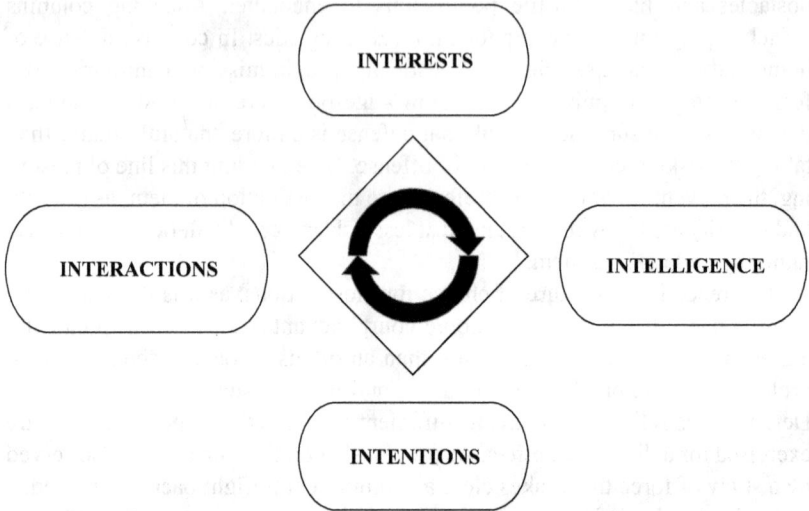

Figure 4.2 4 INT diamond

2. Players illuminate their views of the domain by their use of *Intelligence*, the integrative understanding of the dynamics of concern. Intelligence can be interests-based, focused on how to defend or expand one's empire, or can be strategy-based, assessing which goals are desirable and achievable and which actions are best to undertake.
3. Intelligence also involves gauging the *Intentions*, or the planned moves and ultimate goals of other actors within the domain. Especially challenging is trying to assess the true intentions of rivals, as they may cloak their intentions with ambiguous, guarded statements or hidden maneuvering. Conversely, surfacing and confirming the kindred intentions of allies can promote alliance-building and the collective enlargement of interests. With informed knowledge of the strategic domain, what remains are the actions to fulfill one's interests.
4. *Interactions* are the acts of engagement within the domain. Of these acts, interventions are the scope of willful actions taken to fulfill one's interests, encompassing all forms of power and influence. Effective interventions cause purposeful changes to the dynamics and configurations among actors and factors.

The resulting accomplishments or failures can alter conditions in subtle to dramatic ways, creating a need for ongoing assessments of domain conditions and pathways to goals. Interests, either fulfilled or denied, generate new assessments about options available and what new goals might be pursued, creating an ongoing cycle between ambition and action.

Notes

1. Rosabeth Moss Kanter, *Confidence: How Winning Streaks & Losing Streaks Begin & End* (New York: Three Rivers Press, 2006), 26–62.
2. Michael E. Porter, "How Competitive Forces Shape Strategy," *Harvard Business Review*, 59(2) (May 1979): 137–145.
3. Alex Campbell, "Turning a Scandal into a '-Gate'," *BBC News Magazine*, May 11, 2013. www.bbc.com/news/magazine-22464422 (accessed Aug. 22, 2019).
4. James P. Rubin, "The in Your Face Diplomat," *Politico Magazine*, May 12, 2019. www.politico.com/magazine/story/2019/05/12/richard-holbrooke-biography-review-history-analysis-226871 (accessed Aug. 22, 2019).
5. Henry A. Kissinger, *White House Years* (Boston: Little Brown, 1979), 1222–1229, and *Years of Upheaval* (Boston: Little Brown, 1982), 228–235.
6. Roberta Rampton and David Brunnstrom, "Upbeat Trump Welcomes U.S. Prisoners Released by North Korea," *Reuters*, May 9, 2018. https://uk.reuters.com/article/uk-northkorea-usa-prisoners/trump-welcomes-u-s-prisoners-released-by-north-korea-thanks-kim-idUKKBN1IB0AI (accessed Oct. 18, 2018).
7. Associated Press, "North Korea Says It Will Suspend Nuclear and Missile Testing," Apr. 20, 2018. www.bostonglobe.com/news/world/2018/04/20/north-korea-says-has-suspended-nuclear-and-long-range-missile-tests-plans-close-nuclear-test-site/5DfEj6znIxclpfOGMRXhfO/story.html (accessed through Boston Globe, Oct. 18, 2018).
8. Federal Reserve Board, "Remarks of Chairman Alan Greenspan to the American Economic Association," *News Release*, Jan. 3, 2004. www.federalreserve.gov/boarddocs/speeches/2004/20040103/default.htm (accessed Oct. 18, 2018).
9. U.S. Centers for Disease Control, "Psychology of a Crisis," [slide set], n.d. www.au.af.mil/au/awc/awcgate/cdc/psy_of_crisis.pdf (accessed Oct. 18, 2018).
10. President Lyndon B. Johnson, "Remarks at a Dinner Meeting of the Texas Electric Cooperatives, Inc.," May 4, 1965. www.presidency.ucsb.edu/documents/remarks-dinner-meeting-the-texas-electric-cooperatives-inc (accessed Oct. 29, 2018).
11. Samuel P. Huntington, "The Clash of Civilizations?" *Foreign Affairs* 72(3) (Summer 1993): 22–49.
12. Sharon-Lise Normand, "Tutorial in Biostatistics. Meta-Analysis: Formulating, Evaluating, Combining, and Reporting," *Statistics in Medicine* 18(3) (1999): 321–359. doi: 10.1002/(SICI)1097-0258(19990215)18:3<321::AID-SIM28>3.0.CO;2-P. PMID 10 070677 (accessed Oct. 18, 2018).
13. John Forbes Nash, "Non-cooperative Games," *Annals of Mathematics* 54(2) (1951): 286–295. doi:10.2307/1969529 (accessed Oct. 18, 2018).
14. Graham Allison and Philip Zelikow, *Essence of Decision: Explaining the Cuban Missile Crisis*, 2nd ed. (New York: Longman, 1999), 13–54.
15. Thomas Schelling, *The Strategy of Conflict* (Cambridge, MA: Harvard University Press, 1981).
16. Federal Reserve System, "Policy Statement on the Scenario Design Framework for Stress Testing," 12 CFR Part 252, Regulation YY; Docket No. OP-1452 (effective date Jan. 1, 2014), 5–10. www.federalreserve.gov/bankinforeg/bcreg20131107a1.pdf (accessed Oct. 18, 2018).
17. Allison and Zelikow, *Essence of Decision*, 356–366.
18. Robert S. Norris and Hans M. Kristensen, "Nuclear U.S. and Soviet/Russian Intercontinental Ballistic Missiles, 1959–2008," *Bulletin of the Atomic Scientists*, 65(1) (2009): 62–69. doi:10.2968/065001008
19. Alvin Z. Rubinstein, *Soviet Foreign Policy Since World War II: Imperial and Global*, (Cambridge MA: Winthrop, 1981), 169–175.
20. Leon J. Rosenberg, "Project Evaluation and the Project Appraisal Reporting System," Report to US Agency for International Development (July 24, 1970), part II: 1–18. https://pdf.usaid.gov/pdf_docs/PNADW881.pdf (accessed Oct. 19, 2018).

21. Patrick Wintour, "John Kerry Gives Syria Week to Hand over Chemical Weapons or Face Attack," *The Guardian* (UK), Sept. 9, 2013. www.theguardian.com/world/2013/sep/09/us-syria-chemical-weapons-attack-john-kerry (accessed Oct. 20, 2018).

22. Anne Gearan, Karen DeYoung, and Will Englund, "Syria Says It 'Welcomes' Russia Proposal on Chemical Weapons," *Washington Post*, Sept. 13, 2013. http://wapo.st/18ItsNi?tid=ss_mail&utm_term=.1be59c9a0495 (accessed Oct. 20, 2018).

23. Michael R. Gordon, "U.S. and Russia Reach Deal to Destroy Syria's Chemical Arms," *New York Times*, Sept. 14, 2013. www.nytimes.com/2013/09/15/world/middleeast/syria-talks.html (accessed Oct. 20, 2018).

24. Helene Cooper, Thomas Gibbons-Neff, and Ben Hubbard, "U.S., Britain and France Strike Syria Over Suspected Chemical Weapons Attack," *New York Times*, Apr. 13, 2018. www.nytimes.com/2018/04/13/world/middleeast/trump-strikes-syria-attack.html (Oct. 20, 2018).

25. Allison and Zelikow, *Essence of Decision*, 224–230.

26. Strobe Talbott, *Endgame: The Inside Story of SALT II* (New York: Harper, 1980), 22.

27. National Commission on Terrorist Attacks upon the United States, "Chapter 5—Al Qaeda Aims at the American Homeland," *The 9/11 Commission Report*, July 22, 2004. www.9-11commission.gov/report/911Report_Ch5.htm (accessed Oct. 20, 2018).

28. James Sebenius, Nicholas Burns, and Robert Mnookin, *Kissinger the Negotiator: Lessons from Dealmaking at the Highest Level* (New York: HarperCollins, 2018), part II ("zoom-out")—part III ("zoom-in").

29. Edgar Snow, *Red Star over China: The Classic Account of the Birth of Chinese Communism, Part V—The Long March*, revised ed. (New York: Grove, 1968), 185–208.

30. X [George Kennan], "The Sources of Soviet Conduct," *Foreign Affairs* 25(4) (1947): 566–582.

31. Richard Neustadt and Ernest May, *Thinking in Time: The Uses of History for Decision-Makers* (New York: Free Press, 1998), 111–133.

32. Office of the Director of National Intelligence, "What Is Intelligence." www.dni.gov/index.php/what-we-do/what-is-intelligence (accessed Oct. 20, 2018).

33. "Swiss Army Undertakes Biggest Military Manoeuvre Since Cold War," *swissinfo.ch*, May 1, 2018. www.swissinfo.ch/eng/society/defence-exercises_swiss-army-undertakes-biggest-military-manoeuvre-since-cold-war/44087192 (accessed Oct. 20, 2018).

5 The Line System for Domain Analysis

In the previous chapter, lenses are described as one conceptual tool that both filters and focuses incoming information and defines them in a way to be better understood. As a conceptual tool, lenses act to clarify and to magnify, thereby imparting clearer mental images about noteworthy features found on the strategic domain. By connecting imagery with memory, conceptual lenses work as a psychological tool in bringing about heuristic approaches to the domain, succinctly highlighting those actors and factors of importance to one's interests and arranging them in understandable patterns.

To reiterate, heuristics are practical approaches to reach a vision or solution quickly and efficiently, relying on techniques that connect the workings of the inner mind with outside reality. Language is a rich source of heuristic models, as words are human creations made to label phenomena and make them understood to all people. In the English language, the word *line* is a simple, clear, and versatile descriptor that attaches well to many commonly known objects and conveys a meaning that can be envisioned. Understandably, *line*'s versatility then makes it a natural add-on as a suffix to describe linear like qualities in other fields. *Line*-compounded words, such as *baseline, skyline, fault line*, and countless others, are heuristic nuggets, conveying their meanings compactly and visually. These "line-words" make for memorable markers within frameworks.

The featured line-words are selected for their ability to describe various elements of the strategic domain. Some work well in describing the arrangements of actors on the domain, whereas others depict characteristics of factors. Some line-words stand on their own meaning, as they are applied to the domain. Others have been modified and adapted for a particular purpose. Several key line-words will be used in frameworks described in the upcoming parts elaborating the strategic goal and the strategic plan.

For added heuristic value, the line-words will be grouped according to how well they fit in describing either domain factors or actors, with acknowledgments that several overlap both categories. For conciseness, they will be described in a glossary-style manner. Some line-words have close associations with each other, so they will be discussed more or less as a cohort within a category.

Line-Words for Domain Factors

Skyline

This is the wide-angled lens perspective, taking in the birds-eye, big picture point of view. It takes in information in a top-down fashion, going from the macroscopic to the microscopic. The advantage of the skyline view is that it can appreciate larger patterns unseen from the ground-line. A disadvantage is that items discerned at this level tend to be more abstract and thus more ambiguous in nature. The skyline perspective is particularly robust as it is a level with which one can gain an overview of other line-patterns on the domain. Maps and other forms of overview graphics are mainstream ways in which the skyline viewpoint is captured.

Boundary Lines

These lines classically demarcate geographic or political borders within or across recognized entities such as nation-states. Their presence and configuration are usually determined by legal authority or by international agreement. Disputed boundaries can be flash-points for conflict and war, often stemming from antiquated, unresolved claims or from newly arising economic pressures, such as those involving fishing grounds or seabed mining rights.

Baselines

These are the originating conditions that act as a reference for the measurement and assessment of a goal-seeking campaign. Standardized baselines aid the use of like comparisons; for instance, in economic analyses baseline years for a statistic like inflation rates are established to create consistency across analyses done at different times and by different researchers. For individual projects, baselines are the starting points, the "before conditions," against which comparisons can be made during and upon completion of the effort.

Trend Lines

These lines trace the pattern movements of a particular process or dynamic. In analytics, they are frequently derived from regression analysis of data points. Trend-lines possess much persuasive power when they depict movements in a vivid manner. They can cause the viewer to make projections based on past data for direction, speed, and momentum. Such implications can be acted upon to either anticipate the extension of the trend or in defense of a trend with negative connotations. Still, caution must be applied to the message portrayed by trend lines, as underlying dynamics may suddenly change or responses by other parties may upend previous assumptions.

Fault and Stress Lines

Borrowed from geology, these words refer to lines that result from grand forces coming to act in opposition to each other, revealing stark rifts and fissures between two or more sides. Readily applicable to human-centric forces as well, fault lines are portrayals of the divisions created by colliding factors. On maps, fault lines can identify areas where conflicting juxtapositions might exist between countries with rival ideologies, such as between the Cold War blocs in Europe. Stress lines can indicate where conflicts are in development, building slowly over time. Recognition of where such lines are occurring can guide action to resolve them. A country with simmering ethnic strife, as a hypothetical case, might be mapped showing the regions where ethnic groups abut one another, laying forth areas where peace brokering might intervene.

Dividing Lines

A natural progression from fault lines, dividing lines separate the actors and factors into distinct groups, characterized by some shared trait, such as a common language, socio-economic class, religious affiliation, and any other communal factor. Dividing lines can also illustrate how groups are separated by fundamental disagreements. Controversial issues drive polarizing opinions, often spurring the rise of factions and interest groups to press their points of view. Electoral research uses various means to identify patterns of voting through selective criteria, and place dividing lines upon maps to distinguish voter groups and their distribution. Such lines help to discern patterns of affiliation and inclinations, thereby shaping candidates' approach to identified groups.

Battle Lines

When conflicts arise, they are often fought along fronts as an attack confronts a defense. The colliding fronts coalesce along into distinct battle, clash, or firing lines. Whereas battle lines of war are clearly understood, battle lines can be a conceptual representation of wars fought elsewhere in civil society. Legal fights, for example, involving pivotal cases or different classes of plaintiffs can be seen as virtual battle lines between heartfelt principles or competing industries. Whether literal or figurative, battle lines compel attention as starkly opposed forces fight for critical stakes that could be won or lost by a small margin.

Ground Line

Whereas the skyline viewpoint is one of verticality, from top to down, the ground-line perspective of the strategic domain is one of horizontality, from one side to another, across horizons. It is a natural point of view that engages the

Table 5.1 Four elements of the ground view

GROUND ELEMENT	DOMAIN FOCUS
FOREGROUND	*FRONT AND CENTER ISSUES*
BACKGROUND	*CONTEXTUAL AND CONTRIBUTORY ISSUES*
ABOVE GROUND	*VISIBLE AND OVERT*
UNDER GROUND	*HIDDEN AND COVERT*

innate understanding derived from sight and sight-lines. The ground-line view is that of being "up front and personal," gaining insight from direct observation. The *REEDS* mnemonic rosters five principles of self-reliant observation: Rely upon yourself, Experience it yourself, Explain it yourself, Do it yourself, and See it yourself.

The ground-line vantage point resonates the most among people for its closeness to actual events and personalities. Different aspects of the ground-centered perspectives yield a four-element framelet. Table 5.1 disaggregates the ground-line view into four commonly understood vantage points. The foreground holds those issues that are actively engaging one's attention, perhaps an ongoing stream of activities or an acute problem that requires solving. The background is what holds those driving factors that may have brought about the current situation, or the historical chain of events leading up to the present. The above-ground perspective is the realm of the readily perceivable, especially those actors and factors that are in active engagement. The underground, or below-ground, perspective is the realm of the hidden, unperceived factors, often instigated by intentional acts of concealment.

As the ground-line perspective is the one with the highest degree of vividness from a human perspective, it is the most common basis for the generation of persuasive storylines. First-person narratives convey stories often in personal, authentic heartfelt tones. Whereas no one person could hope to capture the entirety of a complex issue, individual ground-line stories can add "color" to otherwise dry analytical assessments. A collection of such stories can add to a mosaic of descriptions that can reinforce a hypothesis, or they can add "spikes" of unique angles upon the body of understanding that could add up to discernible patterns.

Line-Words for Domain Actors

The elaboration of lenses in line-word form that discern the patterns of characteristics among the players of a domain follows:

Player Line-Up

An adapted term from sports, this line-up is the roster of identifiable and capable players participating in a strategic game, striving to attain interests while defending their own, interacting with each other with calculated deliberateness.

Tribal Lines

In parallel to dividing lines, which separate two or more sides to an issue, groups of people may define themselves in such a way as to constitute a virtual "tribe." Tribes in the socio-political mold are those who are linked together to a cause or point of view, and are often so infused with their shared values that they act and think with a high degree of congruence, even as they are scattered far apart as an ideological diaspora.[1] Members in one tribe of an issue may band together and confront members of an opposing tribe in various forums, such as talk shows and at electoral events.

Line of Authority

Within any organization, there are allocations of responsibilities and gradations of powers, both formal and informal. Powers can be distributed along hierarchical lines, with higher levels holding authority to direct those in lower ranks. Such chains of command, typically ascribed to the military, can also apply within civilian organizations. Identification of the lines of authority is a form of domain intelligence in determining how powers are assigned and to which individuals.

Line of Succession

Closely aligned to lines of authority, succession lines are established by formal rules and procedures in bequeathing organizational authority upon the passing of a top leader. The U.S. government has a specified line of presidential succession centered upon roles and levels of seniority in Cabinet and heads in Congress.[2] Succession in monarchies such as the U.K. and Saudi Arabia relies upon rules and traditions tied to blood lines, the familial and relational bonds between and within generations.[3,4]

Stakes "On the Line"

A central motive for actors on the strategic domain is working to advance and protect their interests. When interests are at risk to be won or lost, such stakes are said to be "on the line," evoking the image of a tenuous high wire act which could tip in unpredictable directions. Stakes comprise the total value that is available to be won in a given situation. Such value could be in a tangible form, such as money or natural resources, or they could be intangible, such as prestige and morale. Stakes can exist within and across different timeframes, from the immediate to the indefinite future. Stakes are not only the specific prizes for achieving objectives, they include broader strategic implications for all parties as well. The presence of stakes creates a dramatic tension among competing parties, stoking appetites and provoking maneuvering for advantage.

Bottom Line Interests

Derived from accounting, *bottom line* refers to the net profit, what remains after all costs are deducted. Over time, it has attained a figurative meaning to indicate the net benefit underlying all interests in general. To invoke the bottom line is to cast attention upon the end result, a focus that alludes to the discounting of all other intervening issues and factors.

Leash Lines

The defense of one's own interests is a primal, instinctual duty for leaders. In service of deterring inbound threats and averting adverse conditions, leash lines represent ways designed to constrain would-be aggressors or to prevent any one entity from becoming dominant.

Interlocking alliances with intricate provisions and joint mechanisms are one means of enmeshing powerful players and moderating behavior. The U.N. Security Council, for example, endows each of the five permanent members (U.S., Russia, China, France, and Britain) an inviolable veto power, giving each an ability to wield blocking power against resolutions it disfavors, thus incentivizing multi-party negotiations to find common ground.[5]

Leash lines can constrain the behavior of organizations acting in civil society. The force of government rules and regulations are a formal source of limits, but organizations are also constrained by other factors, such as cultural norms, professional ties, and evolving societal values. The rise of environmentalism has influenced companies to become "more green" in their practices, reducing insensitive practices, such as ocean dumping, that were mainstream not long ago.

One four-element acronym that describes key leash lines is *ROPE*: *restrictions*, the substantive bounds placed around a particular activity; *obligations*, the set of indebted actions owed to others as the performance of a duty or fulfillment of mission; *prohibitions*, the banning of certain practices justified by a compelling rationale; and *expectations*, the standards set for the purpose of converging action toward a particular result.

Tripwires or Trigger Lines

Tripwires are lines implanted in an environment which are set to emit a warning signal when triggered by an encroaching enemy. Physical and electronic tripwires are manifested in heavily defended militarized borders, such as the 250 km buffer zone between North and South Korea, with each side poised to go to war should the other side be seen as crossing over to attack.[6] Tripwires can also be set for deterrent purposes at the geopolitical level: NATO lays down a military-political tripwire by expressing its core principle of collective defense to mean that an attack against any NATO member will be construed to be an attack upon the alliance as a whole.[7]

Bright Lines

In legal and regulatory circles, bright lines are objective, separating criteria, typically in binary format such as "yes-no" or "present-not present," that determine whether a particular law, rule, or regulation would apply. Bright lines are intended to clarify matters for the benefit of both regulator and those being regulated, so that implementers of the rule can apply criteria fairly and consistently, and that those subjected to the rule know what is or isn't permissible, and thus avoid penalties or pursue other paths.

Bright-line tests have been applied to how houses are taxed in New Zealand, for instance, with different rates applied depending upon when a house was purchased and for how long it has been owned, both conditions centered upon objective information—the date of purchase and the date of sale.[8]

Red Lines

In strategic affairs, the red line has become a memorable declaration of prohibition directed against an aggressor, drawing the proverbial "line in the sand" that enemies are told to dare not cross. The universally known color of the stop sign instinctually conveys the message of "halt or else."

Case in point: Calling upon the world to sanction Iran for its nuclear weapons program before it became operational and irreversible, Israeli Prime Minister Benjamin Netanyahu at the 2012 U.N. General Assembly invoked the red line as the necessary, clarifying step to prevent Iran from advancing any further:

> The relevant question is not when Iran will get the bomb. The relevant question is at what stage can we no longer stop Iran from getting the bomb. The *red line* must be drawn on Iran's nuclear enrichment program because these enrichment facilities are the only nuclear installations that we can definitely see and credibly target. And I believe that, faced with a clear red line, Iran will back down. And this will give more time for sanctions and diplomacy to convince Iran to dismantle its nuclear weapons program altogether.[9]

Another example of a red-line declaration in statecraft is when President Barack Obama in 2012 warned against Syria's escalating tactics against rebel forces and civilian populations:

> We cannot have a situation in which chemical or biological weapons are falling into the hands of the wrong people. We have been very clear to the Assad regime but also to other players on the ground that a *red line* for us is, we start seeing a whole bunch of weapons moving around or being utilized. That would change my calculus. That would change my equation.[10]

The implication was clear that should Syria use chemical or biological weapons, the U.S. would respond. When Syria was declared by the U.S. as having used such weapons against civilians in two separate episodes in 2017 and 2018 in defiant flouting of the Obama declaration, a military strike was immediately ordered by President Donald Trump as a punitive measure for each incident.[11,12]

Red lines, in making an if-then proposition starkly clear, also set expectations in at least two ways: First, that if a line is indeed crossed, then a triggering action will and must be taken. In this way, a red line can constrict the menu options down to a single choice: to respond or not to a breach. Failure to take action after a red-line breach risks the declarer being cast as bluffing or feckless. Second, a red-line declaration is an implicit license for a foe to conduct actions all the way up to but just short of the trigger, allowing that foe to maximize gains while staying technically compliant.

Former State Department Mideast negotiator Dennis Ross spoke of this flaw in regards to Syria: "I think you want to be careful how you describe red lines, because one consequence of defining red lines too narrowly is that it sends a message to the Iranians: 'We can do everything up to that red line,' and that may not be what you want."[13] In this way, a red line can become twisted into becoming a loophole.

Yellow Lines

The weakness of red lines lies, ironically, in their starkness and hair-trigger promises, affording foes to know, on an equal footing with all others, the self-constricted conditions and options imposed upon one's own position. To widen the circle of conditions and options available, and to create a buffer ahead of a red line, a yellow line might be deployed as an indicator more peripheral to a vital concern, analogous to how baseball field warning tracks signal to outfielders chasing outbound fly balls that the home-run wall is being approached.

A hypothetical yellow line in the Syrian crisis might be defined as the discovery of precursor ingredients known to be closely associated with such weapons. An extension of the concept would be to construct a concentric series of yellow lines, with some deployed along different dimensions of a problem, such as economic or political, thereby creating a more nuanced response architecture with gradations of warnings surrounding a red-line trigger. Yellow lines can serve as pre-ultimatums, with warnings escalating in quantity, rapidity, and intensity as more tripwires are crossed.

Green Lines

If red lines are meant to deter an undesired action, green lines are proposed as ways to facilitate cooperative action by proposing conditions that, if met, would trigger a beneficent or de-escalating action. If applied to Syria, a hypothetical green-line proposal might be to offer accommodative flexibility for fleeing refugees should the Syrian regime definitively rid itself of chemical weapons. Green lines can also be constructed in such a way as to create "safe harbors" or "hold harmless" situations in which met conditions are reciprocated with grants of additional time for negotiations or de-escalatory measures. For their cooperative characteristics, green lines are kindred to good-faith gestures, confidence-building measures, and the proffering of carrots rather than the wielding of punishing sticks.

End of the Line

Warnings may be issued but ignored or flouted. Slights may be felt but absorbed without complaint. Grudges may be borne but kept hidden. Grievances may be pressed, in some historical cases over generations, but not adjudicated. However forgiving and accommodative people might be personally, conditions and interests may dictate a response at the institutional level and discharge an accumulated burden. An end-of-the-line situation is one in which a party is aggrieved to the point whereby it can no longer tolerate any additional indignities. The potential for destabilizing backlash increases if pent-up emotional pressure compounds itself without avenues for relief through communication or diplomacy.

In 2017, a Saudi Arabia-led coalition of its Mideast allies suddenly imposed diplomatic and economic sanctions against Qatar over its alleged ties to Iran and its exercise of influence in the region over many years. After nursing a complicated and convoluted complaint, the Saudis chose to lash out at Qatar apparently without forewarning or any use of red or yellow lines, resulting in a regional crisis that also surprised U.S. leaders, who were relying upon the region's stability as an asset for other diplomatic goals.[14] A different, less destabilizing scenario might have arisen if grievances were tied to yellow lines, giving fair warning that, from the Saudi perspective, the end of the line was approaching.

Lifelines

The normal interchange among nations and among organizations at large involves exchange of favors, goods, and services in ways that improve the interests of trading parties. Buyers get what they lack and sellers are paid for their surpluses. An equilibrium of interdependencies is achieved through the balance of incentives. However, at times an equilibrium can be disrupted by any number of catalysts ranging from war, disaster, or disease, and the previous bonds of interdependencies can dissolve into sets of new dependencies, impacting people, organizations, and countries alike. Those in a position to offer aid may extend help, through organized lifelines, to rescue and sustain lives and livelihoods. Among nations, lifelines can come about in the form of ongoing economic assistance, military supplies, development programs, and other forms of technical or humanitarian assistance.

Seldom do these arrangements have a purely charitable character: In the transactional environment of nations, there can be both explicit and implicit expectations for some favorable treatment in return, such as vote trading in certain diplomatic forums, acquiring geo-favorable military basic rights, or undertaking other forms of "log-rolling," or trading favors across deals or sectors.

In geopolitical history, lifelines have been extended to save allies mired in exigencies, as the U.S. did for Britain and the Soviet Union through the Lend-Lease programs during World War II.[15] Economic lifelines extended by Russia to Cuba in the 1960s and 1970s aimed to keep Fidel Castro in power and thus sustain his influence in the Americas.[16] In recent years, Cuba and Venezuela extended lifelines to each other to mutually reinforce their own fragile economies, including oil-for-health arrangements by which Venezuela exported its oil and imported Cuban health workers to man hospitals and clinics.[17,18] As the HIV/AIDS crisis loomed across sub-Saharan Africa, U.S. President George W. Bush authorized a multi-billion dollar aid package that became an essential medical lifeline to countries and individuals affected by HIV/AIDS.[19]

Line of Argument

Affecting change in a crowded, competitive strategic domain in which all players are defending and asserting their interests is a task that compels the skillful and artful use of persuasion, the ability to align people and events for the betterment of one's own interests. With entities' positions and interests so varied, the means and methods of persuasion are likewise diversified, even personalized down to the individual leader's own set of skills. Some of those approaches are described as lines of argument or as chains of logical reasoning.

Hard Line

Political scientist Joseph Nye cleaved sources of influence into two main camps, that of "hard-power" and of "soft-power."[20] Concisely, hard power is centered around the application of coercive and implied threats; soft power is exercised through cooperation and collaboration. Accordingly, the animating application of hard power is the "hard line" approach. The hard line is seen as a rigid, vigorous, doctrinaire application of power or assertion of a point of view. The intensity of argument is often conflated with the merits of what is being touted, reinforcing the factor of emotionality in hard line approaches.

The hard line is also manifested in the mobilization of hard-power assets, which might be called the *Three M's: money, military*, and *materials*. The hard power calculus is reducible to raw comparisons of players' stockpile of the three M's, with scant regards paid to soft power, such as diplomatic overtures, interpersonal chemistry, or moral suasion. An emblematic quote is attributed to Joseph Stalin who, upon hearing Winston Churchill's earnest yet convoluted argument to him about the high-minded desirability in promoting good relations with Catholics in the post-war world order, interjected with tough-minded brusqueness and dismissiveness: "How many divisions does the Pope of Rome have?"[21]

Soft Line

Soft power, as explained by Nye, is rooted in the common bonds that naturally form across societies, such as ties of culture, language, history, and respected institutions involved in health, education, and social welfare. Whereas the desired effects of such bonds may be too diffuse or too variable to be identifiable as concrete objectives, soft power, through its ability to bridge people through civic ties and shared aspirations, can shape prevailing attitudes and unify expectations toward central goals and values.

Whereas the Three M's of hard power—money, military, and materials—are subject to physical limits and the constraining force of scarcity, soft power has an expansive, horizontal quality derived from its intercultural reach. With the population growth, economic advances, and technological interconnectivity, soft power has a sustainability beyond what might be expected by its diffuseness. The ever-accelerating "wiredness" of the world that amplifies any voice with immediate effect, portends the accelerating influence of societal and cultural leaders, i.e. advocates and online personalities adept at social media, relative to conventional leaders in the hard-power fields.

The soft line is pertinent in the interpersonal dynamics between leaders. Those who persistently and insistently negotiate with a hard-line approach will typically elicit a reciprocal hard-line response from counterparts. Not surprisingly, the clashes between hard liners results in hardened positions and hardened attitudes that impede progress, perhaps irretrievably so. Soft-line techniques in negotiation, seeking common ground, exchanging a first set of concessions, inviting third-party intercession, exploring hypothetical solutions, and other ameliorating moves, can mollify otherwise recalcitrant parties enough for them to see the broader context of their positions and induce them to consider a solution that is win-win rather than win-lose.

Soft-line approaches add a degree of added complexity and nuance that, ironically, can make executing the soft line harder than what it would seem by its name. Soft line tactics demand extra effort to "read between the lines," or glean insights from what is left unspoken, as well as to delicately "walk a fine line" astride sensitive positions, some of which may even exist within one's own camp.

The Party Line

A contributing force to the assertion of the hard line is the allegiance to the party line, the doctrine promulgated by a directing authority. Doctrines are composed sets of orthodox principles of convincing strength and clarity that motivate adherents and spur outward proselytization.

In negotiations with outsiders, compromise may be anathema, seen as dilutive and subtractive to core principles, making ultimate agreements much harder to achieve. Those who represent the institution confront the difficult choices of remaining "in line" with the party line, finding ways to "cross the line" in outreach to counterparts, or "breaking out of the line" by risking alienation to one's patron.

By engaging other actors on the strategic domain, one benefits in knowing their party lines for important signals and clues about their intentions, interests, and interactions. Shifts in orthodoxy are just as important, as they add insight on new factors and motives. During the Cold War, Western intelligence agencies spent considerable effort parsing the messaging of previously hidebound powers—for example China, North Korea, and Russia—to better understand the evolution of their ideologies and their underlying drivers.[22]

Parties on the Borderline or on the Sidelines

Lines of argument are intended not only to maintain one's base of adherents or to defeat opponents but to enlist those who are undecided or uncommitted. Those on the borderline are those said to be "on the fence." In modern elections, such fence-sitters who could be persuaded to choose one side or another are typically called "swing voters." As their perceptions and opinions are persuadable, they can be the most voluble and fickle. As those on the borderline, nations, legislators, or voters are the pivotal groups to win over in closely fought contests, but they can demand a high price for their support.

Another prime object for persuasion are those who are on the sidelines, those who feel disenchanted or disenfranchised, such as those in poverty or those enduring discrimination. While those sidelined from society may feel shunted aside, an effective outreach effort that rallies them with emotional resonance and that works toward their interests may result in their enlistment back to the mainstream. Many social programs are directed at underprivileged groups with the aim of providing a vital need so that they can participate meaningfully within their communities.

Summary of the Strategic Domain

The strategic domain is the dynamic setting on which actors and factors interact in ways that facilitate or frustrate one's agenda to achieve vital goals. Given its complexity, the strategic domain requires ways to perceive and assess it in effective and efficient means. Heuristic conceptual tools such as frames, frameworks, and lenses provide ways to organize and structure these arrangements of players, their powers, and their purposes. By simplifying perceptions of the domain, it becomes easier to identify objectives, opportunities, and obstacles.

What lie ahead are the conjoined tasks of establishing strategic goals and designing the plans to achieve them.

Notes

1. Amy Chua, *Political Tribes: Group Instinct and the Fate of Nations* (New York: Penguin, 2018), 1–12.
2. Presidential Succession Act 1947, as amended, 3 U.S.C. § 19—Vacancy in offices of both President and Vice President; officers eligible to act, *80th Cong.* (1947). www.law.cornell.edu/uscode/text/3/19 (accessed Oct. 20, 2018).
3. Government of the UK, "Succession." www.royal.uk/succession (accessed Oct. 20, 2018).
4. Mark Mazetti and Ben Hubbard, "Rise of Saudi Prince Shatters Decades of Royal Tradition," *New York Times*, Oct. 15, 2016. https://nyti.ms/2e6PDHT?smid=nytcore-ios-share (accessed Oct. 20, 2018).
5. United Nations Security Council, "Voting Systems and Records." www.un.org/en/sc/meetings/voting.shtml (accessed Oct. 20, 2018).
6. Andrew Jeong, "Defense Scale-Down on Korean DMZ Raises Security Risks, U.S. General Says," *Wall Street Journal*, Aug. 22, 2018. www.wsj.com/articles/defense-scale-down-on-korean-dmz-raises-security-risks-u-s-general-says-1534922390 (accessed Oct. 20, 2018).
7. North Atlantic Treaty Organization, "Collective Defense—Article 5," updated June 12, 2018. www.nato.int/cps/en/natohq/topics_110496.htm (accessed Oct. 20, 2018).
8. Inland Revenue of New Zealand, "Extension of the Bright-Line Test for Residential Property," updated Mar. 29, 2018. www.ird.govt.nz/news-updates/brightline-extension.html (accessed Oct. 20, 2018).
9. Arshad Mohammed, "Key Portions of Israeli PM Netanyahu's U.N. Speech on Iran," *Reuters*, Sept. 27, 2012. www.reuters.com/article/us-un-assembly-israel-text/key-portions-of-israeli-pm-netanyahus-u-n-speech-on-iran-idUSBRE88Q1RR20 120927 (accessed Oct. 20, 2018).
10. Ben Rhodes, "Inside the White House During the Syrian 'Red Line' Crisis," *The Atlantic*, June 3, 2018. www.theatlantic.com/international/archive/2018/06/inside-the-white-house-during-the-syrian-red-line-crisis/561887/?utm_source=feed (accessed Oct. 20, 2018).
11. Michael Gordon, Helene Cooper, and Michael Shear, "Dozens of U.S. Missiles Hit Air Base in Syria," *New York Times*, Apr. 6, 2017. www.nytimes.com/2017/04/06/world/middleeast/us-said-to-weigh-military-responses-to-syrian-chemical-attack.html (accessed Oct. 20, 2018).
12. "Joined by Allies, President Trump Takes Action to End Syria's Chemical Weapons Attacks," *White House Press Release*, Apr. 14, 2018. www.whitehouse.gov/articles/joined-allies-president-trump-takes-action-end-syrias-chemical-weapons-attacks/ (accessed Oct. 20, 2018).
13. Ben Pauker, "Interview: Dennis Ross," *Foreign Policy*, Jan. 20, 2012. https://foreignpolicy.com/2012/01/20/interview-dennis-ross/ (accessed Oct. 20, 2018).
14. Patrick Wintour, "Gulf Plunged into Diplomatic Crisis as Countries Cut Ties with Qatar," *The Guardian*, June 5, 2017. www.theguardian.com/world/2017/jun/05/saudi-arabia-and-bahrain-break-diplomatic-ties-with-qatar-over-terrorism (accessed Oct. 20, 2018).
15. U.S. Department of State Office of the Historian, "Lend-Lease and Military Aid to the Allies in the Early Years of World War II." https://history.state.gov/milestones/1937-1945/lend-lease (accessed Oct. 20, 2018).
16. Mervyn J. Bain, "Cuba-Soviet Relations in the Gorbachev Era," *Journal of Latin American Studies*, 37(4) (Nov. 2005): 772. doi:10.1017/s0022216x05009867
17. Juan Forero, "Cuba Perks Up as Venezuelan Foils Embargo," *New York Times*, Aug. 4, 2006. www.nytimes.com/2006/08/04/world/americas/04cuba.html?smid=nytcore-ios-share (accessed Oct. 20, 2018).

18. Chris Arsenault, "Cuban Doctors Prescribes Hope in Venezuela," *Al Jazeera Online*, Dec. 31, 2012. www.aljazeera.com/indepth/spotlight/venezuelaelection/2012/10/20121039242915607.html (accessed Oct. 20, 2018).
19. Ed Stoddard, "Former U.S. President Bush Touts Signature Africa AIDS Program in Botswana," *Reuters*, Apr. 4, 2017. www.reuters.com/article/us-africa-bush-idUSKBN1761LJ (accessed Oct. 20, 2018).
20. Nye, *Soft Power*, 11–18.
21. Aleksandr Bangersky, "How Many Divisions Does the Pope of Rome Have?" Voices from Russia blogsite. https://02varvara.wordpress.com/2009/12/10/how-many-divisions-does-the-pope-of-rome-have/ (accessed Oct. 20, 2018).
22. Patrick Cockburn, "R.I.P. Kremlinology," *Washington Post*, Feb. 14, 1998. www.washingtonpost.com/archive/opinions/1988/02/14/rip-kremlinology/1977f8b6-841e-45bc-9c0c-087136cfcbe8/?utm_term=.0f7cb9e4d661 (accessed Oct. 20, 2018).

Part 3

The Strategic Goal

6 Assessing Capabilities

In Part 1, *strategic mission* was defined as the pursuit toward an enduring cause by people animated by shared values. In Part 2, *strategic domain* was defined as the contextual universe in which that pursuit is implemented. In Part 3, the desired end-state that fulfills the pursuit, designated here as the *strategic goal*, will be described by an overarching principle, be shaped by the availability and extent of capabilities, be further structured with a new multi-element concept called "goal-crafting," and then be specified even more precisely within that concept by a novel formula incorporating a series of four line-words.

Consistent with and in support of an entity's strategic mission, the strategic goal is a prospective achievement that, if and when attained, yields specified benefits to be shared among designated stakeholders. The goal ultimately chosen is a confluence of the decision made regarding an objective among all available opportunities and of the judgment made regarding the capabilities needed to reach the goal. Both the aim and the pursuit should be aligned with the values and ideals of the entity and its defined stakeholders. Stakeholders are those groups and individuals who are directly involved within the entity, such as workers, managers, and leaders, as well as those in a broader external circle who are affected by the entity's operations and mission at large, such as shareholders, neighborhoods, governments, and the public in general. As stakeholder circles can widen exponentially, the entities themselves should define the circle that best encompasses their chief constituents.

In assessing its strategic domain, an entity looks out onto a landscape teeming with actors and factors. It seeks to accomplish aims that allow it to survive and to fulfill its ongoing agenda, the roster of priorities it deems vital to its mission and values. The full range of achievements worthy of consideration on its agenda can be said to demarcate its *aspirational horizon*, or alternatively, the *horizon of opportunities*. This conceptual horizon, a feature on the strategic domain, consists of a variety of forward destinations, with each point of arrival attached to both a cost and a benefit. As an opportunity horizon holds so many choices, with differing cost-benefit propositions, an entity needs to use constraining criteria to narrow the possibilities to a select few, and then to sharpen its deliberations further to identify its next best goal. Impending dangers might also loom on the landscape as a perceived *threat horizon*, against which a parallel assessment can be made on the dangers posed and the efforts and costs required to confront them.

Behind these horizons are the vistas beyond what is achieved, designated as the *end-state conditions*, wherein lie the new configurations of actors and factors. Entities work toward achieving end-states that embody all of their intended consequences; however, the pervasiveness of risk factors, especially randomness and resistance from other actors, can result in many unintended consequences becoming realized in the new end-state.

There are two dimensions of an opportunity horizon to consider as a hypothetical line of achievement: its proximity to an entity (how close in or far away) and its breadth (how horizontally wide or narrow). In this model, opportunities closer in are deemed easier to achieve than those farther away. From this it follows that a simple task is closer in, while a complex job is farther out. A wide horizon holds more opportunities than one that is narrow, a quantitative characteristic. Accordingly, ambition can be construed to be an appetite to take on tougher tasks as well as to do more of them, escalating in risk in both qualitative and quantitative dimensions. Risk appetite is inherently a psychological, subjective factor rooted in inner drive and ego, which can complicate external efforts to assess a leader's full scope of intentions.

What else is necessary to carry out one's ambition is the possession and the effective exercise of *capabilities*. Capabilities are the available sets of assets and human talent, individual and collective, that can be activated and organized toward purposeful actions. As a class, they constitute the instruments or equipment with which willful ambition wields power toward a specific aim. Capabilities can be tangible, in the form of tools and technologies, or they can be intangible, in the form of knowledge and emotional skills. Capabilities can work in the present, serving current operational needs, and they can be reserved for contingencies and emergencies.

As capabilities serve upon the direction of their owners, they possess generic and fungible qualities, making them available for innumerable tasks. With these flexible attributes, capabilities are a major factor in defining an opportunity horizon by determining the ease or difficulty of achieving a particular objective, by expanding or limiting the raw quantity of possible objectives, and by intensifying or dampening risk appetites to take on greater and more rewarding challenges. The extent and qualities of capabilities then become instrumental in the broader development of strategy by establishing clearer sets of destinations and by undergirding confidence about reaching them.

Figure 6.1 illustrates the basic relationship between capabilities and the opportunity horizon. If beginning capabilities are at a modest level, they have a fairly limited reach and can attain only a truncated range of objectives. However, if capabilities are expanded in quantity and quality, then the collective reach of these new assets is extended farther out, making the opportunity horizon broader and deeper.

One way by which capabilities clarify what is possible is by exercising them in drills and simulations. Through testing, one gains a vivid understanding of a

EXPANDED OPPORTUNITY HORIZON

**LIMITED
OPPORTUNITY HORIZON**

| REACH OF EXPANDED
CAPABILITIES |
|---|

| REACH OF LIMITED
CAPABILITIES |
|---|

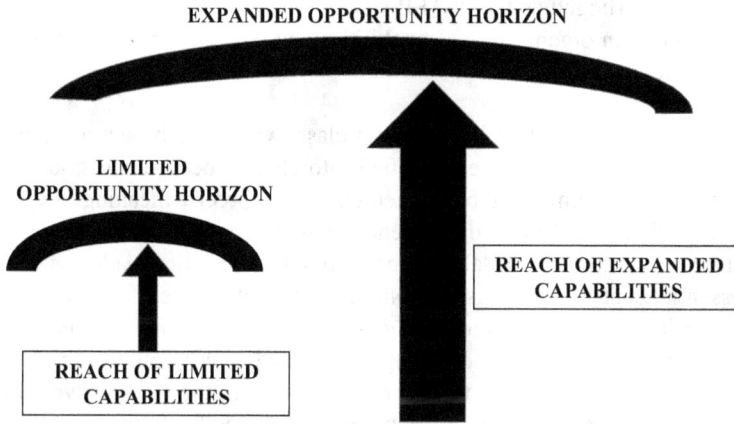

Figure 6.1 Capabilities and opportunity horizon

capability's operational reach, its extent of effective functionality. It is crucial to understand a capability's "can-do vs. can't do" point, better known as its breaking point. Up to the breaking point, the probability of success is high, but beyond that point the probability of failure rises. Bracketing the breaking point is the probabilistic gray area, the zone of murkiness where variability and randomness reflect high uncertainty about what works in a given scenario.

Repeated cycles of testing-improving can improve confidence about the breaking point and reduce surrounding unknowns. Military exercises in particular are conducted to gain a valuable realm of "self-intelligence" about the performance strengths and weaknesses of equipment, units, and individuals. Through testing, leaders are able to transform their theoretical and hypothetical beliefs into practical, validated knowledge that can be fed back for further improvement. Exercises and tests can also serve a strategic purpose: Showcasing one's rising capabilities projects an image of strength and commitment among allies and adversaries alike, and gives credible backing to intentions, whether declared or implied.

An acronym that encapsulates the testing of operational reach of capabilities is *STEP*:

> The first element is the *set-up*, the assembly of components and personnel to engage in the assessment process, along with sets of questions to be asked and answered.
> The *test* is the gauging of an idea to identify an asset's point of maximum attainment within specified conditions.
> The *exercise* is the application of test results and accompanying learnings in real-world conditions, along with any other points of strengths and weaknesses.

The *proof* is the knowledge gained and validated by the test-exercise series. Altogether the "STEP-wise" approach promotes one's awareness of an organization's capabilities and encourages their use toward strategic aims.

The word *capabilities* describes an asset class, which is a broad, open-ended category. If it could be further specified into clearer, better-understood components, then the term could be applied with more precise meaning. As previously described, capabilities overall encompass the range of assets that can be construed as equipment available for activation by a directing leader, as well as the essential contributions arising from the talents of people.

To break down *capabilities*, a generic term, in a more memorable way, a linguistic sleight of hand is used to separate the two words conjoined within it: *capacity* and *ability*. For this model, *capacity* implies the quantitative, objective characteristics of a piece of equipment, such as the lifting power of a rocket. In parallel, *ability* implies the qualitative, subjective characteristics of people, such as the negotiating prowess of a cabinet minister or the work ethic of a project team.

What follows is a simple heuristic equation that breaks down capabilities into two basic components, capacity and ability, that can further trigger a series of nesting constituents:

CAPABILITY = CAPACITY + ABILITY

with *capacity* assigned to mean assets that are instrument-oriented, such as tools and technologies. These can include the base, elemental forms of hard power, such as money (purchasing power), military forces (fighting power), and materials (manufacturing power). From higher vantage points, capacity can include various organized arrangements such as projects, campaigns, and enterprises.

Furthermore, capacity can be subdivided into two functions:

CAPACITY = (GENERATIVE + ABSORPTIVE) FUNCTIONS

or as a comparable alternative,

CAPACITY = (OFFENSIVE + DEFENSIVE) FUNCTIONS

whereby the generative functions are those outbound actions into the strategic domain intended to impact other actors. The absorptive functions are those defensive-oriented actions taken to confront inbound encroachments from actors, such as alerting a defense network or activating reserve units on standby. Accordingly, the terms *generative* and *absorptive* can be substituted with *offensive* and *defensive*, respectively, and still retain the outbound vs. inbound dichotomy.

Ability, the second yet equal half of the capability equation, is assigned to mean the realm of human-oriented attributes related to work and effort. Ability is the set of human talents of specific value to an entity's mission, which is nurtured and harnessed by leaderships as an imperative organizational task.

Human ability can be divided into two contributions:

$$ABILITY = SKILL + WILL$$

with *skill* being the contributions made from the rich realm of personal talents. Skills can be broken out as an E-series framelet:

$$SKILL = EDUCATE \mid EVALUATE \mid EXERCISE \mid EXPERIENCE \mid$$
$$EXPERTISE$$

The second contribution made by people is the uniquely human attribute of willpower, the drive and determination to see tasks to completion through all conditions fair or foul. Willpower might be understood in three dimensions:

$$WILL = PUSH + PULL + NUDGE$$

Push is the drive to move events, or fellow people, forward toward a desired outcome. Pull is the persuasive power to draw in, or enlist, other actors in the strategic domain to one's cause. Nudge is a newly described scope of behaviors, compiled in a book of the same name authored by economists Richard Thaler and Cass Sunstein, centered around a softer style of persuasion through known psychological prompts.[1] By arrangement and by design, the placing and sequencing of such prompts, or nudges, can comprise a "choice architecture," with which organizations can guide constituents toward better outcomes on their own accord, rather than their reliance upon directives and other hardline approaches to affect change.

When seen as an additive product of all preceding elements, capabilities is a compendium of both techno-centric and human-centric halves, modeling the more prosaic relationship between apparatus and personnel. A modified version of the heuristic equation becomes:

$$CAPABILITY = (OFFENSIVE \text{ AND } DEFENSIVE) \text{ } CAPACITIES +$$
$$HUMAN \text{ } (SKILL + WILL)$$

By simple substitution, the equation can be extended into an even longer train of factors with all the additional subcomponents. Similarly, by simple conceptual extension, the capability equation can point out the direct implications of ambition: Setting aspirations to reach ever higher achievements means acquiring greater amounts and more classes of assets as well as enhancing one's reserve of human capital, including pragmatic skills and the intangible skills of willpower, the reservoir of emotional fortitude.

The build-up and maintenance of capabilities in service of ambition and interests can be costly, consuming many forms of capital involving money, time, and talent. Direct expenditures of time and resources subtract from the pool of assets that could serve other aims. The implication is that once activated, resource-consuming operations deplete options because they generate opportunity costs. Building and maintaining organizational capabilities also consume leadership capabilities by demanding the skill, time, and attention of managers and supervisors.

The totality of costs attached to capabilities creates a pressure for organizations to achieve goals that are worthwhile and to do so effectively and efficiently. Organizations, by investing in essential capabilities, take on the challenge to attain outcomes that represent a return on invested capital. The outcomes imperative is weighted differently between private and public sectors: Private companies are primarily focused on profit as a return on invested financial capital, whereas public and non-profit entities are keyed to results that matter to their values and missions, inclusive of both tangible and intangible effects. Thus it could be said that private entities chiefly seek "income," whereas public entities substantially seek "outcome" as the dividends from their capabilities.

A heuristic equation that expresses the satisfaction derived from these sources of success looks like this:

INCOME + OUTCOME = WELCOME

with INCOME being the measure of benefits, OUTCOME being the results of effort, and WELCOME being the degree of emotional satisfaction that arises.

To summarize, the assets of organizations are the means with which they operate and function. More significantly, organizations seek to assemble and acquire such assets they deem essential for them to achieve designated goals and to ultimately fulfill their mandated mission. The most essential asset for any human organization is the people themselves—they bring particular skills, energies, and the determination to succeed. Organizations also need instruments, the tools with which particular tasks are implemented toward an intended result. Altogether the duality of humans and tools, of psychology and of technology, is what constitutes the core capability of organizations. Assembling and motivating these forms of capital is as much a part of strategy as the implementation itself.

Note

1. Thaler and Sunstein, *Nudge*, 83–102.

7 Goal Crafting

The drive to achieve results in order to fulfill a mission and to redeem the costs involved in securing organizational capabilities means that there is an ever-present imperative to specify what those achievements are and what benefits will arise. Defining those answers makes clear what a pursuit entails and if the stakes in play are worthwhile. The set of clarifying answers, the value proposition, is embedded in the construction of the strategic goal, which is a composite of specifications, in varying degrees of preciseness, for what is to be achieved, what is to be gained, and what is to be invested.

In constructing a proposed strategic goal, a basic process of design must be undertaken that reflects a complex judgment about the domain, capabilities, difficulties, and rewards. To reduce the complexity and lay forth an elemental process for setting a strategic goal, the skill of *goal crafting* is introduced. Goal crafting is a deliberative, reasoned method for the structuring of a desired aim in ways to make the necessary requirements understandable among stakeholders. This chapter lays forth four basic processes of goal crafting: *shaping*, *formulating*, *classifying*, and *sourcing*.

Shaping Goals

To shape a goal is to substantiate one's interests in a way that gives them a form that is well understood by others in order to enlist their efforts. It is a commitment to bring to light what the leader believes is a mission-fulfilling achievement, bringing it forward out of the many possibilities available.

In shaping goals, one needs to balance two conflicting forces: clarity and opacity. The pervasive inhibitor of action is vagueness. When events are beclouded by uncertainties and when directions are issued in ambiguous terms, the natural human reaction in those situations is to slow down, even stop, and await clarifying details. Opaqueness, whether by intent or accident, muddies one's mental vision of what is going on or what is being communicated, resulting in an inhibition of one's desire to take action for fear of making mistakes or becoming disadvantaged in some way. Hedging behavior divides attention and depletes energy of personnel, weakening their resolve and morale.

Yet for all its detractions, vagueness still persists in the rhetoric of description and of persuasion. It remains because unfolding events of the world can be turbulent, clouding perceptions to a degree often described in military terms as the "fog of war." Overstating clarity when it does not exist undermines confidence in those who express inaccuracies and also risks taking action toward the wrong dynamics. Discussions regarding sensitive issues are frequently done in diplomatic settings in an oblique, respectful manner so as to avoid triggering emotional reactions that may debilitate substantive talks. In the modern era of instant-cycle, mass communications (messages of persuasion, particularly in politics) are often couched in broad-stroke, impressionistic ways to reach the largest possible audience. The risk to campaigners is that high specificity of content would limit a message's reach and induce opposing arguments.

In contending with these countervailing factors in deciding what goals to achieve, leaders constantly face a *precision decision*: how to walk a fine line between providing either too much or too little detail for the conditions at hand and for the stakes involved. The precision decision involves judgment of the tradeoffs between specificity and optionality, conditions that act inversely to each other. A high degree of specificity implies fewer remaining choices, whereas a high degree of generality in thought and rhetoric retains a wide appeal. Committing to a particular course of action or to a specific conclusion means foregoing alternative paths or interpretations.

As goals are a spur to purposeful, beneficial actions, and as actions ultimately involve the commitment of capabilities in both tangible and intangible forms, the prevailing principle in strategic affairs is to drive toward specificity as interests and urgency escalate. The synchronicities of personnel and materiel in preparations and operations require intricate planning and execution. Ambiguities would inject confusion and doubt among implementers and create conditions for breakdowns and potential chaos.

In navigating the choices along these gradients, the strategist must know the ways to hone in on the right level of specificity while retaining a palpable understanding of the surrounding domain or the "big picture," much in the style described by negotiation expert James Sebenius as the ability to "zoom in or zoom out" at key points in diplomatic interactions.[1]

Heuristic, or rule-of-thumb, methods in adjusting one's focus from the vague to the specific include the concept of a "policy aperture," which allows the perceptual viewing of an issue along various degrees of breadth and depth. A wide aperture lens takes in the broad, thematic features of an issue; a narrower aperture lens zooms in on that which is more operational, perhaps at the level of a project or campaign, and the sharpest lens hones down to the pinpoint level of detail, such as identifying specific individuals undertaking specific tasks with specific tools.

Other ways to envision the focusing process from the vague to the specific is to "come down from cloud-talk to the ground-walk," an homage to the adage of "seeing beyond the forest to the trees." Adapting the direction-destiny-destination framework introduced in Part 1, another method of sharpening focus is to convert notions of destiny into points of destination, translating that which resonates emotionally to that which can attained operationally.

Yet another way is to arrange a series of conceptual lenses, introduced in Part 2, to perform four honing functions:

> *Confine*—establish a first series of bounds to an issue
> *Define*—propose a working understanding of what exists about a matter
> *Refine*—adjust the definition to suit particular conditions
> *Streamline*—enhance the understanding even further by simplification to an instinctual, "gut" level

Arguably the most important, and consequential, precision decision to make in a strategic context is to visualize the desired end-state conditions and how the new landscape of actors and factors would be altered after successfully achieving a goal. The precise articulation of the end-state and how that benefits one's interests then establishes a chain of assumptions of how those conditions can be achieved, what capabilities are needed, and what emanates into the future. With clarity, assumptions can be judged on how realistic they are and what actions might be needed to bolster those assumptions deemed wanting in some way. Thus, defining the strategic goal, the culmination of intent, becomes the first and essential step in establishing the triumvirate between the end-state, assumptions, and capabilities.

Formulating Goals

The word *formulating* has *formula* at its root, denoting the deliberative, stepwise construction of a product or a result from elemental components. If one advances the premise that a strategic goal is a compound proposition of achievement and resulting value and that it is an essential reference for the basing of assumptions and the calculating of needed capabilities, then it follows that a standardized formula in defining the strategic goal would promote a wider common understanding of its importance and how it can be constructed.

In 1981, management consultant George T. Doran introduced a pioneering framework for the establishment of a goal. His use of the acronym SMART encapsulated five desirable attributes of a goal: Specific, Measurable, Achievable, Relevant, and Time-bound.[2] Doran's concise and memorable formulation, with some modifications contributed by others, won widespread acceptance among business and organizational leaders as a useful primary template for setting a goal.

To complement Doran's contribution, a new Four-Line Framework is introduced for defining a strategic goal that is in keeping with the use of line-words throughout the Strategic Policy Design framework. The Four-Line Framework is an approach to constructing goals using criteria that directly challenge strategists to drive toward clearer specifics.

The Four-Line Framework for a strategic goal consists of the following:

1. Finish Line
2. Deadline
3. Pay Line
4. Headline

Figure 7.1 demonstrates how these four elements are related to each other. Fundamentally, getting to the finish line and doing so by a designed deadline is a strategic goal's most essential element. Reaching the finish line liberates value along a pay line, which encompasses both tangible and intangible forms of benefits. The accomplishment also has headline value, or a "whole-of-entity" prominence in the organization's history worthy of recognition.

What follows is an elaboration of each element in turn.

1. Finish Line

Also interchangeable with "goal-line," the finish line is simply the specified end point for an organized effort, such as a project or a campaign. The end point should be defined in such a manner as to be objectively understood by the community that takes interest in its completion. A public goal, such as the restoration of safe, clean drinking water to all the residents of the city of Flint, Michigan, after its water supply was stricken with lead contamination is clear and compelling enough to be understood by the entire citizenry in that community, whereas a highly specialized technical goal such as "the completion of the Roux-en-Y gastric bypass surgery for recalcitrant gastro-esophageal reflux disease" would be best understood by medical professionals.

A finish line that is objective should be verifiable, designed so that both the goal and the accomplishment can be ascertained in a truthful, consistent manner. Many goals are verifiable through perception of the normal human senses, especially the sense of vision, which underscores the adage that "seeing is believing." However, many technical objectives are beyond the perceptual

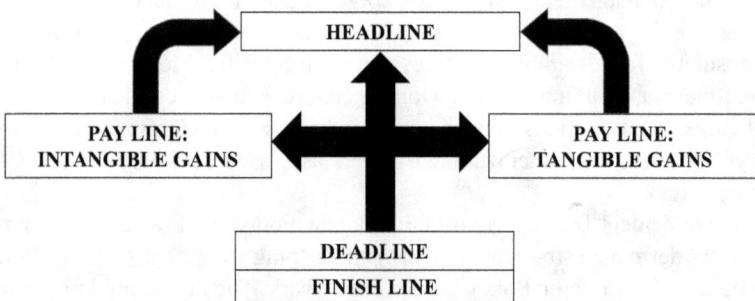

Figure 7.1 Four lines of the strategic goal

range of the normal human sensorium and require specialized instrumentation for verification, such as satellite-based detectors designed to spot military
movements.

Especially challenging are finish lines that are subjective in nature, particularly those involving emotions or opinions. One approach to assess subjective
topics is to emplace quantitative measures as a means to gauge progress to an
approximate extent. Consumer confidence surveys and public opinion polling
are examples of using statistical methods to track movements in peoples' senti-
ments and attitudes.

Yet there are other subjective goals of a deep emotional resonance that
resist all means of sensorial or technical verification. The goals articulated, for
example, by iconic and historic leaders, such as those espoused by American
civil rights leader Martin Luther King, Jr., who fought for racial equality at a
time when systemic discrimination persisted, are verified "within the heart" by
those who embrace his enunciated ideals.

Whereas the goal line establishes the ultimate target for implementers to
reach, it also sets a reference point that planners can use to gauge what capabilities are needed and at what amounts and to establish interim milestones that
measure progress across stages. The goal line is the necessary marker for both
inductive ways of planning, namely how achievements could affect the broader
effort, and deductive ways of planning, namely how the chosen goal determines
what is needed to reach it. In other words, the goal line helps planning in two
directions: forward from the starting line onward, as well as backward from the
goal line toward what conditions and resources exist in the present.

2. Deadline

Time is a universal force endowed upon all that exists, yet it depletes incessantly and irreversibly. Whereas the timespan of living beings is finite, the
timespans of organizations can last indefinitely, giving people a platform to
initiate causes within one's own lifetime and sustain them for following generations. The ability of entities such as governments and corporations to exist
in near-perpetuity grants them unique powers, beyond the ability of any one
individual or even one generation, to conduct trans-generational planning and
to pursue strategic goals of lasting importance. For example, the Great Wall of
China, the grand defensive bulwark that snakes across China's north-central
midlands, was sporadically built in sections became contiguous as successive
dynasties added to the linear network, providing bases for their ancient armies
to counter invading forces.

In our modern era, time is managed and allocated as an instrument of pragmatism, serving as an essential parameter for meting steps within processes, procedures, and projects. The setting of time boundaries and divisions in the form of
deadlines, checkpoints, and stages is an exercise of authority, especially when
that authority is backed by an ability to reward or to punish when deadlines are
met or not. The judgment of time available across a portfolio of interests drives

prioritization whereby urgent matters rise to the top of the agenda and others are shifted according to what remaining time budgets will allow. Time units, such as per-annum, biennium, per-diem, and the like, are the baseline metrics for measuring progress and for standardized cross-comparisons of performance among peers and rivals.

In designing a strategic goal, setting the deadline is a calibrated decision in conjunction with determining a finish line. A time boundary in place exerts a pressure to perform in an inverse relationship with the time made available: A short timeframe imposes a pressure to act urgently and intensely, whereas a distant time marker can induce "action depressurization," resulting in vulnerability to distraction and procrastination. The time boundary for a strategic goal establishes the overall "action density," or the proportion of activities undertaken within a time frame.

Setting the deadline is an act of balance and of nuance: The right deadline is at the balance point at which the time budget is sufficient to reach the finish line at a pace that is effective and efficient for personnel, but not so lengthy as to cause wastage or diversions. The act of nuance lies in setting a deadline with reasonable brevity that signals seriousness, even urgency, of purpose to stakeholders. As all stakeholders are invested in various ways in the mission of the organization, their natural inclination is to see as many goals achieved as quickly as possible and thus maximize return on their contributions, including their own time. However, too much time pressure may demoralize the personnel implementing projects, risking breakdown ("tempo tantrums") and defections, so a leader must gauge how well teams perform under time pressure, both from within their units and across to other collaborating units.

Professions with incessant high-pressure/high-performance demands, such as the military and emergency first-responders, are keyed to the synchronies of intermeshed units, with their lexicons laden with time-linked words such as *tempo*, *cadence*, *timestamps*, and the "*tick-tock*" of intricate operations. On the pathway to the goal line, the timeline is the determinative schedule of action that allocates time among tasks and roles, making clearer what supervisors need to do in managing their teams.

Ultimately, imposing a deadline is an action-forcing event, and doing so in a deliberative manner catalyzes a series of cascading actions in two important directions: (1) outward to the domain of stakeholders and kindred organizations who gauge deadlines as signals of commitment to one's mission, and (2) inward among the community of implementers who parse the time budgets allocated to them and create timelines best suited for their actions. The accumulated body of knowledge earned from work under pressure and carried over to following generations is often appreciated as hard-won, time-tested experience.

3. Pay Line

A line-word adapted from the line that traverses the reels of a gaming slot machine, *pay line* indicates the winning alignment of factors that releases rewards according to a pay table. This sleight of semantics aside, in this goal-crafting framework, *pay line* is used as a code word to evoke the benefits that arise from reaching the finish line, completing a campaign of effort. The rewards of success are expected to deliver upon the premise and the promise of the strategic goal. To motivate action toward the goal and to justify risks along the way, the benefits of winning should be specified to a degree understood to all those involved.

Rewards fall into two categories: tangible and intangible. As elaborated earlier, tangible outcomes center around so-called hard-power assets involving things such as land, money, commodities, and like items that are observable and verifiable. These items are fairly easy to describe and to uphold as motivators because, as items that only exist in finite amounts, they are inherently scarce and thus become valuable. Once acquired, tangible assets may be consumed, stored, traded, sold, or converted into still other forms of assets, enhancing their value further by their fungibility.

The second category of rewards, the intangibles, are more challenging to uphold as a prize because they hold no physical form; they exist mainly in the intellectual and emotional realm of values, ideals, principles, and beliefs. Although there are major intangible assets that are commercially valuable, such as intellectual property, celebrity status, professional reputation, and brand name recognition, what motivates a grander audience are the intangible rewards that are emotionally fulfilling. They can be elusive to define, not only because they defy observability and verifiability, but because they can be defined by a wide range of sincerely held interpretations. It is not surprising that the intangibles provoke the most intense arguments and debate their definitions and how they can be valued even in terms of emotional satisfaction. The aim of working toward a "just and lasting peace" in the Mideast, for example, has yet to gain any commonly accepted working definition among negotiators as to what that entails and what benefits of such a peace would bring to each party.[3]

In a manner that made clear how principles can be envisioned and enunciated compellingly, Martin Luther King, Jr.'s iconic "I Have a Dream" speech, his clarion call for civil rights at a time when discrimination still ran rife in 1963, invoked the foremost and loftiest principle of American governance in this way: "I have a dream that one day this nation will rise up and live out the true meaning of its creed: 'We hold these truths to be self-evident: that all men are created equal.'"

Upon speaking that passage, King then crystallized how equality can be achieved in a manner understood by all: "I have a dream that my four children will one day live in a nation where they will not be judged by the color of their skin but by the content of their character," and then King furthered that ideal by envisioning a compelling everyday scene: "One day . . . little black boys and black girls will be able to join hands with little white boys and white girls as sisters and brothers."[4]

By bridging high principle with a vivid depiction, King made his own strategic goal, the securing of equal rights, broadly understood and emotionally resonant, and he masterfully identified how the benefits would manifest themselves.

The pay line of a strategic goal is centered upon attaining interests by accomplishing specific goals with a promised yield of substantive and fulfilling gains. Whereas tangible gains are readily envisioned and described, equally if not more important are the intangible gains, which when reaped from compelling, hard-fought achievements fulfill the needs of human beings to feel in harmony with their principles and ideals.

4. Headline

Adapted from journalism, a headline is the declaration of the significance and prominence of an event or accomplishment. The headline is a marker of both noteworthiness and newsworthiness of reaching a goal as well as its ramifications for the future. Headline is also an interpretation about the relevance of achievement within a broader context, as seen through any variety of conceptual lenses. In designing the strategic goal, the preceding *line* elements of goal line, deadline, and pay line provide substantive underlying ideas for the declaration of the goal's overarching claim. Reaching a particular goal line may be the first time anybody has made such an achievement; doing so within a particular time measure may have been the fastest ever; and the unlocking of a goal's value may provoke great joy to all. The headline reinforces and uplifts that which has transpired in the pursuit and attainment of the goal.

Whereas a journalistic headline is written by a news professional who typically looks at events from a detached, third-party perspective, the headline for a strategic goal is crafted and articulated by an insider's, first-person interpretation of a goal's meaning and impact. This is a well-honed task for those working in corporate communications and public relations. Whereas self-interest is naturally easier to express, a leader who can articulate an additional perspective on the connectivity of the goal to societal trends at large further enhances the appeal of the organization's mission. For instance, a hypothetical headline for a healthcare company might take the form of: "New FDA-approved Vaccine against Disease 'X' Launches Today in Developing Countries, Injecting New Hope for Vulnerable Populations."

In creating prospective headlines, one can draw upon a variety of dimensions, or characteristics, that underscore the significance or prominence of an event or accomplishment. These include:

> *Metrics and Statistics*: quantitative outcomes, either at maximum or minimum, that are beneficial; statistical outcomes that are major outliers, such as going well beyond average.
> *Symbolic and Historic*: outcomes that are first of their kind, events of reconciliation, ceremonial rituals, pioneering breakthroughs.
> *Dramatic and Climactic*: outcomes with high emotional engagement, David vs. Goliath style showdowns, triumphal peak accomplishments,

victories over malevolent actors or factors, events and situations that release primal emotions, such as relief or joy.

Catalytic and Enzymatic: outcomes that provoke chain reactions, spark new ways of thinking and doing, cycles of pro-action and reaction.

Rhetorical and Political: momentous speech events, outcomes that change formal and informal power relationships, altering or preserving balances of power.

Like the other elements of the strategic goal, a well-chosen headline serves a pivotal purpose between internal and external communities. To personnel a headline highlights the meaning of an accomplishment and serves as a point of inspiration; to outsiders a headline declared upon success is a point of validation of a strategy and of the overall mission.

Altogether, the Four Lines of a strategic goal—Finish Line, Deadline, Pay Line, and Headline—are interconnected by their mutual reinforcement of each other, are calibrated so that a judgment on one element can be assessed in relation to the others, and are designated to be meaningful to both insiders and outsiders.

A historical example of the classical use of the Four Lines in goal-crafting was President John F. Kennedy's historic declaration in 1961, amid tensions with the Soviet Union, of American commitment to win the space race by reaching the moon first. Before Congress, Kennedy vigorously declared:

I believe that this nation should commit itself to achieving the goal, before this decade is out, of landing a man on the moon and returning him safely to the earth. No single space project in this period will be more impressive to mankind, or more important for the long-range exploration of space; and none will be so difficult or expensive to accomplish.[5]

With that, Kennedy concisely identified his Finish Line: landing a man on the moon with safe return; his implicit Deadline of 1969, the last year of the 1960s; and his Headline: a crowning, historical achievement made possible by the strenuous work of the project teams.

With costs escalating since his declaration and debate ensuing about the value of the goal, in 1962 Kennedy traveled to Houston, Texas, the nascent home of the U.S. space complex, and asserted what he believed the Pay Line would be, first in lofty ideals, then in pragmatic terms better understood by the general public:

We choose to go to the moon in this decade . . . not because they are easy, but because they are hard, because that goal will serve to organize and measure the best of our energies and skills, because that challenge is one that we are willing to accept, one we are unwilling to postpone, and one which we intend to win. . . . The growth of our science and education will be enriched by new knowledge of our universe and environment, by new techniques of learning and mapping and observation, by new tools and computers for industry, medicine, the home as well as the school.[6]

Kennedy's crisp and compelling message, entwining the practical dimensions of success with its inspirational promise, gave impetus for a massive acceleration of the space program, culminating in a successful first moon landing in 1969, fulfilling the pledge to win the race, and also spur new aerospace industries. The Kennedy goal design, however sub-consciously structured at the time in the Four Line manner, is one that concisely conveys the sense of mission, the clarity of achievement, and the practicality from benefits earned.

Classifying Goals

Strategic goals are chosen to fulfill purposes that are as varied and expansive in their content as the leaders' scope of interests. The means of accomplishing them, however, through sets of capabilities are more restricted as the realm of assets is subject to real world constraints, such as costs and scarcity. The divergence of ever-higher aspirations from available capabilities enforce the necessity of making choices that optimize the benefits sought while shepherding assets, time, and options. In making choices and trade-offs, knowing what kinds of goals exist helps a leader to articulate the most appropriate objective for a given situation.

What follows is a proposed "goal taxonomy," a set of primary ways with which to classify goals into various types and purposes.

Priority VIPs

A goal can be stratified into levels of importance. A prime objective is the target end-point that is considered essential for a campaign's success, as it is perceived to yield the most important, even vital, benefits. The prime objective can be considered as the "must-do, must-win" achievement with capabilities assigned accordingly. A campaign might include secondary objectives that are in parallel to, or in back-up of, the prime objective. Secondary objectives are those considered "might do" if circumstances allow or if the prime objective is not accomplished. Once a project is underway, reserve objectives provide flexibility in case surprises arise and allow for a partial win, recouping at least some value for the resources expended. Additional levels, such as a tertiary level, can be added for any other peripheral, discretionary purposes, such as acquisition of additional information during the mission, performance data, post-mission tasks, and similar "nice-to-do" items.

Military strategists at the U.S. Army War College stratify the intensity of national interests into three primary VIP tiers:

> *Vital*—those interests that are critical to the survival and functioning of a nation-state.

Important—those interests that are substantial and connect to the critical functioning of the state.

Peripheral—those interests that are non-vital and, while still of value to a community of stakeholders, are of secondary priority in a traditional political-military portfolio of issues and actions.[7,8]

Basic tiering of priorities fosters a thinking of how best to allocate resources across competing priorities within a strategic agenda, whether for an army, a nation, or even a small civic group. Even if surprise events upend prior assumptions about the value of lines of action, a foundational assessment of strategic needs leads to a more rational and justifiable allocation than otherwise might happen without such a deliberation.

Simple vs. Compound

For clarity, the Four Line Framework has been described herein as possessing a single, narrowly defined objective. In a fast-moving world filled with complexities, strategic goals could be designed with multiple objectives with similar values and virtues. Compound goals are those with two or more end points being pursued, such as one objective aimed at reaching a specified quantity and the other aimed at attaining a level of quality. The multiple end points might be sequential, in parallel, or in branched arrays. Obviously, complicated "goal packages" imply needing greater capabilities along with sophisticated managerial and technical skills to execute successfully. Clinical trials for prospective drugs, for example, are typically designed with multiple end points to test the drug's ability to reach certain effectiveness and safety levels, an effort that gauges how medicines can have multiple effects within the body.[9]

Short-Term vs. Long-Term

Time is always of the essence in strategic affairs. Whether it is assertive action toward a goal or a defensive action to protect an interest, all forms of activity (i.e. projects, campaigns, operations) involved in those actions consume time. A standard dividing line between what is considered short-term or long-term is one year, a common business standard. At one extreme, emergencies and downside surprises require a rapid response with very little or no time buffer, resulting in very high action densities. In standard situations, short-term operations mean that consumed resources will need to be replenished and personnel will need to be relieved, creating more necessary lines of action. To contend with the intricacies of here-and-now operations, Japanese industrial manufacturers invented "just-in-time" production cycles, which synchronize the input-outputs of each link of a supply chain.[10]

Long-term goals have inherently lengthier time buffers, meaning that, in general, adjustments can be made well ahead of actions, but the challenge is keeping a workforce motivated. Personnel involved in long-term projects encounter boredom and distractions if they are not engaged frequently enough. Long-term projects left on "auto-pilot" on a chronic basis are prone to slow kinds of decay and depreciation that can escape casual notice. Counter moves to these dynamics can include creating short-term sub-projects to engage personnel and conducting vigilance systematically by use of risk-control frameworks.

Offense vs. Defense

With capabilities, one can take action, by going on offense, to change conditions in the exterior domain and to influence actors and factors. This might be done along a gradation of cooperative stances, from fully collaborative on the pacifist end of the scale to overtly hostile on the militaristic end.

Alternatively, one can take action to protect one's own conditions from inbound aggressors or threatening conditions. Like in offense, defensive moves can range from routine surveillance to pre-emptive military strike against a foe deemed poised to attack. In strategic affairs, the inflection point between an offensive stance and a defensive one relies upon the judgment of other actors' intentions, their true course of future actions. Gauging their intentions would require assessments of their realm of interests for motives concerning taking actions in either posture.

Offensive intent is correlated with the degree of expressed ambitions and any maneuvering consistent with those expressions. But offensive intent can be carefully hidden, in the way that Saddam Hussein carried out his surprise invasion into Kuwait, sparking the Gulf War of 1990. As he was amassing his forces along the Kuwait border, Hussein made no mention of his intentions to anyone in the diplomatic arena, betraying no hint at his meeting with the U.S. ambassador to Iraq just a few days prior to the attack.[11]

Defensive intent can be complex to assess, as protecting one's own territory and assets seems natural enough, but sometimes unbridled defense in the nuclear era can lead to unintended consequences: As the build up of American and Soviet anti-ballistic missile (ABM) capabilities grew in the late 1960s to early 1970s, each nation's race to escalate missile blocking power against the other was deemed destabilizing, as that would actually encourage an offensive preemptive strike from the side who most fears that their outbound missiles would be neutralized by an opponent's defensive anti-missiles. This realization led to a restriction of ABM in a treaty signed in 1972 between the two superpowers that codified mutual vulnerability to each other's missile forces.[12]

Objective vs. Subjective

Objective goals are those that can be perceived by the human senses or by instrumentation. They can be further subdivided into two basic types, tangible and intangible. Tangible items are objective, in the sense that they are "objects" that are verifiable and well understood by almost anyone. Subjective aims are those that are perceived more by psychological perception or by belief systems. Intangible assets are vulnerable to wide variations in perception, acceptance, and verifiability as they stand as concepts, values, or emotional states. The concepts of peace and freedom, for instance, can be interpreted in many ways, and their presence or absence in a given situation can likewise be debated vigorously by those with differing yet sincere beliefs.

Whereas objective aims are more readily identifiable, subjective aims may require the use of a proxy, or an indicator, to gauge progression toward or regression away from a specified goal. Opinion polling is one way of assessing prevailing attitudes about an issue in a numerical way, with the results used to shape influential messaging.

Statics vs. Dynamics

Static aims are those that involve a singular achievement, such as winning a ball game or earning a diploma. These have a binary characteristic: either one achieves the goal (and its prize) or one does not (and loses the prize). They also are centered upon objects in their inert condition, not being substantially changed by being acquired. In contrast, goals involving dynamic situations are those that seek to influence things in motion or in interaction, such as processes and procedures. Industrial goals frequently involve process improvement, in which steps are intricately coordinated with each other to reduce cost and time. Reform goals in policy often focus upon changing antiquated or flawed procedures, such as those discovered in the administration of social programs or in the criminal justice system.

A "meta-dynamic" is one that involves the interactions of a grand system, such as an environmental ecosystem. By convenient example, goals in climate change policy seek to counter the detrimental effects of human processes in the air, on land, and at sea, thus preserving to the extent possible the earth's own natural processes and rhythms. Implementing such policies can mean concerted efforts at successive, cascading levels involving the practices and behaviors of entire industries, specific companies, and ultimately individuals. The desired end-state is the sustainability of the earth's dynamics at large, a goal complex enough to require an expansive series of dashboard indicators that include measures of pollution levels, temperatures, and seasonal onset dates.[13]

Goal Preferences

As organizations are as diverse as their missions, the types and characteristics of goals they pursue will likewise fall into the previously described categories. The basic division of organizations, between public and private sectors, slants members to choose goals with characteristics in line with their identities. Public sector organizations, in general, select goals with a longer-term horizon, with more subjectivity than objectivity, and are more defensive or cautious in nature. In contrast, private sector companies in seeking profits select goals that are near-term, with more objectivity than subjectivity, and are more offensive or assertive in nature. Of course, there is no exactness to the qualitative characteristics of the goals selected, and both sectors evolve their goal characteristics over time: More private sector companies are adopting corporate social responsibility (CSR) principles, whereas public sector agencies, especially state-owned and government-sponsored enterprises (GSE) with a hybridized mandate to serve the public by undertaking business functions, will be expected to earn money at least at a break-even basis in order to sustain themselves and retain political support. Examples of state-owned or chartered enterprises include national oil companies, airlines, and credit banks; government-sponsored enterprises are typically specialized American finance agencies such as Fannie Mae and Freddie Mac in mortgages and Farmer Mac for agricultural loans.

CSR principles are adopted by companies committed to ethical and socially cognizant ideals in the course of their businesses, so that the pursuit of profit does not violate greater equities in societies and cultures at large.[14] Adopting important subjective CSR goals in business helps establish a "social license to operate," thereby enhancing its standing and averting potentially detrimental practices that could hurt the company and society-at-large in the future.[15]

Sourcing Goals

Taxonomies create the compartments, as those described previously, into which goals are assigned by their primary characteristics. Whereas categories might be considered as useful organizational baskets, they do not supply the ideas for the goals themselves. Hence, the remaining element of the goal-crafting technique is to identify some primary sources for goal ideas.

As there are multitudes of ideas for possible targets of achievement, funneling the possibilities down to a practical number provides a starter menu for consideration. Incorporating many of the factors discussed previously, the acronym *ICED TEAS* compactly rosters several key pressuring factors which spur the thinking of new goals.

What follows is the ICED TEAS roster of goal sources:

Interests
Competition
Expenditures
Defenses
Time
Expectations
Aspirations
Standards

Interests

Interests are the sets of stakes which spur entities into purposeful action and form the basis for defined goals and the campaigns to reach them. Put another way, interests are the scope of one's wishes, wants, and needs, and the degree to which they are fulfilled or not determines the intensity of drive to satisfy these appetites. When a vital interest of a nation, such as its energy supply, is being met, then that nation can turn to fulfill its other concerns. If, however, supply needs are not met, then the country is pressed into identifying goals and strategies that turn a state of deficiency into a state of sufficiency. Interests are primary organizational motivators, as they help determine what constitutes a desirable end-state and thus what goals need to be achieved.

Competition

Other players sharing the strategic domain may act to acquire interests to the detriment of all. The strain from struggle and conflict arising from competition can create a need to confront an aggressor or to escalate one's own strengths. The stimulus of competition, when modulated and regulated, can be healthy; the Olympian motto of *Citius, Altius, Fortius* ("Faster, Higher, Stronger") captures this spirit in its quadrennial venues. Competition invariably involves comparisons, in the form of rankings, ratings, and role models. Elite colleges worldwide strive to move up in rankings to gain stature and retain the best students and faculty. Investment banks compete for multi-billion dollar deals that are scored in the industry's "league tables." Online rating sites now assemble consumer opinions for just about any retail outlet ranging from restaurants to car dealerships. Role models, those people who are the pinnacles of their profession, notably in sports, attract admirers who improve their game by inspiration and emulation. Goals can be developed by establishing a target achievement among a field of competitors, such as moving up in rankings to a particular spot, or by rising to become a company known as the "best of breed" in a sector.

Expenditures

Obtaining and holding assets even in reserve consumes money, time, and attention. "Burn rates" create pressure to perform, to use assets and, ultimately, to win goals. As staying static, or being passive, incurs costs but achieves nothing, the natural impetus would be to adopt a purposeful goal that has a chance of earning a return on consumed capital. Whereas "sunk costs," which are the irreversible and irretrievable costs paid in the past, would be excluded from certain calculations about future economic choices, they can color the viewpoints of stakeholders to place added pressure on leaders to try to earn them back. In armed conflict, casualty counts of lives already lost, wounded, or missing create powerful political pressures to either engage further to justify the intangible human cost already paid or to truncate further involvement to limit any further cost. Such was the basic dilemma of American policy toward the Vietnam War: either to fight to win decisively or to withdraw and avoid further bloodshed from a war perceived by many to be peripheral, even detrimental to long-term U.S. interests.

Defenses

Active, engaged entities will have attracted talent and capital to carry out their mission. A prime interest for them is the protection and preservation of their resources in whatever arrangement they might be. Entities will also have sets of existing interests pertaining to their mission, ranging from formal agreements and contracts to ongoing interactions and operations to informal, tacit understandings with other parties; these systemic processes perform the essential everyday functions that keep the entity "alive." As such, these intricacies can be vulnerable to disruption by breakdowns or malfunctions. From these vulnerabilities arise the need for defensive objectives, the specification of goals pertaining to the shielding of existing assets from external and internal risk factors.

When complex dynamics are writ large, broad ecosystems of countries, societies, and industries have an interest in maintaining a stable and predictable equilibrium among each other. When conditions are steady, assumptions made about cause-effect relationships tend to hold truer than under conditions of turbulence. Stability makes planning and various forms of "political investments" more attractive and more likely to be implemented with confidence. Such an equilibrium creates a mutual interest for all participating parties to protect not only their own individual equity but the integrity of the grand system in which it is a member. Defensive objectives for a broad ecosystem would identify current points of vulnerability, but also assess how the system might evolve and result in new sets of protections.

Time

Time markers set boundaries that bracket spans of time like bookends. Familiar calendar units, i.e. days, weeks, months, and years, are widely used and defined denominators for determining the rates of actions or items, such as per day and per year. There are indefinite, looser descriptors of time that give an non-numeric approximation of intervals, i.e. *era, epoch, generation, season,* and *lifetime,* among others. Each group of time markers, definite and indefinite, is associated with the definitive character of an object; in general, tangible and objective items are measured in time with definitive markers, whereas intangible and subjective items are "assigned" to the indefinite time descriptors. In this way, analytics are heavily centered on examining things and processes in such ratios as "miles per hour," "five percent growth per year," and so on, whereas events with an emotive character are framed in such terms as "an opportunity of a lifetime," "a generational shift," and "the golden era," among many others.

In goal-crafting, selecting the appropriate time marker for the proposed goal-line's underlying objective-subjective character is necessary exercise of judgment. A key step is to gauge the sufficiency of one's capabilities to accomplish the goal within the proposed timeline. The deadline itself should be assessed to determine what consequences would ensue if the goal is not accomplished by then; that is, does anything truly "go dead" past the deadline?

In the old days of newspapering, a reporter's article that missed its deadline would simply not be published due to the physical processes involved, resulting in the loss of value to the public for information lost, to the paper for having fewer columns of substance that day, and to the reporter for the effort wasted. In an analogous manner, the selection of the deadline ought to be considered in light of the real detriments that might result, as well as the availability and the authority to impose penalties for deadline infractions. A deadline that has no real downside if missed, or that cannot be backed with a meaningful set of sanctions, is one that becomes inconsequential and unenforceable, and thus becomes arbitrary in nature.

Goals of a subjective nature, especially those with high emotional resonance, are frequently phrased in indefinite time descriptors, but emphasis can be added by touting an achievement as being significant, prominent, or even historic for that chosen timeframe. Thus, for example, someone who is elected as the first woman president of the United States can certainly frame that accomplishment as being historic along many timeframes: lifetime, generational, even epochal. An added task for subjective aims with indefinite time bounds is declaring a tangible goal that crystallizes the subjective aim, then establishing a timeline for working toward sub-goals. In this way, the intention to fulfill ideals is bridged to implementation, giving managers sufficient grounds to develop an action plan.

Expectations

These psychological pressures arise from opinions and beliefs imposed, either by oneself or by others, on what is to be desired or achieved. Inbound expectations, those directed by others toward oneself, can originate from any quarter, from supervisors to peers to employees. Likewise, outbound expectations, that which is directed from oneself toward others, can be imposed upon any community or individual, wherever they may be. Any citizen, for instance, can impose his or her expectations on the performance of government, societal leaders, and fellow citizens.

In strategic affairs, expectational pressures are directed at the attainment of results that matter to the mission and values of a community. Because achieving results is the duty of leaders and managers, it becomes their task to define a strategic goal and an accompanying schedule for action. Success or failure in achieving designated goals is consequential not only for the direct results desired but for the onward reputation of the entity and its leaders. As expectations act as a standard for performance, the results are judged in comparison to those expectations in whatever way they may have been formulated. Results exceeding expectations are held in high regard; those that fall short are held in disappointment, with the former enhancing, and the latter weakening a reputation.

A proposed heuristic equation that represents this dynamic is the following:

REPUTATION = RESULTS – EXPECTATIONS

where results are the change between that which existed at the start of a campaign and that which came about as an outcome at the end. This change can be expressed as:

RESULTS = (END STATE) – (BEGINNING STATE)

These two relationships emphasize the need for action that creates a positive difference and to manage expectations so that such promises are realistic and attainable. Setting expectations too high may take the shine off of real accomplishments that pale in comparison to original promises. Setting expectations too low, in an effort to artificially boost a reputation through a tactic known as "sandbagging," undermines credibility when original promises are deliberately made to be leapfrogged. Whether by accident or design, miscalibrated expectations cause future promises to be questioned for the sincerity of underlying intent. A properly calibrated set of expectations is based upon one's accurate knowledge and assessment of capabilities, conditions on the strategic domain, and the reasoned probability of success. Winning goals in that manner both burnish a reputation and enhance credibility, contributing to a track record that further boosts confidence among stakeholders.

Aspirations

Ambition is an innately human drive to secure vital needs and to attain a betterment of one's standing in the world and of the conditions in the world itself. It is an animating force within individuals and communities alike, empowering a near limitless universe of dreams. The wellspring for aspirations taps into three primal, uniquely human, drives:

1. *Inspiration* is the inner mental "ignition" that sparks new insights and ideas.
2. *Imagination* is the envisioning of the world in new and sometimes radical ways.
3. *Innovation* is the drive to introduce new ways of thinking, doing, and being.

These three channels of human expression combine in ways to generate an appetite to reach new frontiers. With such drives, the horizons of opportunities grow wider and farther, and the realms of possibilities grow taller and richer. To fulfill the dreams of reaching the frontier boundaries, new destination goals are set and new capabilities are raised to empower the journey forward.

Aspirations lead into three additional classes of goals: *Idealistic, Realistic,* and *Pragmatic*. Each class has its own characteristics and importance in public life.

Idealistic goals are infused with values that fulfill deep and substantive emotional needs. Freedom, dignity, and equality are among the many within the universe of positive values. Pursuit of those aspirations relies upon winning a series of goals that are emblematic of those ideals, giving evidence of commitment toward a cause and of competence in implementing a winning strategy. A pinnacle of idealistic goals can be accomplishments of historical noteworthiness, establishing a basis for lasting legacies that re-inspire following generations. Public sector organizations, by virtue of their mission to provide for the common good, tend to incorporate a higher degree of idealism in the choice and rationale of their goals.

Realistic goals are those attainable within the bounds of available capabilities and prevailing conditions. An initial set of aspirational goals in this realm is to build out one's capabilities, such as expanding technologies or training personnel. Another set of goals is to improve the performance of capabilities, such as enhancing effectiveness and efficiency of mechanisms or the workings of people. A further extension of pragmatic goals is to influence the actors and factors on the strategic terrain. The ultimate goal in realism is achieving a strategic goal that liberates gainful benefits worthy of the effort. Companies in the private sector—in pursuit of profit and doing so in an operating environment of real, tangible factors—are predominantly realists in their goal selection process.

As the world is complicated and the nature of problems melds both realism and idealism in endless combinations, it would be expected that goal crafting is rarely an either-or, black-white, exercise. After all, even profits won by a corporation have ripple effects across societies, even beyond borders. High ideals such as equality in the workforce have tangible consequences in hiring policies and calibration of salaries. A bridge between these two poles is the approach of pragmatism. Pragmatism, for the intent of enriching the dichotomy, is the ability and willingness to work within realism in order to achieve goals that are both practical and emotionally fulfilling. In other words, pragmatists are willing to work within constraints presented by the strategic domain (such as costs, laws, and balances of power) to achieve their ideals, and can adapt to changing domain conditions in order to ultimately fulfill emotionally meaningful goals.

Pragmatic goals, therefore, are those that may be tempered, or moderated, from the highest possible achievements, taking into account available capabilities and domain conditions. Such goals recognize that even partial achievements, or those phased over time, are still worthwhile even if they fall short of the zenith. Pragmatic approaches, by seeking tangible and identifiable gains that can be shared, can retain sufficient support among various stakeholders, which can be critical during difficult times. To implement such approaches requires negotiators with experience to identify the realistic ways a deal could work and with the credibility in knowing how each party's interests are aligned within the realism-idealism spectrum.

Standards

These are forms of expectations that come about through the course of experience, tested knowledge, and social norms. They too can come in two main varieties: tangible and intangible. Tangible standards abound in technical sectors, which unify professional tasks and ensure consistency. Benchmarks are more detailed reference standards in performance that are intended to provide a target for practitioners to strive toward in the course of conducting work.

Intangible standards are those that arise through social norms, which are in turn influenced by the cultural factors. Norms take shape in standards of behavior that become prevalent within a community, such as customs, courtesies, and traditions. Some norms can take a "soft" form such as tacit understandings, which are behaviors that are expressed without the need for prompts. "Harder" forms of social norms requiring backing of authority include more formalized rules, such as those which govern institutions and organizations.

Strategic goals for social policy are aimed at sustaining norms, or they can be aimed at changing norms to supersede those found to be outdated or even detrimental. The American civil rights movement, for example, was aimed at securing stronger voting rights in places where such rights were obstructed or simply denied.[16] That movement also sought to transform informal social norms to eliminate discriminatory attitudes and to replace them with values of inclusiveness.

Risks in Goal Crafting

Goals are created to unite achievement with a benefit. They are motivators that enlist efforts and energies to achieve and reap the gains. For basic personal goals, an individual might gauge the values of available objectives and then choose whether or not to expend their time, efforts, and costs in pursuit. Individuals have a simple menu from which to choose: go or no-go, with the consequences of that person's choice accruing chiefly to themselves.

However, in the realm of complex, high-stakes, strategic situations, goal-setting is typically exercised by those possessing the authority to do so namely, high-level leaders and their designees. Those in charge, especially within formal, hierarchical organizations, can wield goal-setting as an instrument of power over those beneath their authority. As with any other forms of power, goal-setting can be wielded for either beneficent or malevolent intent.

Within organizations, people are enmeshed in working relationships that make it more difficult than what is possible in private life to simply reject goals or exit the group. People are substantially tied to the actions and directives of superiors and are usually inclined to accept and implement what is ordered. But leaders also have the direct authority to impose their will upon subordinates through the managerial powers they possess: the ability to hire and fire, set pay and benefits, evaluate work quality, and many other mandates. When assertion of authority goes beyond what is needed to implement tasks, and when authority is wielded as personal power without regard to mission or ideals, the likelihood of corruption and corrosive practices rises. An organizational eco-system can become denigrated into an "ego-system" in which good judgment is displaced by personal prerogatives imposed upon the less powerful, particularly subordinates.

With such powers and with the general disposition of people to follow authority, goal-setting can be mismanaged, misapplied, or even misused. Goal-setting is seen as well within the scope of leadership duties and is rarely challenged by subordinates, so when questionable goals are declared and pursuing actions are launched, there are usually too few countervailing forces to reverse or to ameliorate them. Goals can be set not for the greater good but for selfish, indulgent purposes, and asymmetrical power relationships will compel those in the under-command to do a rogue leader's bidding. As a consequence, organizations and nations can be led down a path to substantial wastage and even wide-scale harm.

History is replete with disastrous goal-setting, particularly those imposed during wars and conflicts that have cost millions of lives, engendered deep suffering, and affected the course of nations: For example, during World War II, Nazi Germany's brutal campaign to vanquish the Soviet Union, carried out by massive surprise attacks through military Operations Barbarossa and Typhoon, ultimately failed to reach the defined strategic goal of capturing Moscow and additional swaths of eastern Russian heartland before the onset of the winter of 1941–1942. Instead, the campaign outran supply lines, bogged down at the outskirts of Moscow, and became a failing quagmire that killed millions of soldiers and innocent civilians.[17] That goal and many others of questionable military value, such as the subsequent aim to capture Stalingrad for propaganda purposes, went unopposed because Hitler's absolute clench over his command and control lines precluded his generals from altering his impulsively driven strategies and tactics. As a result his unchecked impulses, compounded by miscalculations and the unanticipated ferocity of Russian counter-attacks, horrifically culminated in escalating death tolls and wanton destruction across the entire German-Russian battle theater.

Goals spawned from hubris are also found in modern civilian life. In everyday business, overbearing goals in the form of onerous sales quotas, overly difficult specifications, unrealistic timetables, and under-resourcing of needed capabilities can create internal rifts, overt and covert dissension, debilitation of morale, and legal liabilities arising from lawsuits and governmental interventions. Starting in 2013, a series of media articles spotlighted the consumer banking practices at Wells Fargo, an American bank. In an attempt to boost fee revenues, the bank imposed upon its branch employees aggressive sales quotas that resulted in numerous instances of unauthorized accounts being opened and products being ordered without customer authorization.[18,19] The ensuing public relations firestorm and regulatory sanctions forced the bank to stop its system of branch sales goals and pay heavy fines.[20,21]

With the aggregation of power resident in countries and organizations compounded by the authority delegated to leaders to set goals, the prospects are rife for "goals gone wild," as one critic noted, whereby goals are laid forth indiscriminately or are imposed with such dominant self-interest as to create alienation and demoralization among stakeholders.[22]

When leaders are empowered with the cache of "carrots and sticks," they get to decide who gets carrots and who gets sticks and in what proportion that yields a desired result. When sticks predominate in goal-setting, they create a pathway experience akin to a "forced march" rather than a collaborative journey. Whereas principled leaders look to establish goals that win results and serve broader, beneficial purposes, the concentration of power and authority can lead to goals specified to back an ulterior motive.

In what ways might goals become misconstructed? Using the Four Lines framework for strategic goals, a starter set of wayward methods can be identified.

1. Finish Line

The designated end point of a goal is the initial target for a campaign of effort. Underlying that choice are assumptions about the degree of difficulty in reaching the goal, the forecasted conditions, and the capabilities needed. Over-optimism about the goal and capabilities, whether by design or by ignorance, can produce a false sense of attainability resulting in personnel working with insufficient resources or within a state of complacency. When conditions are harsher than expected, morale can plummet and the credibility of leadership is then undermined. Under-preparations weaken effectiveness in the field and can result in clogged and confused lines of supply and communications.

Goals can also be changed, or re-specified to account for new conditions, or used as a way of coaxing more work out of personnel. This move is often called "moving the goal posts" (or the goal line). A campaign toward a simple, straightforward goal may become transmuted into a difficult, complex goal, in what might be deemed an organizational "bait-and-switch" maneuver. Once a campaign has incurred sunk costs, it can be psychologically difficult to back away mid-stream, and such costs can be used to justify renewed effort in a different direction. In complex negotiations, a side might demand a concession that, once granted by the other side, not only fails to quench further demands, but spurs new demands. The other side, having "paid" a concession as a price already, may be inclined to pay with more concessions in order to achieve the goal of an agreement.

Goals act as destination end points for efforts, and often formally mark the points of termination of campaigns. With all the focus and attention upon reaching a goal, reaching the arrival point becomes a time of celebration. Afterward, built-up emotional energy is dissipated and personnel are released for other projects. For projects needing a level of sustainability for contingencies, rapid demobilization upon goal attainment can make planning for following phases more difficult. After World War II ended, the relaxation of tensions resulted in a rapid downsizing of Allied militaries but not so of Soviet forces, which Joseph Stalin maintained at robust levels in order to maintain his domination of Eastern Europe.[23] In everyday terms, just as a campaign to reach a goal can rally people in a structured, concerted effort, the actual winning of the goal releases that collective energy but may result in the foregoing of additional opportunities or in the under-preparedness toward ongoing risk factors.

2. Deadline

The ability to set deadlines is a fundamental power within organizations. What makes deadlines consequential is the application of sanctions if they are missed or the bequeathment of rewards and praises if they are met. With this inherent advantage, those in leadership can structure directives nearly unilaterally, including those directives involving the setting of deadlines and timelines.

As with the specification of goal lines, over-optimism can creep into the assumptions about the time required to accomplish a task. An erroneously optimistic outlook results in deadlines that are too short, consequentially leading to compressed timetables. Such crowded timetables have very high "action densities" with many actions and operations occurring within a unit of time. When action densities are too high, errors in execution and in coordination can ripple across a campaign might debilitate efforts and lead to ultimate failure.

Overly short deadlines also risk the diversion of resources into high-action density projects to the detriment of long-range opportunities. If deadlines were set in accordance with achieving a balance between effectiveness and efficiency, resources could be allocated rationally across the field of opportunities. Overly high rates of resource consumption in projects with improperly set deadlines can lead to a compounding of losses; first, from the wastage within the project itself and secondly, from the depletion of assets for other projects, making them vulnerable to failure.

3. Pay Line

As reaching a goal means achieving a set of benefits that can be distributed among stakeholders, it stands to reason that this is a goal element that can be subverted. Again, over-optimism about the rewards to be reaped upon victory can raise expectations among implementers. But if such rewards are found to be below expectations, or even to be non-existent, then implementers would be duly angry and upset that their efforts did not pay off as promised.

Goal rewards can also be misspecified in the expected mix of tangible and intangible benefits that are thought to result from success. The promise of a goal package that has a high ratio of tangible to intangible benefits would be expected to have many enlistees, as the tangible rewards can include money and promotions for individuals or vital resources and territory for nations.

A campaign that yields little in the way of tangible benefits exposes the intangible benefits—a sense of accomplishment, appreciation, prestige, group morale—to being cynically dismissed or rejected.

Goal packages that have a high ratio of intangible rewards relative to tangible rewards, such as philanthropic and volunteer work, are also subject to the force of expectations. As people often enlist for humanitarian-oriented work to uphold ideals, fulfill psychological needs, and reinforce notions of identity, they have invested much of their emotional energies into being involved and being appreciated at the end point. Should the campaign end without some realization of the emotional rewards, participants can leave feeling unappreciated.

An aggressive form of subverting a goal's pay line is the expropriation of rewards upon goal completion, or the distribution of benefits in ways that contravene what was originally promised. Many multinational companies have been induced to invest substantial financial amounts in support of developing countries' economic goals, only to have their assets, once on the ground and operating, expropriated by governments or to be subjected to harassment and corruption. Governments have also exercised their sovereign powers to initiate debt restructuring in ways that imposed losses to creditors, which act as a means of expropriation.[24]

4. Headline

Reaching a goal is important not only for the benefits that might accrue to the achievers but the accomplishment is also a marker or milestone of prominence and significance in the history of the entity. Like what can happen with the other benefits, fame and recognition arising from goal attainment can be misattributed to those in a position for self-promotion rather than to those who actually did the work. Internal reward structures may be such that those who can attach themselves to successful campaigns can seize onward opportunities, so claiming exaggerated or undeserved credit is incentivized. As with other forms of organizational perquisites, headline grabbing can be seen as the prerogative of and for those in charge.

With the rostering of some of the basic ways by which goal-setting can go wrong, the question then becomes how such risks can be reduced. Whereas the underlying basis for questionable usurping behaviors will persist, namely the concentration of authority and the power to allocate reward or sanction to a favorite few, there are approaches that principled leaders can use to reduce inadvertent goal mis-specifications and that help organizations establish an environment in which goal-setting is transparent and broadly beneficial.

One overarching approach is to undertake "contextual goal-setting." This is a philosophy that considers decision-making at large to be supported within a governing environment that minimizes compartmentalization and promotes communication, coordination, and collaboration. For the task of goal-setting, a contextual approach would take into account the stakeholder community and their needs and expectations; the grasp of knowledge regarding existing capabilities in resources, equipment, and personnel; and the guiding values and ideals of the organization. With an objective understanding of assets at hand and the sincere appreciation of the subjective feelings amongst internal communities, the specification of a Four Line strategic goal can become more aligned and harmonized to the overall organizational mission.

Within contextual goal-setting, a set of "guardrails" might be put in place to prevent unilateral goal-setting. Such guardrails might include a regularized system of oversight and questioning by a third party or by a board of directors. Another guardrail might be a set of "red lines" and gateways that prohibits unilateral goal-setting without a series of evaluations or approvals. Still another method is to establish a system of cross-accountability for goals, with leaders being held accountable to stakeholders and workers for principled goal-setting, with rewards and penalties assessed accordingly and applied by a non-leadership group. Although such arrangements may add more complexity, they may be appropriate in entities with large, complex strategic goals and with sufficient organizational capabilities to manage its contextual environment. For smaller entities, a body of widely propagated standards might be developed for principled goal-setting so that adherence to or detractions from those standards could be readily assessed.

Summary

Organizations are created to translate their mandates into enduring, purposeful missions and the achievements that would fulfill that charge. Goals are the aims that are substantiated into a reasonably defined, well-understood set of individual parameters that altogether creates a package of aims or targets. A strategic goal is proposed as a set of four elements that incorporates an outcome that defines success (Finish Line), the expected schedule needed (Timeline), the necessary rewards (Pay Line), and the emotional or historical significance of success (Headline). Such a formulation allows for a goal to be standardized and to provide prompting of the key elements. As the range of possibilities for achievements are innumerable, the chapter identified some basic groupings in terms of character, time frame, and tangibility. Ideas and inspirations for goals can arise from a variety of practical, interests-oriented sources and the resulting strategic goal can have both idealistic and realistic characteristics. As the legitimacy of articulated goals stands on the healthy and vibrant interchange of the people within organizations, caution is needed to make sure that abuses of power do not result in the degradation of goals for selfish, rather than noble, purposes.

Notes

1. Sebenius, Burns, and Mnookin, *Kissinger the Negotiator*, part II ("zoom-out")—part III ("zoom-in").
2. George T. Doran, "There's a S.M.A.R.T. Way to Write Management's Goals and Objectives," *Management Review* (AMA Forum), 70(11) (1981): 35–36.

3. U.N. Security Council Resolution 242, Nov. 22, 1967. https://documents-dds-ny.un. org/doc/RESOLUTION/GEN/NR0/240/94/IMG/NR024094.pdf?OpenElement (accessed Oct. 20, 2018).

4. Martin Luther King, Jr., Research and Education Institute, Stanford University, archived speech text, Aug. 28, 1963. http://okra.stanford.edu/transcription/docu ment_images/InVol8/630828-005.pdf (accessed Oct. 20, 2018).

5. John F. Kennedy Library and Museum, "Special message to Congress on Urgent National Needs, 25 May 1961," Speech text in online archives. www.jfklibrary. org/Asset-Viewer/Archives/JFKPOF-034-030.aspx (accessed Oct. 20, 2018).

6. National Aeronautics and Space Administration, "Text of President John Kennedy's Rice Stadium Moon Speech," Sept. 12, 1962. https://er.jsc.nasa.gov/seh/ ricetalk.htm (accessed Oct. 20, 2018).

7. H. Richard Yarger and George F. Barber, "The U.S. Army War College Methodology for Determining Interests and Levels of Intensity," U.S. Army War College, Carlisle Barracks, Carlisle, PA, 1997. Adapted from Department of National Security and Strategy, Directive Course 2: "War, National Policy & Strategy" (Carlisle, PA: U.S. Army War College, 1997), 118–125. www.au.af.mil/au/awc/awcgate/ army-usawc/natinte.htm (accessed Oct. 27, 2018).

8. Graham T. Allison and Robert Blackwill, "America's National Interests: A Report," *The Commission on America's National Interests*, July 2000. www.belfercenter. org/sites/default/files/legacy/files/amernatinter.doc (accessed Oct. 27, 2018).

9. U.S. Food and Drug Administration, "Multiple Endpoints in Clinical Trials, Draft Guidance to Industry," Jan. 2017. www.fda.gov/downloads/drugs/guidancecom plianceregulatoryinformation/guidances/ucm536750.pdf (accessed Oct. 20, 2018).

10. Len Calderone, "The Benefits of Just-in-Time Inventory," *ManufacturingTomorrow online*, June 1, 2017. www.manufacturingtomorrow.com/article/2017/05/the-benefits-of-just-in-time-inventory/9734/ (accessed Oct. 20, 2018).

11. "U.S. Messages on July 1990 Meeting of Hussein and American Ambassador," *New York Times*, July 13, 1991. www.nytimes.com/1991/07/13/world/us-messages-on-july-1990-meeting-of-hussein-and-american-ambassador.html (accessed Oct. 20, 2018).

12. Talbott, *Endgame: The Inside Story of SALT II*, 21–22.

13. U.S. Global Change Research Program, "Indicators." www.globalchange.gov/ browse/indicators (accessed Oct. 20, 2018).

14. United Nations, "The Ten Principles of the UN Global Compact." www.unglobal compact.org/what-is-gc/mission/principles (accessed Aug. 24, 2019).

15. Morrison, John, "Business and Society: Defining the 'Social License," *The Guardian*, Sept. 29, 2014. www.theguardian.com/sustainable-business/2014/sep/29/ social-licence-operate-shell-bp-business-leaders (accessed Aug. 24, 2019).

16. Civil Rights Act of 1964, signed into law by President Lyndon Johnson July 2, 1964. www.ourdocuments.gov/doc.php?flash=true&doc=97&page=transcript

17. Drew Middleton, "Hitler's Russian Blunder," *New York Times*, June 21, 1981. www.nytimes.com/1981/06/21/magazine/hitler-s-russian-blunder.html (accessed Oct. 24, 2018).

18. Bethany McLean, "How Wells Fargo's Cutthroat Corporate Culture Allegedly Drove Bankers to Fraud," *Vanity Fair* (May 31, 2017). www.vanityfair.com/ news/2017/05/wells-fargo-corporate-culture-fraud (accessed Oct. 24, 2018).

19. E. Scott Reckard, "Wells Fargo's Pressure-Cooker Sales Culture Comes at a Cost," *Los Angeles Times* (Dec. 21, 2013). www.latimes.com/business/la-fi-wells-fargo-sale-pressure-20131222-story.html (accessed Oct. 24, 2018).

20. Michael Corkery, "Wells Fargo Fined $185 Million for Fraudulently Opening Accounts," *New York Times*, Sept. 8, 2016. https://nyti.ms/2co9hQK?smid=nytcore-ios-share (accessed Oct. 24, 2018).

21. Jim Puzzanghera, "Wells Fargo is Eliminating Retail Sales Goals after Settlement over Aggressive Tactics," *Los Angeles Times*, Sept. 13, 2016. www.latimes.com/business/la-fi-wells-fargo-sales-20160913-snap-story.html (accessed Oct. 24, 2018).
22. Lisa D. Ordonez, et al., "Goals Gone Wild: The Systemic Side Effects of Over-Pre scribing Goal Setting," Harvard Business School, Working Paper Number: 09–083, Jan. 2009. www.hbs.edu/faculty/Publication%20Files/09-083.pdf (accessed Oct. 24, 2018).
23. Rubinstein, *Soviet Foreign Policy Since World War II*, 72–73.
24. United Nations Conference on Trade and Development (UNCTAD), *Sovereign Debt Restructuring and International Investment Agreements*, IIA Issues Note, No. 2, July 2011, 5. https://unctad.org/en/Docs/webdiaepcb2011d3_en.pdf (accessed Oct. 24, 2018).

8   Heuristic Cascade
of a Strategic Goal

The strategic goal serves to articulate a target for achievement, one that is beneficial in terms of creating change through expressed, verifiable results, but also one that ennobles the spirit of those involved or invested in the mission. Through the Four Line Framework, a template is provided so that a goal can be structured in such a manner to provoke the deliberation of its content and its broader significance.

To reinforce the centrality of a strategic goal in the pursuit of an entity's mission, a new heuristic equation is introduced that integrates many of the elements and principles previously discussed. The equation, when disaggregated into its contributing parts, can also serve as a prompt to unwrap these elements and display them in wider arrays.

Although these heuristic equations take on mathematical form, they are not literal mathematical operations but rather impressionistic statements that aim to highlight interrelationships among the elements. In this sense, the multiplication function denoted as "X" can be seen as an amplifier or a necessary condition for its partner element; the additive function denoted as "+" suggests a cumulative relationship of one element contributing to the values and actions of the other elements.

As a campaign, reaching a goal is conducted with a specific purpose in mind: to impart an "impact" that improves upon what has existed in the past and that yields valuable benefits upon achieving the goal.

Because of the intricacies involved in elaborating the conceptual, interconnected relationships, a numbered step-wise approach is as follows:

1. Recall from an earlier explanation in Part 1 that the following equation described impact:

    IMPACT = RESULTS × VALUATION

    with RESULTS = (END STATE - BEGINNING STATE), or the change in conditions achieved,
    with VALUATION = (END VALUE - BEGINNING VALUE), or the change in value achieved in both tangible and intangible ways.

2. A strategic goal is formulated to identify an impact that fulfills one's scope of interests. This relationship can be expressed as:

STRATEGIC GOAL = IMPACT × INTERESTS

with the multiplier sign used to indicate each element amplifies the other, and because setting either term to zero means the chief value of the strategic goal is negated if an effort does not make an impact or serve an interest.

3. By substituting IMPACT in step 1, the equation expands to:

STRATEGIC GOAL = (RESULTS × VALUATION) × INTERESTS

4. Achieving results is a function of having capabilities and using them, so:

RESULTS = CAPABILITY × IMPLEMENTATION

with the multiplier sign used because by setting either term to zero means no results are achieved if there are no capabilities or if they are not being implemented.

5. Implementation is a process involving preparations and then activating a plan through operations:

IMPLEMENTATION = PREPARATIONS × OPERATIONS

with the multiplier sign used again because by setting either term to zero means implementation cannot occur without either planning preparations or conducting operations.

6. By substituting IMPLEMENTATION from step 5 into the RESULTS equation:

RESULTS = CAPABILITY × (PREPARATIONS × OPERATIONS)

7. Further recall that capabilities are a conjoining of having the means, thorough tools, or technologies that extend human abilities:

CAPABILITY = CAPACITY + ABILITY

8. By substituting CAPABILITY from step 7 into the RESULTS equation from step 6:

RESULTS = (CAPACITY + ABILITY) × (PREPARATIONS × OPERATIONS)

9. Further recall that interests are a span of wishes, wants, and needs:

INTERESTS = (WISHES + WANTS + NEEDS)

10. By substituting both RESULTS from step 8 and INTERESTS from step 9 into the STRATEGIC GOAL equation from step 3:

STRATEGIC GOAL = (RESULTS × VALUATION) × INTERESTS

STRATEGIC GOAL = IMPACT x INTERESTS

WISHES | WANTS | NEEDS

RESULTS x VALUATION

TANGIBLE | INTANGIBLE

CAPABILITY x IMPLEMENTATION

PREPARATIONS | OPERATIONS

CAPACITY + ABILITY ➡ **SKILL | WILL**

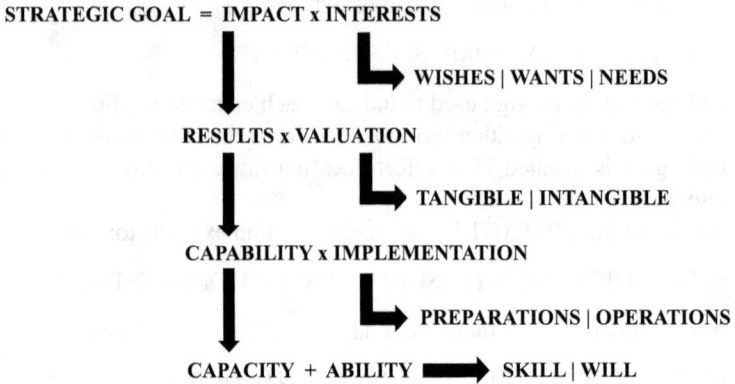

Figure 8.1 Strategic goal cascade

becomes:

STRATEGIC GOAL = (CAPACITY + ABILITY) × (PREPARATIONS × OPERATIONS) × VALUATION × (WISHES + WANTS + NEEDS)

11. An even fuller elaboration would incorporate the components of human ability:

ABILITY = SKILL + WILL

so that the finalized cascade would be:

STRATEGIC GOAL = (CAPACITY + SKILL + WILL) × (PREPARATIONS × OPERATIONS) × VALUATION × (WISHES + WANTS + NEEDS)

To show these interrelationships in a visual manner, the diagram below shows how the concepts cascade down to a granular level through the use of substitutions in the way shown above.

Figure 8.1 demonstrates that the strategic goal equation, when fully disaggregated, shows a positive correlation between the significance of the goal with the contributory components, and that raising the levels of any component on the right-hand side of the equation enhances the achievability and desirability of the goal.

Summary

The strategic goal is the culmination of effort put forth by a campaign to reach an achievement of compelling value. That value is defined by the potential benefits that emanate upon reaching the desired end-state. Whereas tangible benefits fulfill critical and vital needs, intangible benefits as expressed in emotional bonding and the sense of unity from partaking in a challenging journey add psychological sustenance to all involved in the long-term mission of an entity. By applying goal-crafting skills and the Four Line method, a balance between tangible and intangible gains can be incorporated into the final design of the strategic goal.

Now that the strategic goal has been characterized, the next task is to assemble the means to reach it through a strategic plan.

Part 4

The Strategic Plan

9   The POSTERS Roadmap
to the Goal

The strategic goal embodies the innate drive within people to achieve that which is sustaining in the realm of pragmatism and that which is fulfilling in the realm of idealism. To succeed in the world of what materially exists, the goal demands a degree of precision, particularly in specifying the end-point of an effort, its destination. To succeed in the world of the emotions, the goal demands a degree of resonance, those feelings that emanate upon reaching the destination and that fulfill a shared sense of destiny. The strategic goal, then, activates the force of ambition and establishes what is at stake.

The strategic goal is not set in the abstract nor in isolation, but within an ever-dynamic environment teeming with real world conditions, with many intrusions and obstructions. Limitations of what exists physically create conditions of scarcity and the consequent zero-sum behaviors of competition, negotiation, and often aggression. The strategic domain is the terrain upon which multitudes of actors move about according to their own logic of self-interest, aligning within or disentangling from each other by calculated necessity. Prevailing domain factors, in the form of broader societal trends, exert additional complicating pressures.

Once the strategic goal is articulated and the strategic domain is understood, what remains to be charted is the strategic plan: the activation and deployment of capabilities to reach the goal in a deliberative and directive manner. The strategic plan is the template for action that is the connecting pathway between what conditions currently exist at the starting line, the beginning-state, and what is desired at the finish line, the end-state.

In a familiar sense, a plan can be plainly described as a journey of action between an origin and a destination. But because of the special rewards attached to a strategic goal, a strategic plan can be described in a more robust, motivational style. In the way that the strategic goal is a declared "proposition of value," the strategic plan is a "proposition of experience," an excursion onto a complex terrain that portends extensive and intensive engagement with the actors and factors encountered along the way.

Implementation of a plan makes two important contributions: the first is the obvious and necessary effort in reaching the goal and reaping the benefits. The second contribution is more nuanced yet is highly relevant for building long-term institutional capabilities: the gaining of "experiential intelligence," the body of knowledge, skills, and insights gleaned from the full extent of efforts and interactions. Those learnings, inclusive of mistakes, become assimilated into an organization's history and serve as a foundation for future improvements.

In elaborating on the elements of a strategic plan, several more line-words will be introduced, either singly or within a cohort, consistent with the frameworks previously described within the strategic domain and the strategic goal.

As striving toward a goal across complex, even hostile, policy terrain can be arduous and risky, and involve many unique and novel situations, leaders often rely upon *guidelines*, accumulated wisdom that conveys useful "rules of the road" to follow during a journey. Guidelines are typically conditional, or premised on certain events or situations being present in order for the advice to be useful. Guidelines, like any other form of advice, can become crutches that could undermine one's own judgments if they are relied upon excessively. General guidelines, when overly applied without adjustments, can become hard-and-fast rules, locking in lines of thought and behavior and creating vulnerabilities when novel situations arise. It remains a matter of judgment to discern when the right circumstances apply to a set of guidelines and when to make adaptations when presenting circumstances stray from the norm.

To embark on a journey is to undertake three basic steps: depart one's origins, travel across a terrain, and arrive at a destination. In strategic affairs, the journey is exponentially more complex with the mobilization of large-scale assets, proliferation of actors and factors, presence of significant stakes in play, and ever-shifting conditions. To distill the complexities of a plan with strategic implications into a simpler, understandable model, a three-element, travel-centered heuristic is introduced:

JOURNEY = CAMPAIGN + ROADMAP + VEHICLE

with CAMPAIGN embodying the organized, directed effort that is charged to win a prominent goal, ROADMAP defining the way forward with accompanying contextual information, and with VEHICLE representing an assembled set of capabilities, also known as an organizational "apparatus," being activated and driven forward.

The ROADMAP itself consists of the "path line" plus a series of interim objectives along the way, which altogether comprise the string of achievements embodied by a campaign.

The path line is the line-word used to denote the main route, the chief pathway, from the starting line to the finish line of a strategic goal; in other words, it is the track that defines the way forward originating from an existing state of affairs, traversing a domain of forces and factors, and converging upon a desirable end-state, or the "promised land." The path line is the trail that guides the primary actions of initiation, mobilization, and implementation.

A campaign's path line to the strategic goal consists of the following components.

Starting Line

This anchors the initial conditions at the outset of a campaign, including configurations of assets, obligations, personnel, and any strengths or weaknesses. These configurations make up the "beginning state" that is to be transformed into new configurations upon attainment of the end-state. The starting line of conditions is also the baseline, or the line of reference, against which progress is measured and compared, much in the style of "before and after" photos that portray stark contrasts.

On-Ramp or Entry Ramp

This is where action begins to accelerate, involving preparatory steps just ahead of the full campaign. Once preparations are complete, the on-ramp phase is an acceleration movement onto the main highway of the campaign's strategy, with the cadence of actions intensifying.

Lines of Action

Also known as lines of effort in the U.S. military or lines of play in the world of sport and games, lines of action are streams of work done along major categories, specialties or geographies, such as finance, personnel, communications, or a certain zone.[1] A line of action can be a conventional, pre-planned series of tactics or it can be an improvised set of responses in reaction to a surprise. Any action series is what a leader deems as the best course to undertake in a given situation. A typical line of action involves a work stream composed along a "*Five A*" linear structure:

1. *Actor*, the person or unit assigned an active role in an organized effort
2. *Asset*, the enabling equipment used by the actor
3. *Aim*, the goal or purpose of the actor's effort
4. *Action*, the tasks and tactics undertaken
5. *Achievement*, the fulfillment of the specified end point

There are three key points of assessment within a line of action: the *decision point*, the designated time for making a significant choice among presenting options; the *checkpoint*, a designated spot during the campaign when progress is assessed for any needed adjustments, and the *chokepoint*, the problem area(s) where the campaign becomes significantly hampered, such as supply chain bottlenecks or where opposing actions by rivals have taken hold.

Off-Ramp or Exit Ramp

This is the downshifting zone as the campaign nears completion; with either success or failure reasonably ascertained, one can determine how to de-escalate or disengage one's actions in order to reallocate resources to other priorities.

An exit strategy also entails knowing what post-goal actions are needed to consolidate gains earned and to prepare for still other goals.

Finish Line

Interchangeable with *goal line*, this is the end point that defines success in the strategic goal and marks the official termination of a campaign. As one of the integral Four-Line elements of the strategic goal, the finish line is the point at which the effort bears its fruit and confers emotional meaning and satisfaction for those involved in the pursuit.

Timeline

This is the timetable for action across all phases of the campaign, leading to the specified deadline for reaching the strategic goal. The timeline maps out the main course of action for participants and the operational schedule for key projects or sub-campaigns. The timeline is designed to produce a pace deemed most effective and efficient for personnel and equipment alike. As a form of organizational choreography, the operational tempos of projects involving the spacing and pacing of activities are often synchronized with the tempos of other projects so that their outputs and inputs can be intermeshed, the products of one project becoming ingredients for another.

The terminology of time expressed in the world of games and sports often transfers fluidly into the lexicon of strategic affairs. When opportune, a campaign undertakes slow-down tactics to "buy time" or "play for time," as a means to delay unfavorable events or gain new options. In situations when a rival faces time pressure, a competitor might choose to complicate matters in order to "run out the clock" and force opponents to make concessions.

A nuance of time-influenced actions by players is either to obey or to flout the speed limits and speed bumps imposed by external authorities that restrict actions, such as quotas or regulations. Conversely, a key power of one's authority is to impose deadlines and other forms of time regulation upon other players; such tactics are used to allow oneself to catch up, to maintain a lead, or to slow rivals down.

Figure 9.1 demonstrates how the major plan elements fit together and connect to the strategic goal. Both the plan and the goal are integrated into a grander policy architecture in which each element connects to another, and collectively they feed into the overall mission of achieving success and benefiting from the result.

Objectives

The mission of a campaign is to achieve its designated purpose: to reach its finish line. With all the complexities expected to be present on the path line, it would be unusual for a campaign to reach its goal with pure success and

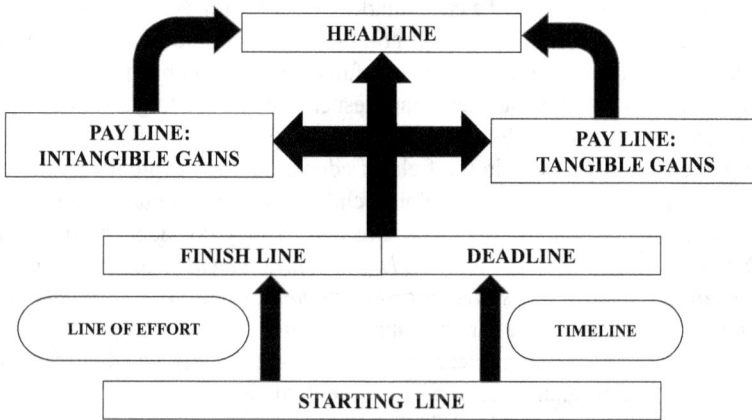

Figure 9.1 Strategic plan feeding into strategic goal

without complications, or to design the path line with absolute certainty that assumptions will always hold. Personnel have limited time spans with which to implement tasks. Unexpected surprises and unanticipated opposition might arise at any time.

The omnipresence of complicating factors adds incentive to segment the campaign into discrete phases and even sub-phases so that capabilities are directed to the right tasks at the right time. A campaign at large could be disaggregated into smaller sub-campaigns, which could be broken down further into mini- and even micro-campaigns designed for very detailed tasks. Compartmentalization segregates both tasks and risks, but it also enables a function of overarching importance to a campaign: the ongoing verification of the chosen strategy and its tactics. As strategy is built upon assumptions about conditions, actors' actions and reactions, and cause-effect chains on the way to the goal, the validity of all those assumptions is tested once a campaign goes live and begins to encounter real-time conditions. What bridges theory with reality and what validates the underlying assumptions of strategy are the presence and placement of *objectives* in the design of a campaign.

Objectives are the targets for attainment by a directed effort. They are the intended results that verify whether or not a tactic or task has worked as intended. For a proposed objective to be deemed objective in its own right, the result must either be observable by the human senses or be detectable by instrumentation. If the result is neither observable nor detectable, then it could be classified as being subjective, a quality that is assessed by other means, chiefly through psychological perception and emotional feeling. The colloquial terms *gut check* or having a *gut feeling* are folk expressions about sensing subjective situations.

A handy way to determine if a nominated objective is verifiable is to apply a *checkmark test* that is premised on a simple yes-no question: If the proposed objective is successfully reached, is the end result or action is clear enough or sufficiently testable to be awarded a checkmark? If so, the proposed objective passes the checkmark test for objectivity. If not, then the proposed objective is either subjective in nature or requires further refinement toward objectivity.

Figure 9.2 shows how the checkmark test can be applied to gauge the objectivity, and by extension, the verifiability of proposed aims. For example, if an organization is working in the field of education, the people involved may choose to devote themselves to helping children in disadvantaged communities learn better in school, a laudable mission. If they consider the mission's objectives to be three broad aims— *1) promoting educational opportunities, 2) improving schools in disadvantaged communities*, and *3) helping children learn better in school*—one can then apply the checkmark test to see if, at present, the end result or action clear enough or is sufficiently testable to earn a checkmark. At first glance, each of the three items is not yet clear enough nor testable. But, if they are refined further to become: *1) create a modern math learning tool at the first grade level, such as a mobile phone application; 2) organize an after-school tutoring corps recruited from recent college graduates*, and *3) raise college aptitude test scores by 10% in 3 years*, they become much clearer by their visibility and, in this case, quantitative measures which lend themselves to a verification process, and thus become "checkmark-able."

Of course, there can be many alternative refinements of those objectives that could pass the checkmark criteria. The checkmark test is a practical way for one to consider an aim couched in general, vague terms and refine it to a higher level of specificity whereby the aim becomes a sharply defined and clearly objective *aim point*. It may take several rounds of refinement to reach a testable level of clarity, but the exercise alone helps implementers to know

PROPOSED OBJECTIVE	CHECKMARK-ABLE?
PROMOTE EDUCATIONAL OPPORTUNITY	✘
IMPROVE SCHOOLS IN DISADVANTAGED AREAS	✘
HELP CHILDREN LEARN BETTER IN SCHOOL	✘
CREATE MATH LEARNING AND TESTING TOOL FOR FIRST GRADERS	✔
FORM AFTER-SCHOOL TUTOR CORPS IN DESIGNATED AREAS	✔
RAISE PRE-COLLEGE TEST SCORES BY 10% IN 3 YEARS	✔

Figure 9.2 Checkmark test

more precisely what aim points their tasks are supposed to reach. In sum, the checkmark test helps ensure that "objectives stay objective."

Whereas the terms *goals* and *objectives* are interchangeable in everyday language, they are assigned distinguishable roles within the frameworks of this volume: *goals* for the ultimate, end points that, if reached, formally signify the termination of a campaign; *objectives* for a broader variety of results within a campaign that add up to the completion of the full goal itself.

In this framework, objectives are the primary units of achievement with which to organize and structure a strategy. Objectives within a campaign can be organized in series, in parallel, by functions, or by any other classification that allows for the recognition of results. At key junctures, objectives are the checkpoints that provide evidence as to whether or not a task or tool is working. If a checkpoint objective is met, it adds confidence about underlying assumptions; but if the checkpoint objective is not met, then assessments can be made as to the reasons why and the forward strategy can be adjusted—a process often referred to as making "mid-course corrections," a reference borrowed from space missions.

The POSTERS Framework

A strategic plan is centered upon implementation, the activation and deployment of resources in pursuit of the goal. In Part 3 of this volume, a two-element heuristic equation was introduced:

$$\text{IMPLEMENTATION} = \text{PREPARATIONS} \times \text{OPERATIONS}$$

For each element (preparations and operations) a supporting series of verifiable objectives can be nested within, creating a specialized checklist for use by planning and implementing teams. By adding still other elements that make up a campaign, one can design a series of objectives within each, creating menus of objectives across the range of campaign components from beginning to end.

The potential to create menus of objectives gives root to a new acronym useful for conceptualizing a campaign:

$$\text{CAMPAIGN} = \text{P.O.S.T.E.R.S.}$$

whereby POSTERS is a series of contributing objectives comprised of the following types:

Preparational
Operational
Stage
Terminal
Evaluation
Results
Supporting

A fully expressed POSTERS-designed campaign encompasses four main pathway segments involving preparations, operations, stages, and destinations, along with two segments that validate the strategy by assessing processes and achievements, and one segment that covers contingencies and complementary actions.

Each POSTERS element has a role and function within the overall framework. What follows is a description of each element.

Preparational Objectives

These are the sets of end-points during the planning process that prepare for the activation of capabilities. In some preparations, additional precursor steps or intermediate products may be needed. Personnel may rehearse and practice skills and maneuvers ahead of the time of action. Precursors and intermediates may then be fed into channels for further refinement, creating a virtual "pyramid of preparation" that peaks with the completion of a finished product or the performance of an action. The series of completed products or readied actions would then be made available for implementation.

Figure 9.3 features a pyramid of preparatory actions with two parallel tracks, one for personnel and the other for the realm of goods and services. Physical items undergo a process originating from raw materials to intermediates to end products. In the realm of personnel, forethought and planning seek to anticipate operating conditions and to calculate needed quantities and configurations of people and assets. Preparations include rehearsals, practices, reconnaissance, and other forms of knowledge-gathering that lead to the actual performance at the designated point of action. Such processes are typically convergent, honing skills and making refinements toward achieving a desired result. In planning, convergence involves making sets of assumptions and then casting aside those found to be unworkable through trial runs and other forms of pre-action discovery.

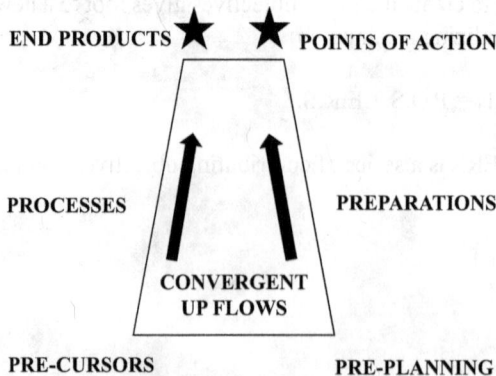

Figure 9.3 Pyramid of preparation

Preparations can be done steadily for the purpose of establishing a sustained state of readiness in defense against threats or surprises. To enhance readiness, scenario-planning backed by unit exercises provides opportunities to rehearse crisis response ahead of time and to identify gaps and vulnerabilities. Preparations frequently involve safety and risk-control checks ahead of an operation or a campaign. Mandatory checklists for airplane pilots and for surgical staff are examples of exacting methods to account for every common need ahead of a unit of action, such as a sortie or a surgical procedure.

Operational Objectives

These are the designated aim-points toward which the actions of an organized effort are directed. The standard unit of action is the operation, which is the set of discrete, identifiable actions carried out by implementers tasked to achieve a specific result or condition. Other units of activity include jobs, projects, campaigns, production lines, and procedures, along with defined work-streams of all kinds.

By incorporating commonly defined inputs, throughputs, and outputs, operational objectives promote standardization within professional planning processes, thereby clarifying the planners' own objectives. For instance, operations typically involve the "*Five Ts*":

1. *Tools*: the instruments with a specialized function
2. *Techniques*: the application of tools as they were designed to do
3. *Tasks*: the units of action that were carried out by individuals wielding such instruments
4. *Tactics*: the actions taken toward a particular objective
5. *Time*: the allocated lifespan of the operation and its component stages

Once activated, an operation's line of action involves common markers such as their initiation, interactions, transactions, and termination. Lines of action and their operational objectives can be arrayed across any number of functions, such as finance, personnel, logistics, or medical. Much of strategic planning looks to mesh the different lines of operations so that their operational objectives are mutually reinforcing and so that each makes a contribution to the attainment of the strategic goal.

In the realm of the military, the operation is the primary unit of action, just as a surgical operation is a primary unit of action for surgeons. Major operations in the military are given code names, not only for security purposes, but to grant a particular action a cohesive character that facilitates communications among insiders. Arguably the most famous military example is Operation Overlord, the World War II campaign unleashed on the beaches of Normandy, France, on D-Day, June 6, 1944. Overlord consisted of a sprawling panoply of vital support operations and sub-campaigns all with their own code names, allowing those working in secret to compartmentalize sensitive information, but also to succinctly convey the gist of what each operation sought to accomplish.[2]

Specialized operations requiring elite levels of skill create unique cultures in which participants bond together from shared history and traditions. The U.S. Navy SEAL teams, for example, constitute an elite culture derived from the rigors and dangers of their jobs, which is predominantly centered upon performing highly specialized and extremely dangerous operations. Strings of operational successes boost morale and further a SEAL team's storied history. It is the clarity and the value of the operation as a unit of action that makes its outcome, the operational objective, an important citation on a military resume.

Operational objectives serve as important performance markers in other professions. In sports, the concept of the operational objective is well illustrated in the team sport of American football. A team on offense is allocated four tries, or downs, to move possession of the ball ten yards. If the team succeeds in reaching those ten yards or more, it is awarded with another set of four downs. The operational objective of the quarterback is to call a mix of plays believed to be the best way to achieve the first down. A successful string of first downs will put the offense in a position to score at the goal line.

Alternatively, an operational objective can also be cast as a tactical objective, the product of a particular maneuver known to yield a consistent result. Many front-line professions, such as law enforcement, train their implementers to select the best option from a menu of specialized tactics for certain situations. In contrast to strategic decisions made by leaders with an overarching, skyline perspective of events, tactical decisions are judgments made by ground-line forces in real time and in reaction to realities encountered during direct engagement.

Whereas most tactics are assertive in nature, many are defensive in nature, in the forms of gambits, ruses, and distractions meant to throw off an opponent or to disguise one's intentions. When complicating circumstances are encountered, tactical objectives could be considered as offshoots from the main drive toward an operational objective, coming into play when improvisational responses are warranted.

Stage Objectives

These are the operational objectives that terminate a major phase of a campaign. For effective management, a campaign is divided into major stages or phases across functions, time periods, sequences, and geographies, among other possible means of segmentation.

Each stage can be considered a mini-campaign, arrayed in serial sets of operational objectives. A stage might be implemented in parallel fashion, with ongoing action across different operations. The military often uses contingency plans for conflicts happening simultaneously in far-flung regions, with each arena of action called a "theater of operation." Another example is a global sales campaign for a multi-national food company involving the major geographical regions it serves, with each regional campaign making adaptations in ad messaging for local cultures.

Stage objectives are notable milestone markers, denoting success at a prominent juncture in the life of the campaign. Milestones reached not only validate a strategy, but they can become the basis for establishing a positive, uplifting narrative of the journey to date. A string of achieved milestones creates a palpable sense of momentum, building excitement and anticipation of further victories to come, and attracting even more participants to the cause. In the way a ground army seeks to win and occupy land territory, winning campaign milestones is akin to securing "psychological territory," providing a base of proven ability that can be translated into additional momentum, engendering a virtuous upward spiral of accomplishment.

Conversely, missing milestone objectives can be demoralizing, especially if expectations are high. An early failure can lead to second-guessing and various forms of "blame casting" about the causes, leading to personnel departures or withdrawal of investor backing in financial situations. Managing expectations in a pragmatic way entails communicating the possibilities of failure along with a commitment to assess any failures immediately and to apply lessons learned toward future improvements.

Terminal Objectives

These objectives are simply the stopping points of a campaign. Interchangeable with the Finish Line of the strategic goal framework, the terminal objective becomes the marker for the official cessation of operations for when the campaign reaches the end point. Such a marker holds added importance by setting expectations about the denouement of the campaign and the winding down of operations. But, the terminal objective need not be rigid nor immovable: At times the terminal objective is changed because of shifting conditions or sometimes by fiat. Other elements of the strategic goal, especially the element Deadline, also can be altered in reaction to new situations.

Abrupt changes in the placement or timing of the end point, often called "shifting the goal line," can jar expectations and set off internal divisions concerning the way forward. The sudden lurching and turbulence that comes about is often described as a "hard landing." A strategic plan that can account for contingencies is one that incorporates a capacity for resilience, providing options known in advance and an avenue for sharing information as the terminus is approached.

A portion of the journey can be allocated to create an "off-ramp," the penultimate segment for an exit strategy. The off-ramp is the avenue for the deescalation of operations commensurate with accomplishments made to that point. It also provides opportunity for last-stage judgments about the certainty of reaching the end point. In this manner, actions and judgments are communicated to stakeholders so that expectations about results are better aligned. In contrast to the jarring consequences of a "hard landing" that can come from under-managing expectations, the smoothness that comes about from a carefully calibrated exit process is often described as a "soft landing."

If a campaign itself is considered as a unit of operations, it can be seen as a modular component in an even broader context. A campaign can be singular in its own right, having a terminal objective that defines its finality. But a campaign also can be part of a wider multi-campaign effort whereby each campaign's terminal objectives contribute to an even grander campaign. Wars are often prosecuted in this way with distinct campaigns across regions, each and together contributing to the drive for ultimate victory.

A campaign can be a part of a perpetual mission that strives ceaselessly toward a highly idealistic goal or toward an indefinite objective with an open timeline. Campaigns dedicated to social ideals such as equality or universality are often conducted as ongoing missions. How campaigns align and interconnect with one another is the foundation of grand strategy, requiring the widest apertures of intellectual and historical perspectives to gauge how actors and factors might play out and how one might choose to "play in."

Figure 9.4 illustrates how the four POST objectives described to this point are arranged among each other: Preparational objectives are pre-campaign aims; Operational objectives are the end points for units of activity such as projects; Stage objectives are the end points for the major phases of a campaign; and the Terminal objective is the formal, finalizing end point of the campaign.

Evaluation Objectives

These are the points of assessment that inform a judgment regarding performance and outcomes. Regardless of the degree of planning and preparations, all situations are inherently unique, with ever-changing conditions by which entities act and their strategies interact in ways never before encountered. In

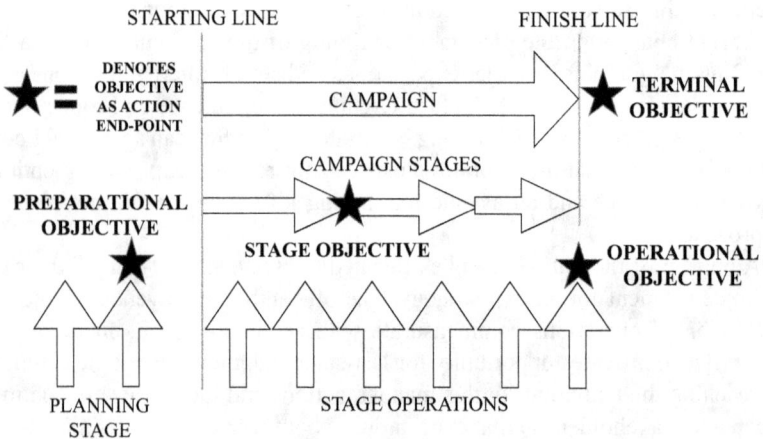

Figure 9.4 POST objectives

taking action toward a goal, the underlying assumptions of strategies become validated or invalidated, with infinite shadings in between. Missing the errors and vulnerabilities emerging from operations embeds blind spots and escalates risk and hazards in future missions.

A commitment to surfacing weaknesses in addition to the strengths and learning how implementers handled unexpected situations is a strategic value unto itself. The knowledge gained from operational actions builds out the organization's *experiential intelligence*, the capability to absorb learnings and to evolve future tactics. Experiential intelligence is distinct from the related notion of institutional memory, which implies a static warehousing of knowledge. Feedback cycle speeds can range from near instantaneous, like that given in coaching from mentor to mentee, to longer-term "post-incident" analyses conducted with deliberative thoroughness, such as past reports issued by presidential commissions investigating major national disasters. Experiential intelligence is a commitment toward a fluid, flexible feedback cycle that acquires learnings through its various means of engagement, assesses them, and applies lessons learned in a deliberative, purposeful manner.

Whereas there are a myriad of evaluation systems used to gauge programs, a basic four-element model of evaluation performs the following actions:

1. To *analyze* is to break down the whole into constituent parts, simplifying relationships to make them more understandable to evaluate.
2. To *identify* refers to the ability to discern and diagnose the key cause-effect relationships underlying a problem or a strength, often requiring specialized expertise.
3. To *synthesize* is to integrate learnings into the existing "playbooks" that entities use to design and implement their strategies.
4. To *modify* refers to the changes and improvements made to processes, personnel, and product in order to enhance effectiveness and boost efficiencies.

This cycle of evaluation acts in response to new realities encountered, provokes thinking on how assumptions have changed, and spurs corrective actions. Just as a driver of an automobile relies upon the instrument readings on the car's dashboard to gauge the operating performance of the vehicle, an organization embarking on the course laid forth by its strategic plan should also gather knowledge about the conduct of its operations. A performance dashboard can be created with any number of metrics and indicators pertinent to an operation, such as units of performance achieved, time per operation, money flows, and many other signals of progress or failure.

A similar concept is creating a master scorecard that captures output and outcomes achieved over time, and comparing those results to past performance or in relation to peers and rivals. Resulting improvements are made not only for the benefit of the organization internally but also for the purpose of enhancing its stature within its field.

Results Objectives

The central purpose of implementing a strategic plan is to achieve results, the outcome of one's efforts. It is the results that matter to stakeholders, as results yield the valued benefits that can be consumed by them or be deployed to other needs. For large, complex campaigns that have expended much time and capital, achieving results is an important fiduciary duty sought by leaders to validate that investments were successful in producing needed returns.

Recall the heuristic equation:

IMPACT = RESULTS × VALUATION
with RESULTS = (NEW STATE - ORIGINAL STATE)
and VALUATION = (NEW VALUE - ORIGINAL VALUE)

With this basic model, an impact analysis must determine if and what results occurred from an intervention and how they compared with what existed at the start. Furthermore, the impact analysis would include an appraisal of what the new state has produced in value, both in tangible and intangible ways, in relation to its original value.

For tangible outcomes, such as money or other items assessed in quantitative measures, these assessments can be straightforward; however, for outcomes and values of an intangible nature, these assessments can be complicated and even hotly disputed.

For intangibles, a variety of means might be used to characterize features that could become measured. They can include the use of indirect measures, such as indicators known to hold a reasonable correlation to an outcome, or survey research techniques to gauge emotional attitudes of people through statistical means.

Although impact analysis has as its central focus the direct consequences of implementing a strategy, it should also take into account the implications of the outcome. A new state of affairs, especially those involving new arrays of interests and tensions, typically sets off a ripple effect in ways expected and unexpected. Such consequences, in turn, would either facilitate or complicate the landscape ahead for an entity contemplating a new strategic goal.

Predictably, discerning all unintended consequences arising from an impact is a Herculean task. Attempts to simplify these scenarios requires work to shrink the universe down to those situations that pose the most concern, such as unexpected vulnerabilities arising in the new state of affairs. One way to truncate ripple effects is to impose a limit of scenarios analyzed so that repercussions are not examined beyond a realistic probability. Another way to limit scenarios is to project likely behavior of people by modeling past actions or by using psychological profiling techniques, as is done by criminal investigators.

Situational analysis can clarify likely outcomes by drawing from history and case studies in which the events or conditions are similar to what has been encountered.

Yet another means of forecasting is to exercise professional judgment of a particular field and use projections on what might happen, such as what an epidemiologist might do in predicting the course of a new, threatening epidemic.

Altogether, assessing whether or not a results objective has been achieved relies upon validating what has been changed by the campaign and determining the beneficial value that resulted. Furthermore, the evolutionary nature of strategic affairs, arising from the incessant change of world affairs, implies an ongoing need for assessing both impact and implications. Impact is the degree of desired change actually realized, and implications are the follow-on consequences that radiate across one's strategic domain, affecting actors and factors alike.

Supporting Objectives

These are the objectives that supplement and complement the value of the main objective by adding to or reinforcing efforts to reach the strategic goal. Whereas primary work-streams absorb the most attention and resources, adjacent efforts aimed at "clearing the brush" or "blazing the trail ahead" are often underappreciated for their contributions. Ancillary actions to provide vital supplies, to establish robust communications, or to service broken equipment are among the many examples by which support operations sustain the mainstream effort.

In military science, the flanking maneuver serves as a supporting action for the main battle group by threatening an enemy's side, forcing it to recoil in response. That reaction enables the main group to execute its plan. The flanking move acts in an intentional choreography with the main campaign, a duet of tactics that together create the maximum chances for success.

Supporting objectives can also "enwrap" themselves about the main objective, widening the impact of an achievement. A U.S. presidential campaign, for example, is fully dedicated to achieving the candidate's victory, yet it might choose to opportunistically invest time and resources into winning majorities in Congress so that the victor would have an even stronger mandate to govern.

Supporting objectives might also take on the form of secondary, or backup, objectives. Should the main campaign falter or even fail, secondary objectives provide the means to still obtain partial value for the mission. Contingencies are often built into scientific and military missions in recognition that volatility and variability can throw off the main mission, putting a high-cost, high-risk project in jeopardy of becoming a total loss. Backup plans salvage value when events go awry, and such diversions can still add to the body of experiential intelligence in ways helpful to future missions.

As the campaign has been highlighted as the featured unit of action in the preceding discussion of POSTERS, it can also serve as an example in demonstrating how the acronym might work as a whole. Once again using the American presidential campaign as an example, one might categorize some of the multitudes of actions taken by a candidate to fall within the POSTERS framework in the following manner:

Preparational objectives: Assemble campaign apparatus, open headquarters, set fundraising target, file paperwork, hire field staff, declare candidacy.

Operational objectives: Travel to key states, meet voters, unleash advertising, court important societal figures, solicit endorsements, place campaign signs, knock on doors, get out the vote efforts.

Stage objectives: Win key primary states, win party nomination, pre-convention and post-convention positioning, pre-debate and post-debate messaging.

Terminal objective: Win majority of states' electoral votes on Election Day.

Evaluation objectives: Assess lines of advertising effectiveness, gauge messaging themes with key voter blocs, analyze impact of candidate's debate performance, measure numbers of voters transported by "Get out the vote" workers.

Results objectives: Assess winning margins across regions and voter groups, determine extent of mandate, identify themes with high voter resonance, identify top promises to implement.

Supporting objectives: Determine extent of "coattail" effect on other candidate races, party wins majorities in legislative houses, exercising power of appointments throughout government, implementing powers on regulation and on international affairs.

From this example, the POSTERS framework captures much of the sequence and priorities integral to a major campaign dedicated to a singular strategic goal, in this case winning an election at a certain time point. As the terminal objective is the same as the Finish Line of the strategic goal, one can further substantiate each of the goal's four lines:

Finish Line: Win majority of states' electoral votes.

Deadline: Election Day, with a timeline starting from declaration of candidacy and inclusive of key events.

Pay Line: Winning presidential powers and ancillary capabilities of the executive branch.

Headline: The significance and prominence of winning the election in light of candidate's messaging and framing of themes; implications for agenda and for relationship across the political and diplomatic communities.

Notes

1. Cheryl Pellerin, "Mattis Details Three Lines of Effort in Memo to DoD Personnel," *DoD News*, Oct. 11, 2017. https://dod.defense.gov/News/Article/Article/1339147/mattis-details-three-lines-of-effort-in-memo-to-dod-personnel/ (accessed Oct. 20, 2018).
2. Maj. John Krysa, "Operational Planning in the Normandy Campaign, 1944, Appendix B, Summary of Major Code Word Operations," Paper for the U.S. Army Command and General Staff College (Apr. 1968), 36–37. www.dtic.mil/dtic/tr/fulltext/u2/a195453.pdf (accessed Oct. 20, 2018).

10 The Line Elements
   of a Strategic Plan

Recall the initial heuristic equation introduced at the outset of Part 4:

JOURNEY = CAMPAIGN + ROADMAP + VEHICLE

Upon completing the descriptions of CAMPAIGN and ROADMAP, the next section examines the characteristics of VEHICLE as the essential means to undertake a path line to the goal.

Whereas the word is a descriptor for a means of transport, *vehicle* has an alternative meaning in the realm of organizational affairs; it can also be translated as an organization's "apparatus," which is the body of mechanisms available to perform functions upon command. Apparatus evokes the equipment attached to a scuba diver, for instance, allowing underwater activity.

In a similar manner, an organization is a type of human-animated "equipment" that is "attached" to a leader in order to implement strategic and tactical directives. In fact, embassies frequently employ "attachés" of various functions in attachment to mainstream diplomatic work; for example, military, agricultural, legal, science, and health attachés commonly advise ambassadors at embassies worldwide about issues in their respective sectors.

Like all forms of equipment, apparatuses are comprised of distinct functioning parts that work enmeshed with each other to act as a whole in a coherent, consistent, and persistent manner. To describe their working parts, a new framework that incorporates several line-words is introduced.

The heuristic equation that describes these contributing components appears as follows:

LINE-UP = FRONTLINES + BACKLINES + LINK LINES

Discussing each of these components in turn:

The Line-Up

Reminiscent of the list specifying baseball players' sequential order in going to bat, the line-up is the roster of policy players with their designated roles and responsibilities. Identifying those individuals and institutions influential to the issue at hand makes clearer the array of powers with which one must contend on the policy landscape. Assembling or obtaining such a roster also engages one's intelligence capabilities, even in basic or innate ways.

A standard organizational chart is a visual way of presenting the configuration of individuals, roles, unit functions, and hierarchical lines of authority. Sometimes these charts are openly and freely available, but often they are outdated or, as is typical in the world of defense and intelligence, they are guarded and classified as secret. When such information is irregular, achieving a clear understanding of internal power structures can be difficult.

The importance of rostering is recognized by militaries worldwide in their institutionalized use of "orders of battle" in delineating the units, either friendly or foe, involved in a particular conflict or mission. An order of battle not only flags the particular unit's name identity, it delves deeper to reveal each unit's key characteristics pertaining to its attributes and capabilities. An elegant military acronym that captures those elements is SALUTE, which rosters a group's Size, Activity, Location, Unit, Time, and Equipment.[1] With the essential, concise information embedded with an order of battle, commanders map out their strategies in ways they believe optimal to achieving their mission. Orders of battle are also important historical documentation of the planning process, incorporating commanders' intentions and assumptions about prevailing conditions and how they changed during the course of the action.

Although many civilian organizations do not have formalized rosters like those that exist in the military, they can develop looser, simpler rosters in what might be called an "order of engagement." A business version could identify all functional units, such as sales and marketing teams to be activated for a major marketing campaign, for example, and could even include a parallel roster of those competing companies expected to react. A hypothetical diplomatic order of engagement for a vote at the United Nations might configure the ambassadorial team, the foreign affairs ministry, and relevant specialists as well as those of key allies and opponents of a measure. A civilian order of engagement, even done informally, provides a common platform for participants to know what "forces" one plans to deploy and what other forces could be encountered on the domain, and to know one's strengths and weaknesses relative to the others. In preparing for an important meeting, an order of engagement could list the speakers, supporting delegations, and expected lines of arguments by parties.

Identifying key players in a line-up is integral to a detailed planning process that includes the "line-item" rostering of necessary resources and actions. A line-item roster can be in the form of a checklist, but it can also be developed further at senior levels to include traditional line-item budgeting slates wherein assets and actions are allocated. Line items and checklists can be organized within each phase of the POSTERS objectives framework to create a choreography for implementation.

Frontlines

These are the teams and individuals assigned to achieve the goal through their direct actions. Once a strategic goal has been set and a plan developed to implement it, the goal-scoring actions are delegated to those "on the ground," either literally or in other practical manners. In performing their duties, front-line implementers directly engage other actors and contend with prevailing conditions.

For example, if a public health agency acts toward a goal of administering polio vaccines to all at-risk children in a given province within a period of one year, then the elaboration of the strategic plan, with quantitative targets and timelines, would eventually be transmitted down to the team level. That team, comprised of nurses and health specialists, would then walk into neighborhoods, engage parents, and directly administer the vaccine to the children. Once administered, each dose successfully administered adds to the campaign's overall goal. The team's work provides the essential on-the-ground, "numeric traction" that translates their specific goal-scoring tasks into definitive progress toward the campaign's goal.

From this insight, a strategic planner can better identify the composition of the front line by asking these simple questions: Who will be implementing the goal-scoring actions? Do their actions and results directly add "numeric traction" to the campaign goal? If one can answer these questions with clear roles and tasks, then the composition of frontline teams facilitates planning for logistics, deployment, support, and many other needs. If one cannot envision the answers, then further refinement of either the goal or the tasks is necessary.

Implementers on the frontline own the ground-line perspective by seeing conditions as they really exist and by acting in accordance with what they encounter. By doing so they are critical contributors to experiential intelligence, that reservoir of gainful knowledge that is learned and earned from direct experience. As noted previously in this volume, those who act at the ground-line earn the authenticity of their direct perspective from the REEDS principles: Rely upon yourself, Experience it yourself, Express it yourself, Do it yourself, and See it for yourself. For teams, the five REEDS principles are pluralized to become "by ourselves," alluding to an experiential bond among them.

Backlines

These are the centers for direction and coordination of the frontlines, typically from headquarters or command centers. The biological analogue would be where the "nerve centers" or the "brains" of the organizations are residing. Interchangeable with the skyline perspective, the backline is at the conceptual altitude high enough to see how the grand scheme of events unfold and is where the platform for authority sits high enough to give direction through firm lines of command and control. This level is where strategy conjoins with tactics, with leaders possessing the supervisory scope of sight to perceive the domain as a whole and the command authority to direct frontline forces to specific places and to carry out tactical orders.

The integration between strategy and tactics implies that the backline is at the confluence for inflows of information and outflows of directives. That integration relies upon the work of the "*Four INTs*": *Interests, Intelligence, Intentions,* and *Interactions,* with which the values and ideals of the organization are assimilated, the broad parameters of the situation are assessed, and the levers of influence are activated.

It is from the backline that leaders play a pivotal role in managing the dual forces of rationality and emotionality. In bridging these demands, leaders assess situations through rationality, gauging, and judging with analytical tools and techniques. They also must practice the art of "strategic emotionality": expressing ways to sustain the motivations of frontline teams by reinforcing their mission, sharing the skyline perspective and boosting their morale.

By exercising power at the nexus of rationality and emotionality, leaders undertake tasks that are both integrative and expressive. One backline task that spans these characteristics is the art and skill of communicating the *storyline*. The storyline is the telling of a narrative of the journey under way. Compelling storytelling is a form of strategic communications in that it conveys the mission ahead, the obstacles to be overcome ("dragons to be slain"), and the ultimate fulfillment in reaching the goal ("reaching the promised land").

The telling of narratives establishes a connective form of history, a linking of what is being undertaken in the present with that which has happened in the past. By upholding acts of courage, heroism, and aspiration, stories inspire those along the frontlines not only to do their best but to establish a bond between what they are doing today with the ennobling values of the heroes in the past. Institutional traditions and ceremonies set a lineage upon which new stories could be told and from which fortitude and willpower for arduous tasks ahead can be kindled.

To motivate, one basic form in telling a narrative in pragmatic terms is to "*gel, tell, sell.*" This is a modern formulation reminiscent of Aristotle's ancient formula of rhetoric: *ethos* (credibility), *logos* (reason), and *pathos* (empathy).[2]

To gel a story is to coalesce an interpretation or a perception about a situation into succinct, instinctually understood concepts or, more colloquially, as talking points.

To tell a story is to express it in ways authentic and skillful, conveying both content and emotional tenor.

To sell the story is to radiate its message in ways persuasive and meaningful, using a judgment between reason and passion.

By whatever structure used, a narrative authentically told connects idealism, the realm of that which is being sought, to realism, the realm of that which now exists.

Link Lines

Link lines are the connecting systems between the leaders on the backline and the implementers on the frontline. Recall the "Three S Triad" introduced in Part 1: Strategic, Systemic, and Specific. By overlaying the line-up of Backline, Link line, and Frontline one can identify the pairings of:

Backline—Strategic
Link line—Systemic
Frontline—Specific

Thus it is consistent and logical that the leaders in the backline have the strategic vantage point, those working in the link line are the systemic connectors, and those implementing on the frontline have specific tasks and specific objectives. Link lines serve both practical and emotive roles: They channel vital resources and relay essential orders down to the frontline. They also remit the implementors' feedback up the line, providing essential information about what is being encountered. Without adequate link lines, the signals to and from the "brains" of the campaign would be disrupted from the implementing "hands and feet."

Figure 10.1 aligns the three element line-up of strategic plan in a ladder with counterparts in the Three S Triad and identifies the similarity of their actions.

As linkages are critical to an organization's performance, they are constituted along specialized functions. What follows are several line words that aptly describe important link line functions.

Supply Lines

Frontlines often consume prodigious amounts of resources, requiring a system for resupply with sufficient capacity to feed inputs and to extract waste and

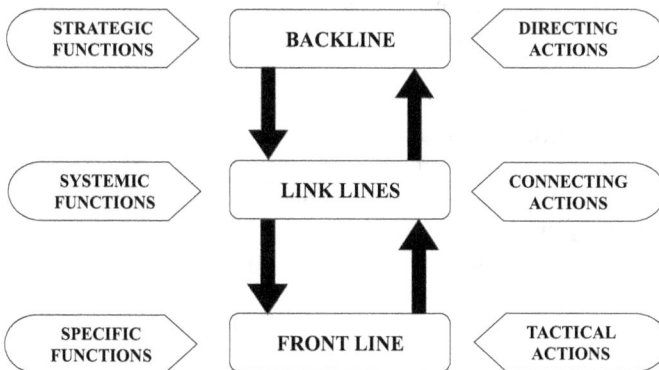

Figure 10.1 Plan-line ladder

by-products. Supply chains are systems that convey material in interlinked segments, providing flexibility in how they are aligned and the distances to which it can extend or contract. Pipelines are rigid physical pipes that are designed for high volume flows; the tradeoff is that they are immobile and require maintenance, making such systems potential targets of high strategic value. Transport lines in all three physical spheres—land, sea, and air—are ubiquitous in their coverage and reach worldwide. A major risk of intermeshed supply lines is that intersections among them can become chokepoints which stifle movements and provoke wide disorder.

Communications Lines

These are the channels by which information is transmitted to and from parties in a network. These transmittal streams encompass all forms of information that are used in tactical, strategic, and intelligence functions: voice, video, audio, data, transactions. Like physical supply lines, lines of communications in physical and cyber space are vulnerable targets. In recent times, cyber attacks have proliferated, causing substantial economic and political damage. A specialized form of communications line is the hotline, a dedicated, private channel that is activated upon the onset of a crisis in order to clarify intentions and to reduce misunderstandings that might trigger a broader, unintended conflict.

Reporting Lines

These are arrangements for how authority flows between the front- and backlines. Frequently described as chain of command, reporting lines can be formalized along rank and other hierarchical arrangements, making clear duties and obligations. Reporting lines enable the orders from a recognized authority to be generated, disseminated, and vested with designated recipients. Conversely, verification of actions flows up the line.

Alternatively, reporting lines can be informal, or be contingent on certain conditions such as emergencies (known as "dotted line" authority), drawing upon casual interactions, friendships, or the existence of a loose "grapevine" of speculative opining. Informal lines can supply irregular but sometimes insightful, even truthful depictions of events that have been excluded from the formal, official lines of communication.

Whether formal or informal, reporting lines must be secure in their integrity in order to assure the authenticity of orders dispatched and received, as garbled or compromised messages can create dangers arising from deliberate intrusions or disruptions.

Lifelines

This colloquially coined term instinctually describes the lines that connect to rescue and emergency functions. Such lines can be of the physical type, such as emergency resupply to regions cut off by strife or hit by disaster, or the release of assets held in reserve upon a triggering action. Lifelines can be of a political stripe, often extended by prominent patrons in differing types of independent-dependent, client-state relationships.

Although virtually all nations deem themselves sovereign and independent, many have fallen into a state of dependency in which they received vital aid from a dominant country in return for some form of political or diplomatic allegiance. Classical examples include the 18th- and 19th-century European empires holding sway over swaths of colonies across the globe.[3] More modern examples include the Soviet-era client states of Eastern Europe and Cuba.[4] In recent years, new forms of lifelines have come into being in the form of humanitarian and medical aid, spurred on in large part by the rise of epidemics such as HIV/AIDS, programs that have saved millions of lives through the provision of medicines and care from donor countries.[5]

Brake Lines

Brake lines are conceptual constraints built into the weave of international relations, particularly among alliances and the workings of international organizations. Alliances are often formed for the purpose of constraining a powerhouse, such as the creation of NATO as counterweight to the Soviet Union. International organizations such as the United Nations and the International Monetary Fund serve as political and financial buffers, respectively, in times of crises and provide a forum for negotiation and amelioration of tensions.

The natural inclination of a strategic posture laden with expensive assets is preparing to go on the offensive, mobilizing forces, asserting prerogatives, and exerting powers in an outbound direction. However, there are many conditions that inhibit full fury pursuit of interests, namely defenses and other obstacles put up by other entities, and one's own set of weaknesses and vulnerabilities. Some countries and organizations subscribe to values that disown aggression and uphold peaceful coexistence, making a defensive posture a preferred policy.

Defensive objectives are intended to avert aggression and protect one's interests when they are threatened. A standing challenge is deciding when and how to take such measures. Making known to all actors in the strategic domain what conditions one considers threatening can act as a deterrent or, at a minimum, as an informed warning to would-be aggressors. Delineation is one means, a declaratory tactic, to set boundaries around a situation to mark those specific circumstances deemed to be of high concern. When used as a warning indicator, delineation establishes limits to one's restraint in response to an encroachment. When delineation is set forth in a generalized, open-ended manner, such lines of demarcation might said to be "soft lines." A declaration to maintain the status quo might be said to be one of "holding the line."

As previously described in Part 2, delineation can take the form of rigidly defined "hard lines," clear yet intractable boundaries that, if breached, dramatically escalate the stakes along with the magnitude and intensity of response. Red lines, bright lines, and trip wires have come into more frequent usage in recent years as declarations of deterrent determination. Although such hard lines may back a defensive posture with a promise of responsive force, opponents may still choose to test those lines in defiance or to claim as much value as possible right up to the line, a situation that risks unintended consequences.

To curb unwanted actions or incentives, brake lines are applied formally by administrative entities with authority to impose and enforce laws, rules, regulations, and sanctions. Hierarchical organizations have lines of authority and lines of command and control that apply such braking tools to internal workings.

Braking forces applied by rivals are intended to hinder one's progress toward a strategic goal. There are at least four ways that such forces can cause turbulence to one's plans: They can be *disruptive*, by outside forces striking into the plan; they can be *eruptive*, by inside forces causing conflicts that rupture the plan; they can be *corrosive*, by inside tensions simmering unchecked; or they can be *corruptive*, by forces from any quarter that betray the mission.

Notes

1. U.S. Marine Corps Training Command, "Combat Orders Foundations B2B0287 Student Handout, Order Format," 12. www.trngcmd.marines.mil/Portals/207/Docs/TBS/B2B 2377%20Combat%20Orders%20Foundations.pdf?ver=2015-08-03-075817-200 (accessed Oct. 20, 2018).
2. Purdue University Online Writing Lab, "Aristotle's Rhetorical Situation." https://owl.purdue.edu/owl/general_writing/academic_writing/rhetorical_situation/aristotles_rhetorical_situation.html (accessed Oct. 19, 2018).
3. Paul Kennedy, *Rise and Fall of the Great Powers: Economic Change and Military Conflict from 1500–2000* (New York: Random House, 1987), 143–191.
4. Rubinstein, *Soviet Foreign Policy Since World War II*, 72–92.
5. U.N. Programme on HIV/AIDS (UNAIDS), "Global HIV & AIDS—2018 Fact Sheet." www.unaids.org/en/resources/fact-sheet (accessed Oct. 20, 2018).

11 Heuristic Cascade of a Strategic Plan

As the strategic plan involves the application of power by an entity with capabilities, and as winning operational objectives on the path line are valuable in generating momentum toward the strategic goal, a series of heuristic equations are constructed in multi-step fashion to demonstrate the components' interlocking relationships.

The Force Heuristic

1. Recall the basic equation:

    RESULTS = (END STATE − BEGINNING STATE)

    which is the change in conditions brought on by a campaign.
2. Achieving a string of successes in quick succession can then be described as:

    MOMENTUM = RESULTS × ACCELERATION

    with

    ACCELERATION = (PACING + SPACING)

    whereby PACING is the speed of effort and SPACING is the distance of milestones on a timeline, which shortens with acceleration and lengthens with deceleration.
3. Thus the fully elaborated cascade equation becomes:

    MOMENTUM = (END STATE − BEGINNING STATE) × (PACING + SPACING)

    which reinforces the concept that achieving gains in quick succession sustains momentum.
4. As an entity comprises itself as a force exercising power to implement action, that relationship can be described as follows:

    FORCE = POWER × ACTION

    with the multiplier sign used because by setting either term to zero means a force is negated if there is no power or if no action is taken.

5. Power (the strategic kind, not the physical property) itself can be composed of two necessary elements:

    POWER = AUTHORITY × CAPABILITY

    with one in AUTHORITY being in possession of a license to act, and CAPABILITY being the implementing apparatus previously described as (CAPACITY × ABILITY).

6. Action is the product of having designs to wielding power in a certain way or toward a particular purpose. This can be described as:

    ACTION = INTENTION × IMPLEMENTATION

    with the previously described relationship:

    IMPLEMENTATION = PREPARATIONS × OPERATIONS

    and

    INTENTION = (TARGET + WILL)

7. Substituting these relationships into the original FORCE equation from step 4, one can derive the following fully elaborated version:

    FORCE = AUTHORITY × CAPABILITY × INTENTION × IMPLEMENTATION

    FORCE = AUTHORITY × (CAPACITY × ABILITY) × (TARGET + WILL) × (PREPARATIONS × OPERATIONS)

Figure 11.1 illustrates that, in essence, force is commensurate to having license to act, having assets, discerning a clear goal, possessing the requisite determination to achieve it, and executing a prepared plan.

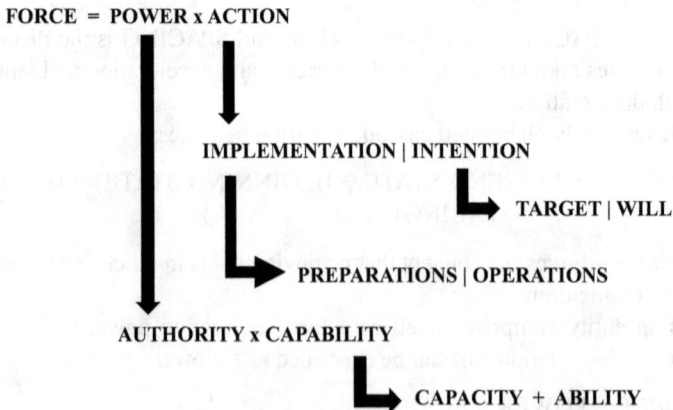

Figure 11.1 Force cascade

The Credibility Heuristic

The interactions of parties as they each pursue goals and advance interests mean many occasions for conflict and the need to resolve them through negotiations. Among the many skills and attributes successful negotiators should possess are experience in producing results ("track record") and the ability to deliver on promises or to back threats ("add bite to the bark").

1. This can be described in the following way:

   CREDIBILITY = CAPABILITIES × REPUTATION

2. Recall that:

   REPUTATION = (RESULTS − EXPECTATIONS)

   and accompanied by the now familiar:

   CAPABILITIES = CAPACITY × ABILITY

   with CAPACITY being the technological proxy for TOOLS + TACTICS and with ABILITY being the proxy for human SKILL + WILL.

3. By further substitution into the CREDIBILITY equation, the cascade unfolds:

   CREDIBILITY = (RESULTS − EXPECTATIONS) × (CAPACITY × ABILITY)

   CREDIBILITY = [(END STATE − STARTING STATE) − EXPECTA-TIONS] × (TOOLS + TACTICS) × (SKILL × WILL)

Figure 11.2 shows in a cascading format that the credibility of a negotiator and his or her positions is reliant on a track record of substantive success and on managing expectations. Credibility is also reliant on having sufficient national or institutional capabilities full of technical and human forms of capital.

Credibility is at the heart of principled, enduring leadership. As the source of trust and believability, credibility is the trait that leaders must possess in order to attract adherents who can contribute efforts and energies to a cause. Without

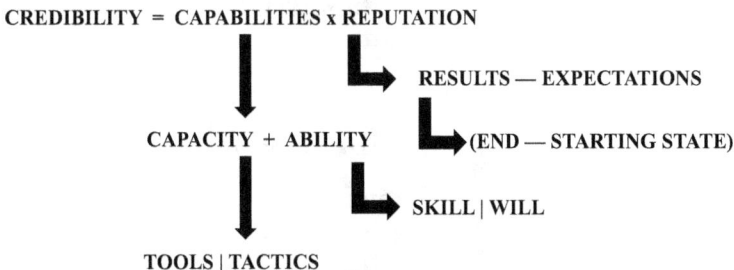

CREDIBILITY = CAPABILITIES x REPUTATION

RESULTS — EXPECTATIONS

CAPACITY + ABILITY   (END — STARTING STATE)

SKILL | WILL

TOOLS | TACTICS

Figure 11.2 Credibility cascade

it, leaders would have to direct by hard-power tactics involving coercion and imposition. Credibility is accentuated by an individual's character and personality, making possible infinite styles and expressions of leadership, with each as unique as the individuals themselves.

The Leadership Heuristic

1. The relationship between credibility and character as contributing traits to leadership can be described as:

    LEADERSHIP = CREDIBILITY × CHARACTER

    with the multiplication sign indicating each factor magnifies the other.
2. Further, if CHARACTER is a composite of two elements, one of mindset and the other of actions taken, that relationship can be expressed as:

    CHARACTER = ATTITUDE × BEHAVIOR

3. Recalling earlier that:

    CREDIBILITY = REPUTATION × CAPABILITIES

4. Then recapitulating the leadership equation and making substitutions:

    LEADERSHIP = CREDIBILITY × CHARACTER

    then becomes:

    LEADERSHIP = (ATTITUDE × BEHAVIOR) × (REPUTATION × CAPABILITIES)

5. Further substitution for REPUTATION and CAPABILITIES yields a final result:

    LEADERSHIP = (ATTITUDE × BEHAVIOR) × (RESULTS − EXPECTATIONS) × (CAPACITY × ABILITY)

LEADERSHIP = CREDIBILITY x CHARACTER

→ **ATTITUDE | BEHAVIOR**

CAPABILITIES x REPUTATION

→ **RESULTS — EXPECTATIONS**

CAPACITY + ABILITY

→ **SKILL | WILL**

TOOLS | TACTICS

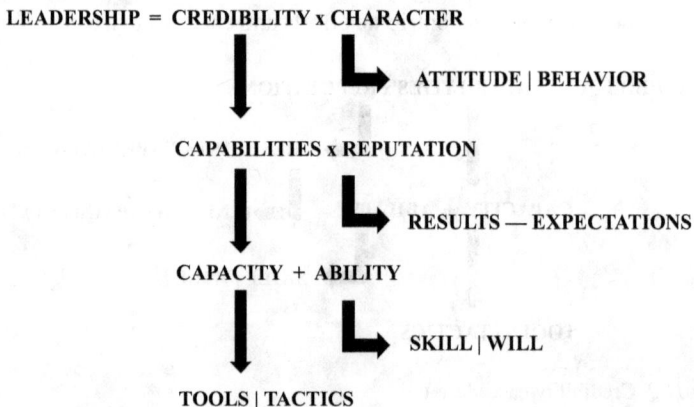

Figure 11.3 Leadership cascade

Through the heuristic exercise shown in Figure 11.3, leadership is a holistic function of personal attributes, commitments, records of accomplishment, and skills involving professional expertise and managing expectations. It involves both objective and subjective attributes, reflecting that core human dichotomy residing within all individuals.

12 Communications Tools

In all aspects of strategy development and implementation, communications is a vital function, as organizations are comprised of people working toward a goal, often amid challenging conditions. Communications is essential to the transmittal of information across and beyond the organization, and it is necessary for the conveyance of intentions, which is what is being contemplated as the future course of action. Without the means to communicate effectively and efficiently, the myriad of professionals tasked to achieve objectives would become isolated from the grand view and become prone to inertia or to acting without coordination.

As organizations pursue their missions on a long-term time frame and seek goals that mainly hew within their technical or professional boundaries, the style and content of communications become shaped by internal cultures. In these working environments, professional vernaculars arise, acronyms are coined, and procedural habits are formed. As conditions evolve and professional staff turns over with the passage of time, organizations rely on internal policies and procedures to standardize communications. In addition, professions and industries adopt standards in order to facilitate the flow and content of information across their communities.

In policymaking, the challenge of finding common standards in communications escalates as organizations proliferate and complexities emerge. Yet if some basic, even rudimentary, standards could be developed as *lingua franca*, bridging technical professionals and broader audiences, then coordination and collaboration should become more effective and efficient. As there are two fundamental realms of communications, verbal and written, this chapter advances a new framework for each realm, one for memo writing and the other for speechwriting, or the development of talking points.

The SOAP and SPIGOTS Framework for Memos

Among the most requested skills by students and young professionals entering public service is to be taught how to write a policy memorandum, and rightly so: Due to its conciseness and timeliness, the policy memorandum is the key vehicle in communicating ideas about an ongoing issue. With the press of events, a leader must rely on the coterie of advisors to import information from the strategic domain and to export directives out to the implementers at the frontlines. Such interchanges must be done with speed, volume, and accuracy, putting a premium on succinctness.

The drive for compactness also means that the substance and layout have to be well-organized and standardized, with categories chosen for their relevance to organizational priorities and internal practices. With the added pressure of deadlines and the modern rapidity of information "spoilage" due to fast-moving events, memos designed with a basic, standardized system save time and also prompt organized thinking well ahead of the actual writing; if an agency's memo always has a section reserved for objectives, for instance, then the coterie of advisors would be predisposed to focusing attention on their definitions and ways to reach them.

A useful framework draws out first-run ideas and places them in categories with a logical order. Once initial ideas are elicited, they can be refined and revised further. Frameworks, by covering common concepts, allow more attention to be focused on the unique problems at hand. Enduring frameworks are versatile, evolving with ever-changing practices and knowledge. They become compact, portable toolkits one can carry into unique scenarios and begin to clarify the factors and forces in play. With such a system, the writing task becomes much easier, and the points made more compelling and effective.

With their diagnostic character, frameworks also promote a habit of organized, structured thinking. As events unfold, having the practiced means to perceive patterns of interests, strategies, and behaviors confers oneself with a near instinctual ability to analyze and synthesize with alacrity and confidence.

This chapter introduces a new practical framework, or template, that guides memo writing. The framework aids in "jump-starting" the flow of ideas when one is at a quandary: staring at a blank piece of paper (or more commonly nowadays, a tablet screen), striving to come up with points of description or action, and facing a looming deadline. The framework is based on an easily remembered mnemonic so that it can be readily "uploaded" mentally and be implemented in short order.

Before delving into the formulas, some desirable characteristics of an effective memo are worth identifying. A memo should strive to uphold the *ABCs* of *Authenticity*, *Brevity*, and *Clarity*. The first "A" could also stand for *Accuracy*, a vital quality; thus, as an instrument of persuasion, a memo should describe externalities accurately and it should reflect the author's true inner judgments in a way that reveals the architecture of one's thinking: how one structures and organizes ideas, how one determines priorities, and how one drives toward results. A memo should also be concise enough to convey ideas with sufficient vividness, and even terseness, to save time and avoid attention fatigue among readers. A memo should strive to clarify matters to the level of understanding of the target readership, which implies the task to recast vague, technical or jargonistic terms into plain and simple language.

Another set of valued attributes for an effective memo is embodied by three elemental tasks: *Description*, *Prescription*, and "*Conscription*." A memo describes the topic at hand with objectivity and in measured tones. It prescribes action by articulating a judgment on what to do and the underlying rationale. It also "drafts" or draws in needed participants by a call to action to implement a plan and to persuade others about the merits of the mission.

In keeping with the approach used throughout this volume, a new heuristic equation for a memo is introduced:

MEMO = SOAP + SPIGOTS

with the SOAP acronym embodying the contents of the topic and the SPIG-OTS acronym representing a quality control checklist.

SOAP Contents

SOAP is a four-element outline that tracks the basic arc of the *Strategic Policy Design* framework, from tracing origins of an issue to identifying desired outcomes to calling for specific implementing steps. Although SOAP elements are described serially, they could be rearranged in other sequences to suit circumstances or adapted in portions and placed into existing templates.

A standard-fitted sequence most congruent with the *Strategic Policy Design* framework is *Situation, Objectives, Assessment,* and *Plan.* The SOAP acronym first originated as a method to structure daily medical patient records, with *S* standing for the patients' subjective expressions about their health at the time of query.[1] Its logical sequence and emphasis on taking action makes it highly adaptable for broader organizational uses. With some modification of the elements and redirection of their meaning to the strategic environment, SOAP finds new, versatile uses here as a template for considering issues in organizational contexts.

1. Situation

This section summarizes the presenting event, or decision, at hand. This is an appropriate section to present background information, emphasizing factors and preceding decisions that directly contribute to present-day circumstances. Succinct historical descriptions of how events unfolded or how interests evolved can convey the progression of an issue over time.

The sets of lenses and frameworks described in the strategic domain portion of this volume offer many ways with which to characterize a situation; for example, pointing out the fault lines separating two opposing sides, the ongoing battle lines being fought between them within their professional arenas, or the red lines that have been drawn in self-defense.

The situation can be presented to populate one's understanding of the strategic domain with the key actors and factors, their interests, and the major stakes on the line. The situational analysis can further delve into forces deployed and strategies employed.

From its descriptive role, the situation section is heavily weighted toward realism and objectivity, thus making this memo portion a natural place for the inclusion of data, facts, figures, and timelines. Here, projections and inferences derived from such information can be used to paint a picture of what might arise in the future.

A situation also has contextual elements that encircle and flow into a partic-ular set of circumstances. Motives behind certain actions, precedents that have tilted decisions in a certain direction, and ongoing relationships and bonds among people are among the many contextual factors that add "color" to an ongoing dynamic and that reinforce an understanding of the situation.

2. Objectives

This section specifies the targets of opportunity now being pursued, or those that have been identified as worthwhile to pursue. The status of progress in reaching toward an objective is important information, as is the achievement of key milestones. Conversely, the status of a project that is falling short of an objective or falling behind a timetable, although often uncomfortable to sur-face, is requisite information for corrective action.

Like situations, objectives also have contextual properties in how they were originally formulated, how they were presented to stakeholders, and what value they are believed to contain. Presenting the tie-ins between objectives, their value, and core interests justifies a case for either continuing toward a particular objective or switching to a new one. Also pertinent are judgments regarding the underlying assumptions regarding the goal and the pursuit; as operations proceed, new realities and unexpected events may upend those orig-inal assumptions and may require their recalibration.

The strategic goal and its four line-word elements, Finish Line, Deadline, Pay Line, and Headline, are natural residents in the Objectives section. Here, the stra-tegic goal can be laid forth along with any of its components. The status assess-ment of a campaign's progress toward its set of POSTERS aims—Preparational, Operational, Stage, Terminal, Evaluation, Results, and Supporting objectives—can illuminate influencing factors and forces in more granular detail.

Adhering to the section's label, a helpful tip is remembering to "keep your objectives objective." That is, strive to make clear the targets to which efforts are being directed and also make clear the desired end-state conditions that a campaign wants to bring about. To aid in precision, applying the checkmark test to a proposed objective can bring about the desired specificity. The check-mark test, as introduced earlier in Part 4, involves seeing whether or not a proposed action or objective is clear enough to indicate with a checkmark. If so, then the test is passed and the item can be deemed objective; if not, then refinements are needed. Ultimately, an objective is objective when it is detect-able by the human senses or by instrumentation.

3. Assessment

This section embodies the evaluation of the situation, mainly as it relates to the campaign toward the goal. By keeping the focus of evaluation on the goal and its pursuit, the memo retains coherence and relevance to the ongoing mission. Evaluation is the process by which one can render a judgment about a certain matter. What informs that process is a wide array of evaluative tools that aim to surface patterns and trends applicable for decision-making. The assemblage of requisite data, charts, graphs, and evidence may require an eye in judging what to include in order to keep the section concise. Too much evidence presented in a disjointed or overly lengthy manner can shorten attention spans and inhibit understanding.

Ultimately an assessment should lead to a reasoned judgment or an opinion concerning the entity's strategic or tactical situation. Upon the point of making a judgment, the assessment process pivots toward making a decision, a choice among options available. A memo at this juncture can either present options and attendant pros and cons for a higher leader to decide, or it can present the options and make a recommendation on what the memo-writer deems the optimal pick.

Assessments, judgments, and decisions are interlinked because a determination of one can influence the outcome of the others. For instance, changing the terms of an assessment, by emphasizing one set of data over another, can lead to different judgments and thus to alternative decisions. For this reason, assessments themselves operate within a context of surrounding factors that drive what is being evaluated and what arrays of outcomes could arise. In other words, assessments frame issues, and the ways they frame can tilt a judgment one way or the other, leading to consequential decisions. A brief statement on the way an assessment was conducted or the basis with which a judgment was applied gives the reader additional contextual factors to consider in the decision-making process.

An assessment that is persuasive in promoting a perspective or pointing to a course of action seeks to enlist those within the organization to make an investment in time, effort, and resources, and, more prominently, to take a role in the campaign toward the strategic goal.

4. Plan

This section is dedicated to the prescription of action, the implementing steps that lead to designated objectives and ultimately to the strategic goal. A plan is the prospective roadmap in taking the entity from the original beginning state, or situation, to the desired end-state. A plan is directive and forward looking: It serves as a prospectus describing how one proposes to convert resources into progress toward goals. A basic unit of progress within a plan is comprised of three serial A's: *Asset—Action—Achievement*. With such links arranged in sequence or in parallel, with outputs of one operation feeding into another, a plan can be constructed with logic and order.

As objectives and goals, when properly constructed with the principles laid forth in this volume, are designed to be tangible and verifiable, the action links pursuing them should also be as such. Again, the checkmark test can be applied to each of the three A's of Asset, Action, and Achievement to determine their objectiveness. If they are clear enough to be observable and verifiable, they pass the checkmark test.

A critical element in planning is the management of time, not only across its totality, the lifespan of the operation, but also within an operation's constituent parts. Policy choreography is the skillful meshing of people, process, and product along with timing of the start-stop points of each operation stage and their tempo, or pacing. That meshing of time and action comes together in various formats, from simple daily schedules to intricate timetables to role scripts for those participating in highly formal events.

The SOAP Menu

The acronym serves as a prompt, bringing forth a wellspring of concepts, when needed for just-in-time circumstances. Although the featured sequence, Situation—Objectives—Assessment—Plan, can be considered a standard default series, there can be a variety of substitutes for each element, depending on industry, profession, or office custom and on individual preference.

Table 12.1 is a roster of possible SOAP element substitutes, yet allowing for still others that could be added.

For example, from the menu presented in Table 12.1, one possible alternative SOAP combination is Strategy—Operations—Actions—Prospects. Still another is Scenario—Opportunities—Argument—Policy. Even with a moderate number of items under each category, there are exponential numbers of combinations that could be devised, out of which a chosen few could fit a given need or be held in reserve to cover commonly encountered situations.

Table 12.1 The SOAP menu

S	O	A	P
scenario	objectives	accomplishments	paperwork
scene/setting	objections	achievements	personnel
security	observations	actions	perspective
situation	obstacles	advocacy	plan
special items	operations	advancement	policy
staff views	opinion	advantages	positions
stages	opportunities	agreements	powers
stances	opposition	aims	principles
standards	options	ambitions	priorities
statements	origins	analysis	problems
statistics	organization	antagonists	processes
status	outcomes	argument	procedures
strategy	outliers	aspirations	programs
sufficiency	outlays	assessment	proposals
suitability	outreach	assets	prospects
synthesis	overview	authority	purposes

Additional members can be added under each letter and even additional category letters can be appended from one's own repertoire of ideas.

The SOAP elements can be interwoven, as a whole or in part, either in straight order or in custom combination, within standing templates. The SOAP menu is not so much a directive but an initial, portable conceptual tool-kit that can be customized, reconfigured, and even dispersed and integrated into other frameworks.

SPIGOTS Quality Control Checklist

Equally important to a memo's substantive content is its professional quality. A memo that is otherwise excellent in content can depreciate in impact if it reaches the reader in poor shape, with misspellings, grammatical errors, ragged edges, and other avoidable flaws. A memo that is polished in its look shows off an overt commitment to professionalism and is much more likely to be read in earnest than one that bears signs of hurriedness and sloppiness. To reinforce the value of a well-edited, well-polished memo in a professional setting, one might adhere to a practical mantra to "put a business suit on your memo." That is, for a formal, professional piece of communication it is a best practice to make it conform to norms and standards with a detailed inspection.

What follows is a new quality control checklist embodied by the acronym, SPIGOTS, which is a complementary companion to the contents of SOAP. (For those unfamiliar with the word *spigot*, a somewhat aging term, it refers to the everyday object commonly known as a faucet, or water tap.)

Spelling

Make use of the ubiquity of spell-check functions within word-processing programs, but double-check for homonyms (words that share same spelling but can have varied meanings, such as the words *lie* and *space*) and for homophones (words that share the same pronunciation but are spelled differently, as *bear* and *bare*).

Punctuation

Review drafts to spot errors or omitted punctuation marks. Make use of available online and software programs that check for punctuation and other grammatical issues.

Information Integrity

Guard against charges of plagiarism with proper citations and adherence to copyright rules and laws.

Grammar

Adhere to rules of grammar of the language used. Consider any needed corrections or improvements in sentence structure, vocabulary, syntax, or tense forms. Make use of available software tools or in-house style guides.

Organization

Break up monotonous blocks of text by creating sections and labeling them prominently. Segmentation not only relieves boredom, but it engages your readers' attention to the flow, logic, and emphases of your analysis and judgment. Maintain the memo's clean, organized look with consistent indentations of paragraphs and by correcting any ragged margins, especially on the left margin.

Typos, Typefaces, and Timing

Do a line-by-line review to find and correct any typographical errors. Reading draft sentences out loud can catch many such errors. Check to ensure that typeface choice abides by the in-house standard and that typefaces are applied consistently. It is critical to abide by deadlines by submitting the memo *on time*. A late memo depreciates in value the instant a deadline is missed, not only by the loss of information to whoever commissioned the memo, but also by the downturn of one's in-office reputation.

Style

A publishing style is a consistent set of rules and formats that promotes uniformity and conformity across books and their authors, creating a known look and feel within a particular publishing realm. Depending upon the content's professional category, i.e. science, math, medical, etc., one should consult the style manual most appropriate for the subject or the entity's internal preference. Prominent style formats include APA, Chicago, and MLA systems.[2]

The Twelve O Roster for Talking Points

Another sought-after skill is how to draft talking points for oneself or for somebody else, such as a legislative aide preparing a senator to speak to a group. As in memo development, there are many worthy templates in use. What is presented is a roster of twelve interlinked elements, combined together in an alliteration of the letter *O*, which can be drawn upon when needed on short notice.

Again, as with the SOAP memo framework, the twelve O's can be used in their entirety or in parts. They can be arranged in straight order or in alternative sequences. They can also be interwoven into existing speech templates. Other elements can be added to the roster from experience or preference. Again, the rostered elements are meant to serve as prompts and suggestions for when one is struggling for ideas, especially in circumstances when a deadline is looming.

Figure 12.1 shows a clock-style arrangement for these twelve elements, with the Opening, naturally, at the twelve o'clock, or noon/midnight, position.

What follows are brief descriptions for each talking point element.

1. Opening

This is the leadoff point that launches the talk. It is customary to introduce oneself and to acknowledge hosts and prominent guests. The opening can identify the central theme of one's presentation and outline the talk's forward path.

2. Overview

This talking point gives a skyline perspective of the issue at hand, describing major trends and current events and how they are playing out in the sector. This point can introduce a historical perspective in describing how past events have shaped the circumstances of today, or it can describe in what ways the current compares to the past. As discussed in Part 2, the strategic domain can be described here with assessments given of the major actors and factors.

3. Observations

This is the sharing of one's perspectives regarding the situation at hand. It is the entry point for the revealing of one's ideas and opinions. The audience will be attuned to how the speaker frames an issue and gauge the speaker's tilt for

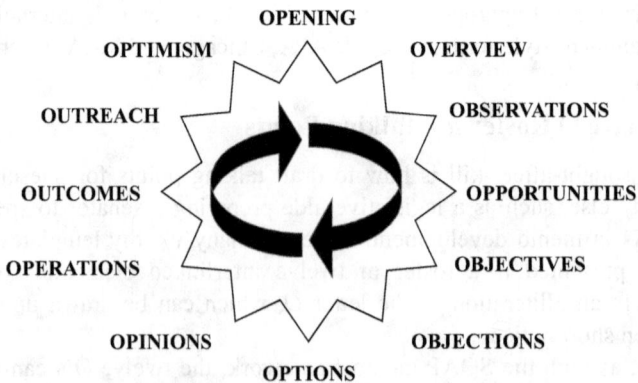

Figure 12.1 Twelve o'clock talking points

or against a particular side or ideology. Observations can range from being highly objective, i.e. just laying forth facts, to being highly subjective, asserting strong, even emotional, opinions about a topic.

4. Opportunities

A natural pivot from one's assessment of the current situation is toward what could be a beneficial improvement, a newer and better situation that could be achieved. An opportunity might be discerned from the mobilization of the group's own strength toward an unrealized goal, or from the identification of the exploitable weaknesses of an opponent, which is a typical talking point in political campaign rallies. An opportunity can be cast as fulfilling an ideal or attaining particularly important interests in either tangible or intangible form.

5. Objectives

This talking point identifies the specific goal worthy of accomplishment that is in keeping with the group's mission and values. It can be specified along the Four Lines of a strategic goal (Goal Line, Deadline, Pay Line, and Headline) in whole or in part. Identifying potential targets for achievement focuses the audience to visualize what a success could look like and what rewards could be reaped.

6. Objections

After declaring worthy objectives, this phase of a talk identifies the counter-case that an opposing side might be making. By sharing what objections are being raised, the speaker gives the impression of being realistic and possessing sufficient confidence to acknowledge that one's cause may not be universally supported. To further underscore one's knowledge of the realities ahead, one can identify key obstacles that complicate a drive toward a particular goal, such as financial cost, a process bottleneck, or an opposing bloc. Once highlighted, a speaker can then "frame an override," or use the presence of the obstacles as a foil to be overcome rather than feared.

7. Options

This point is the identification of the choices available to an organization. It could be framed as a stark binary choice as to whether or not to pursue a particular objective, or it could be presented as a broader menu of choices. In general, the fewer and simpler choices discussed, the more of the audience's attention can be directed to the speaker's reasoning. Discussing options also enlists the audience in the deliberative process and opens up the mindset of participants to consider the different routes laid forth.

8. Opinions

What ultimately drives a talk is its declaration of a purpose and the best route to achieve it. From the opportunities and possibilities, the speaker-leader ought to declare an opinion on what he or she ardently believes to be the best goal and the best strategy. Without a decisive opinion, a talk becomes desultory, an aimless exposition in keeping with a lecture rather than a motivating call to action.

9. Operations

To achieve a goal, action has to be taken in the form of a strategy and its component operations. Striving toward ideals entails taking action. A talk that puts forth even a basic action toward an early objective, or a milestone target, in the form of next steps illuminates for the audience the specific upfront tasks that need to be done, making clear to them how implementation will work. Additionally, the more challenging the goal, the grander and more complex an effort becomes. For sophisticated operations, the organization and its stakeholders need to be enlisted; showing a way forward in pragmatic terms engages their frontline perspectives and makes the case for their direct involvement.

10. Outcomes

The purpose in winning objectives and achieving goals is to fulfill ideals and interests. There is an expectation that for work expended, there should be a worthwhile reward. This talking point elaborates the ultimate end-state, how it might look, what changes would take place, who would benefit, and what the rewards would be. Specifying the desired outcome gives listeners an opportunity to gauge for themselves the value of the quest.

11. Outreach

A speaker alone cannot accomplish the great tasks; he or she simply makes clear the opportunity and provides a way forward. But for goals to become realized, many people need to do their parts. This talking point makes an appeal to the audience to take an action that contributes to the mission, including actions of an intangible nature, such as supporting a point of view. The outreach is often rhetorical, seeking to strike a logical, rational, or emotional chord among the audience.

12. Optimism

The talking point that completes the circle is conveying a sense of optimism, a belief that actions taken and the unfolding of events will ultimately play out in one's favor. Optimism imbues the sense of confidence that enables people to move forward and to endure challenges. Pessimism, on the other hand, is the belief that worse outcomes are looming, a belief that drives people to disinvest themselves from a given situation. The speaker's challenge is divining optimism from a mixed analysis of the world as it is, maintaining realism, and selling a story that is believable and authentic. Not doing so will leave the storyline vulnerable to criticism and cynicism. Ending a talk on a note of optimism brings uplift to the event, and establishes the "hook-end" of the story that rouses an audience in favor of the speaker's world view.

Concluding Remarks About *Strategic Policy Design*

The *Strategic Policy Design* framework approach has been fully elaborated through all of its major components: strategic mission, domain, goal, and plan. The framework introduced new ways of perceiving and organizing contributing elements, employing a number of heuristic hooks, line-words, lenses, formulas, and mnemonic devices that aid in prompting their underlying concepts. The framework introduced practical ways to crystallize thinking about the actors and factors that prevail in a policy environment, to formulate a strategic goal, and to identify clear objectives on a roadmap to that goal. The methodology recognizes the paramount importance of human values in the pursuit of interests by highlighting the tensions between idealism and realism and between intangible and tangible factors.

The use of structure helps to segment the scope of strategic policy into smaller, clearer groupings, and helps to "modularize" policy designs. The framework uses disaggregation as a means to promote aggregation in synthesis— that is, by breaking down complex concepts down to the level that is most understandable, the model enables practitioners to think of new combinations and constructions beyond what has been practiced conventionally. In thinking about strategy, a practitioner can use the framework in its entirety or use pieces in particular, specialized situations. The ultimate aim of the book is to promote new, more consistent ways of thinking about strategic affairs in ways that could yield benefits for multitudes of stakeholders worldwide. It is the abiding hope that this book's mission finds sustained usefulness particularly among young leaders worldwide as they rise into positions of ever-higher responsibility in their home societies.

Notes

1. Lee Jacobs, "Interview with Lawrence Weed, MD—The Father of the Problem-Oriented Medical Record Looks Ahead," *Permanente Journal*, 3(13) (Summer 2009): 84–89. www.thepermanentejournal.org/files/Summer2009/Lawrence_Weed.pdf (accessed Oct. 20, 2018).
2. *The Publication Manual of the American Psychological Association*, 6th ed. (Washington, DC: American Psychological Association, 2010); University of Chicago. *The Chicago Manual of Style*, 17th ed. (Chicago: University of Chicago Press, 2017); *New Oxford Style Manual*, 3rd ed. (London: Oxford University Press, 2016).

Index

Note: Page numbers in *italics* indicate a figure and page numbers in **bold** indicate a table on the corresponding page.

For Product Safety Concerns and Information please contact our EU
representative GPSR@taylorandfrancis.com
Taylor & Francis Verlag GmbH, Kaufingerstraße 24, 80331 München, Germany

9 781032 474694